THE BEST OF
PEOPLE
& FOOD
COOKBOOK

THE
BEST OF
PEOPLE
& FOOD
COOKBOOK

EDITED BY
BARBARA DAVIS

SEVEN SEAS PRESS
Newport, RI.

1   3   5   7   9   KP   /   KP   0   8   6   4   2

LIBRARY OF CONGRESS CATALOGING IN PUBLICATION DATA
Main entry under title:

The Best of people & food.

   Includes index.
   1. Cookery, Marine.   I. Davis, Barbara (Barbara M.)
II. Title: Best of people and food.
TX840.M7B48   1983   641.5'753   83-9523
ISBN 0-915160-56-0

Designed by Irving Perkins Associates

Cover design by Magratten & Wooley

Printed in the United States of America

CONTENTS

FOREWORD

"People & Food" in *Cruising World* was started as a gossip column—who's where and what's cooking—about people cruising on lakes, rivers and oceans around the world. Nine years later, it's still the same.

Over the years we amassed a wealth of recipes and how-to articles sent in by readers and decided to compile the first *Cruising World* cookbook.

Editing this book would have been impossible for me without Lynda Morris, assistant editor of *Cruising World*. Lynda and I selected the recipes (a difficult task), edited and proofread, and finally got the book together. Lynda's hard work and expertise were invaluable. (She's also a great cruising cook!)

Kate Davis, a liveaboard at the age of six and now wrangling horses in the Wild West, did the illustrations. Noreen Barnhart, Jennifer Wright and Joanne Oakes helped with research and development of the book.

The heroes and heroines of this book are the readers who sent in all the marvelously diverse recipes and articles that have been published in "People & Food" over the years and are now in our first cookbook.

Many Thanks!

BARBARA DAVIS
Newport, 1983

CHAPTER 1

COOKING ON A BOAT

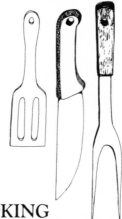

• DUTCH OVEN COOKING

We were planning a 3-month cruise on the Great Lakes, and when I looked below in the cabin, I realized I was about to experience the ultimate in compact efficiency. Since *Snow Goose II* was only 22 feet long and 7 feet in beam, she had limited space and awkwardly shaped compartments in which to stow cooking utensils and food. A 2-burner alcohol stove was the heat source for cooking. My selection of cooking utensils would have to be made carefully.

Our usual menu of periodic fresh foods and ongoing staples would serve us well until the request for something special like a cake was made. An oven was out of the question. The answer was a Dutch oven. Yes, you can not only classically fix stews and 1-pot meals in such a kettle, but you can bake cakes, biscuits, meats and fish, and even pizzas.

Our Dutch oven was made of heavy aluminum and had a well-fitting lid. The snug fit of the lid made an adequate seal for successful baking. The easiest and most delightful treat was baking Snackin' Cake mixes.

We surprised many of our friends when we would arrive by dinghy with a banana walnut cake to share with them for the evening. When our catch for the day didn't bring in any fish, a small can of mushrooms added to a Pizza-in-a-Skillet mix made up for the disappointment. Cinnamon biscuits baked up moist and hot and tasted especially good on rainy mornings.

If we scraped and washed the Dutch oven first, the kettle was then used as a dish pan for the rest of the dishes. Bowls and our 5-cup coffee pot were stacked inside the Dutch oven, then, conveniently, all was stowed.

Lise Olman

• BAKING JAMAICA STYLE

Jamaica is the world's largest producer/exporter of bauxite from which aluminum is refined.

Jamaicans cook most of their food over an open fire; if a meal is cooked indoors, an ovenless stove is used. While cruising in Jamaica, we discovered our first cast aluminum pot. This simple pot was the vehicle for the first of many breads, pies, cakes, quiches, casseroles and limitless other baked foods that we enjoyed regularly, whether at sea or in port.

About 8½ inches in diameter and 3 inches deep, this pot has a slightly convex bottom and a top that fits closely but is not airtight. Though more crudely made, and thus having a more porous surface than most sophisticated models, it is lighter to handle than the pressure cookers that some sailors use, without pressure, for baking. It also has a more easily removed lid.

Cast aluminum doesn't peel, rust, blacken or absorb as much grease and dirt as does cast iron, yet it distributes heat as evenly. Though stainless steel is great for some cookware on a boat, it has poor heat conductivity, causing hot spots, disastrous for baking. Solid, lightweight and easily cleaned, this cast aluminum pot became the perfect oven.

Whether we're baking with the Jamaican pot or our newly-acquired and more smoothly finished Japanese model, we grease the pan generously as one would for baking in a conventional oven. The pots are quite easily cleaned, though the newer one has a smoother and thus more sanitary finish.

Although there has been controversy about pitting in cast aluminum ware and fears about the consumption of indigestible bits of aluminum, recent reports suggest that any trace of the metal that might be absorbed by the body is harmless.

We don't preheat the pan for baking. If we're preparing a casserole, we often use the Jamaican pot first to sauté and then to bake, possibly adding a little extra oil or liquid if the food seems likely to stick or burn. Breads are most often baked for the time specified in the recipe.

Don't be afraid to try a recipe from any cookbook that assumes you are in possession of an ordinary house stove. An oven is an oven. Get acquainted with your stove and estimate at what temperature it is burning. Then you can experiment with an asbestos pad or other such device for slowing the heat without interrupting the even distribution.

Bread is one of the most appreciated results of our baking technique. Whatever the flour, leavening or recipe, the bread is consistently good. It always has good texture and shape, and the crust is the same as it would be in an ordinary oven.

The only difference is in the baking procedure. When baking bread in the cast aluminum pan atop the stove, it is necessary to flip the loaf after approximately ⅔ of the baking time, then continue baking on the other side for the remaining time. The flip is easily accomplished given a properly greased pot, a potholder and a good, flexible spatula or similar kitchen utensil. In this way, the bread will have equally browned crusts, top and bottom, and will bake through thoroughly.

This flip is not required or even advised for fruit breads—banana, blueberry, etc. These are really more cake than bread, and cakes, muffins and brownies should *not* be flipped. They are far too delicate to be tossed over, and it's not at all necessary. If the heat is slow and steady, these items will bake evenly and to delightful perfection.

Cathy Lash

• THE FUEL-LESS COOKER

When cruising, a slow cooker can be a useful cooking device, and one can be constructed inexpensively by using materials that are normally cast off by our overabundant commercial society—a cardboard box and packing foam. Begin by scrounging large pieces of packing foam, perhaps from a local appliance dealer. This is the white stuff that is form-fitted around fragile products for shipping.

Decide on the pan to use as the container. A 3- or 4-quart saucepan with a tight fitting lid works well (your pressure cooker is ideal). Then find a cardboard box sufficiently large to hold the pot and 4 or 5 inches of foam around it. Cut the foam pieces so that they fit solidly in the box. This is your insulation and the success of your cook-box will depend on how well and closely this fits together.

Now comes the most difficult part—carving out the depression to hold the pot. There are really no directions—just manage to get the pot placed in the center of the foam so that there is adequate insulation on all sides, top and bottom. My husband insists he is going to make one the easy way, by stuffing the box with tightly packed crumpled newspaper as insulation, but this is as yet untested.

Now you are ready to try out the cooker. The dishes that can be made in the cook-box are those that generally require a long period of simmering—soups, stews, chowders. There are a couple of things to keep in mind about cooking in this manner. The heat of the pot dissipates very slowly, gently cooking the food. Nothing escapes, either flavor or liquid, as in ordinary cooking. Because of this, it is advisable to use slightly less liquid than called for in the standard recipe.

Prepare food in the ordinary manner, bring ingredients to a boil, and continue cooking for 5 minutes. This will assure that the contents are heated completely through. Place the covered pot immediately into its nest in the box, cover and let sit for 8 to 12 hours. When the proper length of time has passed, the pot can be removed, returned to a boil, and the contents served. The appeal of this type of cooking is obvious to any "galley slave"—tremendous saving of energy, human and otherwise!

When cooking in this manner, one simply cannot be a pot watcher,

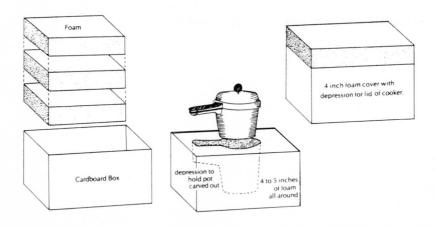

Foam

Cardboard Box

4 inch foam cover with depression for lid of cooker.

depression to hold pot carved out

4 to 5 inches of foam all around

as each time the lid is removed a great deal of heat is lost, making the results uncertain. Just be patient!

I have found that such things as dried beans, lentils, split peas must be precooked longer—30 to 40 minutes. My first bean soup was chewy, but we were so hungry that we ate it anyway.

While cruising, I usually prepare the evening meal while the stove is still going after breakfast. In the tropics you want to do the bulk of the cooking before the heat of the day gets too oppressive. That leaves only the final touches later on before serving the meal.

When I first heard about this kind of cook-box, I thought it was a new idea. Then my mother informed me that her mother had had such a cooker, in which sawdust was the insulation. My grandmother would prepare the evening meal while the woodstove was still hot from breakfast, so as to be able to escape cooking in the heat of a South Dakota summer day. We've come full circle!

Demaris Fredericksen

• HAUTE CUISINE ON TWO BURNERS

The capabilities for haute cuisine aboard a small yacht (assuming that you are not in the middle of a gale) are endless. Many of the great dishes of the great chefs are "top of the stove" dishes. Chinese cooking is a cinch (if you can store a wok) and French gourmet delights, Indian and Pakistani dishes and Italian specialities can all be turned out on a 2-burner stove.

The simplest things that can be used to doctor up canned food of various sorts are sherry and onions. Sherry can be added to canned stews and bouillon. Onions can be chopped and sautéed prior to adding such staples as canned stew, canned hash and the like. Both sherry and onions are simple to store aboard for extended periods of time.

What is needed is imagination, a good spice rack and some basic equipment—a good heavy cast iron skillet, an even heavier cast iron Dutch oven, a couple of good carbon steel chef's knives, a cutting board, a little vegetable peeler, a wooden spoon, trivet, a couple of sauce pans, a couple of wire mesh covers to go over the skillets to prevent grease spatter, a folding wire colander, a whisk (preferably stainless) and a pastry brush. And the wok, if Chinese is your bag. And let us not forget the garlic press!

Jay Stuart Haft

• PRESSURE COOKING

For our cruise down the Blue Danube in a small boat, I wanted time for writing and sightseeing. We were also worried about the availability of bottled butane gas in countries like Hungary, Czechoslovakia, Romania and Bulgaria. We had a simple 2-burner stove with broiler to cook on.

I bought a 6-quart pressure cooker.

After using this magical instrument for a year, I can report that either pressure cookers were made for boats, or boats for pressure cookers. I don't know why it took me so long to discover them—or why they're not standard equipment on every cruising yacht.

Pressure cookers are fast, efficient, versatile, economic and easy to maintain and clean. They also create less heat in the galley because they are "on" for less time—a boon in a small boat on hot summer days.

We didn't use canned food aboard *Lady Fiona,* preferring to shop for fresh produce while exploring each new port. This makes a pressure cooker even more useful—it's a fast medium at the end of a busy day; you can cook dishes in advance, and the high temperature of cooking will take care of any 2- or 3-day old meat (we don't have refrigeration or ice). You can also use cheaper cuts of meat as they are tenderized in cooking.

Their best use is for 1-pot casseroles. You can cook *any* favorite oven casserole in a pressure cooker. It will taste just as good and take ¼ of the time, or less.

The pressure cooker is particularly useful for recipes calling for any kind of dried beans or lentils. When cooking these, I cut the actual cooking time even more by leaving the pressure cooker on full pressure for about 10 minutes, then remove from heat and throw a towel over the whole thing for 1 or 2 hours, leaving the food cooking in the good old Scottish haybox style. The food will still be hot enough to eat direct from the pressure cooker at the end of this time.

In the case of fish, I use a covered dish in the pressure cooker so that it does not lose flavor through over-steaming.

I also bake all kinds of breads, cakes, custards and puddings in the pressure cooker. There isn't much you can't do.

Fiona McCall

• USING THERMOS BOTTLES

We have cruised happily for 2½ years with no refrigeration and often no ice in our ice chest. Of course, this increases our appreciation of cold drinks in port.

When block ice is unavailable, as it generally is in the Pacific, we buy cold milk or juice at the nearest store, hurry it back to the boat in a foam insulated tote bag, and keep it in Thermos bottles until mealtime.

Thermos Bottle Soup

We prefer canned soup, but away from America dried soups are cheaper and more widely available. Instead of simmering for 15 minutes, which is impractical on a kerosene Primus stove, I simply bring water and dried soup to a boil, stir thoroughly to avoid lumps, and transfer to a widemouthed Thermos. Prepared at 1 meal, it is still hot and ready to serve at the next meal.

Thermos Yogurt

This is a good way to consume dried skim milk. Just mix together ⅓ cup milk powder, 1 cup warm water, and a spoonful of yesterday's yogurt (or freeze-dried starter). Fill a widemouthed Thermos with boiling freshwater to heat and sterilize it. Pour out the water and put in yogurt mixture. Leave in Thermos overnight or until thick. Serve with jam or canned fruit.

Liz MacDonald

• CRUISING WITH A TAFFRAIL SMOKER

My barbecue, mounted on the taffrail of *Renaissance,* will hold a 7-pound red snapper that has been cleaned, with the skin removed from the area to be served. Sitting on a rack so the smoke can reach all sides, and resting on foil to make clean-up a pleasure, it is ready to begin 2 hours in a barbecue loaded with briquets and damp hickory chips.

Using 2 thermometers, 1 in the fish, and 1 measuring temperature within the barbecue, I guarantee success. During cooking, the oven temperature will average 300° or more. When done, the fish will "break" in 1 or 2 places along the side, and flesh will be both moist and done.

Serve on the roaster pan with a bed of parsley or other leaves for greens and the slices of 2–3 lemons for added color. Garlic slivers may be inserted in holes conveniently made by the thermometer probe at intervals of 1–2 inches along each side. Alternatively, a mixture of spices and chopped onion can be inserted in the body cavity.

The suitcase-sized barbecue has smoke and draft controls at the sides and on top. It is mounted using the front legs that came with it, braced by one of the other two legs, all secured using U-clamps to the taffrail top and middle rails. When cooking is completed, the holes are all closed and the fire goes out.

Because the fire is contained, one can cook while underway despite heeling, following winds, etc. There must be some limit to this, but ordinary conditions present no problem.

This is the third barbecue I have used this year, and it suits me best. It is a Meco, and I have recently done a 7 pound cod and 11 pound turkey at the same time. (Two hours for the fish, 4 hours for turkey.)

Smoked Turkey

For smoking turkeys I use my special spice mixture: A portion of every seed spice in the spice rack at my grocery store, plus small amounts of oregano, basil, rosemary and sage.

My stuffing utilizes chopped red and green peppers, onion, especially green onions, stalks or tops and all, chopped cabbage, parsley and croutons. I once used leftover tossed salad ingredients, and it worked so well I continue to reflect on that lesson.

In the spring I did a 25-pound turkey for a club party. After carving the bird in pieces suitable for "finger-food," I took my cooking pan, knives, etc., to the boat. A mistake! When I returned the turkey was gone!

Bill Warner

• COOKING IN A CUPBOARD

Moonraker of Fowey had her cooker mounted in a cupboard, and I was so impressed by the advantages of this idea that I have copied it, with minor improvements, on *Ron Glas*. I strongly recommend the idea, particularly to those who cruise in warm climates.

The first advantage is that the heat and smells from cooking are kept out of the accommodations. Two burners working can increase the temperature below decks by at least 10° in warm weather and make the saloon uncomfortably hot. If you want to heat the saloon, then you can leave the cupboard door open while you are cooking.

Another advantage is that it insulates the noise of burners, fryers, etc. —a great benefit when entertaining people aboard.

The slightly greasy deposit that forms eventually on the deckhead above the galley is confined to the cupboard and does not spread.

When you are cooking, the cupboard heats up, of course, so you can warm the plates by placing them anywhere in the cupboard, or dry your socks if you wish. Hang the dishcloths clear of the cooker and you will always have dry cloths for the washing up. You can also keep pans and food warm when they are off the stove.

The cupboard should be wide enough to enclose the cooker, but not the working tops or other parts of the galley layout, and wide enough to lean into to reach plates, pans or whatever may be stowed outboard of the cooker.

My cupboard door is mainly heat-resistant glass so that I can see if the soup is boiling without constantly opening the door. The door must have a catch to hold it open so that it does not bang your elbow just as you are ladling out the soup!

The cupboard requires one opening porthole in the coaming to allow the heat and steam to escape outside, weather permitting, and one permanent "weather proof" ventilator in the deckhead above the stove to allow heat and steam to escape at all times.

I have not found it necessary to have any holes in the bottom of the galley sides to allow air in, but it is possible that some burners might require this to ensure they burn properly.

I have a hanging tray with deep fiddles, suspended above and outboard of the cooker. This holds pans, plates, mugs, etc., both level and warm at any angle of heel, a great boon when serving a meal and there is nowhere level to put anything down.

If you have a Cupboard Galley, you won't even know that the cook is baking, unless you are sleeping on deck next to the galley porthole!

Jock McLeod

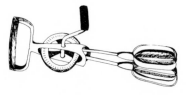

CHAPTER 2

PROVISIONING AND PRESERVATION

• THE LONG-RANGE GALLEY

Knowledge of provisioning and preservation can mean the difference between enjoying fresh fruits and vegetables for weeks at sea and depending entirely on canned stores.

Some fresh foods last best under cool, moist conditions; others need dry, dark and cool. Some may go on the deck topside, others in shaded places or in the hold. Bins and lockers specifically designed and located for preservation of fresh stores should be prepared before they are taken aboard.

Covered deck lockers with louvered sides can be used for those foods that travel best in moderately moist conditions. Some of these are: cabbage, cauliflower, Chinese cabbage and lettuce. They should be wrapped separately in burlap and dampened from time to time. Choose cabbage that is solid and heavy for its size. Cauliflower should be white with no yellow tinge. Lettuce must be firm, the outer leaves green, and the core end sweet-smelling. Lettuce should not be stored next to fruits, for many fruits give off a gas as they ripen, causing dark spots to develop on green leafy vegetables. Oranges and grapefruit store the same way. If heat is so intense that these items start to sweat, shade the bin, but allow air to circulate.

A box of moist sand kept out of the sun is a good place for many root vegetables. Choose all as fresh as possible, with crisp, green foliage. Trim foliage to within 1 inch of the base, as it drains moisture from the root. Small carrots with small cores are sweetest and a dark or discolored stem end is a sign of age. Bury celery in the sand so only the leafy tips are exposed.

Keep potatoes in a cool dark place: They can stand some moisture but light causes green areas to appear and turns them bitter. They should be separated from onions, which steal moisture from them. Keep onions dry and dark. Watch all vegetables for sprouts and remove these from time to time. Pumpkins and hard-shell squash fare well in warm weather if kept dry. When acorn squash starts to turn orange, it is showing its age.

Buy tomatoes while still green or with a slightly pinkish cast, wrap in tissue paper, and keep in a cool spot. Bring out a day or two before planning to use, but never place them in the sun. They should last 6 or 8 weeks. Select mushrooms with tightly closed caps, the smaller the better, and store where it's dark and humid. Broccoli should have compact heads with tightly closed flowers; it will last about 2 weeks if wrapped in a damp cloth and kept cool. Purchase avocados while still hard, with a full stem end, and free of bruised spots. Wrap separately and bring out to ripen. You can accelerate this a bit by placing them in a paper bag for a day or two. Never refrigerate avocados before they are fully ripe as chilling stops the ripening process.

Apples, peaches, apricots and plums last longer if kept dry. A box of sand stored inside the boat helps preserve them—if they are free from blemishes and completely dry before covering. Or, wrap the fruit in paper and store in a covered crock with paper between each layer. Firm, small apples keep better than large ones. Select hard, green pears; they will ripen quickly when you bring them out. Color doesn't always indicate ripeness, but a slight "give" at the stem end shows they are ready to eat. Peaches, apricots and plums should be firm but not green. Enjoy these less durable fruits at their best as they won't last long.

Buy lemons with thin skins that are slightly green. They will last indefinitely if wrapped in foil and kept in an airtight container. Limes can be kept the same way. The ones you buy in the tropics are fat, juicy and delicious.

Other Perishables and Packaged Goods

The longevity of eggs is always of special concern on long voyages, for they are needed in many recipes and are an excellent source of protein. With refrigeration there is no particular problem as they are available in most ports, but for long passages some method of preservation must be used. On *Passagemaker* they were rubbed with petroleum jelly for the 6-week trip from Singapore to Greece and were still edible on arrival. You test eggs by putting them in cold water: Fresh ones go to the bottom; bad ones float; and those that hover in between—well, it depends on how much you want eggs.

In areas where water temperature is below air temperature, quarter-pounds of butter can be wrapped in plastic and kept in a bucket of water out of the sun. Unless the water is over 70°, the butter should stay fresh 3 to 4 weeks. This method of cooling may also be used for such perishables as mayonnaise and sauces after the jars have been opened. But it is best to select small jars of these items so they will be used up quickly.

Hard Italian cheeses such as Parmesan, Provolone and Romano are least perishable because they have the least amount of moisture. In warm weather, keep in a salt- or vinegar-saturated damp cloth in a cool place. In cool weather or when refrigerated, wrap tightly in plastic to keep the air out. Seal Cheddar, Gouda and Swiss with paraffin wax, then coat again after cutting. Processed cheese keeps until opened if kept relatively cool. If mold appears on any cheese, just cut it off; it doesn't affect the taste, nor is it harmful.

Our voyages have taken us across thousands of miles of oceans and into dozens of harbors. They have been a blend of many pleasures: The joy of being at sea . . . the thrill of a landfall . . . the fascination of personal discovery in each new port . . . and always, the continuing gastronomical adventure of savoring the exotic in cooking pots of the world.

Linford Beebe

• THE VIEW FROM BELOW

There is no doubt that a well-provisioned larder within the limits of the boat's storage space and the skipper's tolerance helps avoid "friendly" recriminations between the first mate and skipper.

The solution is to stock basic food items and lots of auxiliary foods such as dried sauces and spices that can be mixed with creativity to arrive at a reasonable facsimile of the desired article.

For non-edibles the same rule applies, i.e., as many multipurpose items as possible.

For both categories, leakproof containers are a must.

Stores

The decision as to what level of stores are kept permanently on board depends upon your personal preference.

For us, groceries for a 6-foot, hungry husband, 2 active children, plus my reasonably sturdy self can be awe-inspiring if brought aboard at one time. I prefer to sneak a bag or two on every time I go aboard during the fitting out season—and then keep it topped up later on.

As well as accommodating a sudden impulse to set off on a short cruise, this approach also minimizes low growls from the skipper on how he'll soon have to raise the waterline—again!

Icebox

Unless you're one of the lucky cruising people who have refrigeration, you'll be forced to cope with keeping the food from going bad without interfering with the main purpose of the icebox, which is, of course, to keep the beer cold.

Freeze as much as you can before you leave and replenish with frozen foods. Cool down the icebox a day before you add your food. Start off with a lot of ice and try to keep the icebox full. The food acts as an insulator.

Keep emptying the water out if you can without opening the icebox. If you can't, try to talk the skipper into installing an electric pump.

Insulate the icebox lids with some type of insulating foam.

Don't buy cube ice if you want it to last a long time. Use block ice and an ice pick for the cocktail hour.

Keep meats and cheese in separate plastic containers. Be especially careful to avoid meat juice in the bottom of the icebox—it makes an awful smell.

Shopping in Ports

This usually occurs *under duress* for a combination of reasons: The skipper is convinced 90% of the food is unnecessary and thinks all that's needed is more ice for the beer—and maybe some peanuts. The first mate is miffed because the skipper thinks it's all unnecessary, which makes her want to *not* get things and *then* see what he does! The kids are complaining because they can't understand why Mommy won't keep ice cream in the icebox. There is frequently a howling gale going on, which makes the skipper and crew even more anxious to keep the shopping to a minimum. So it's a good idea to get it over with as quickly as possible.

Always have a good list. Follow the list—don't impulse-buy. Bring a sturdy carryall and plastic shopping bags along (a lot of small stores don't have shopping bags). When buying meat, try to stick to frozen meat. Buy everyone a treat as blackmail to cut down on the griping. Read your list out loud at the check-out counter.

Take a taxi back if you have a heavy load (or even a medium load—it gets heavy after 3 blocks). If the nice people at the marina where you stop offer you a lift to town—take it. We've even been offered, and accepted, the use of a marina truck.

Carolyn Ross

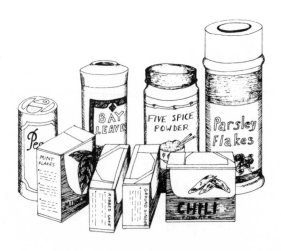

• DECODING CANS

I would like to pass on the usefulness of a Product Identification Code List. Our code list is for Campbell Soup Company products, due to high usage of their items. You can receive a similar list of codes for any brands you use by writing the respective company.

Product Identification Codes are stamped on the can lid. If 3 rows appear, the code is the top row; if 2 rows appear, the code is the last 2 characters of the bottom row. The 2 characters will always identify the contents of the can.

EXAMPLE: <u> 03 </u> (03 = Cream of Chicken)
CEX N3
820

CR C7 (R4 = Cream of Potato)
BY9R4

Invariably, even marking cans with indelible ink fails if cans start to tarnish and rust. I'm not even going to mention how fast labels disappear, so having a list of the codes stamped on the lids ends unpopular surprises.

Reg Hinnant

• SEALING MEALS

My best discovery yet—the Dazey Seal-a-Meal! Our boat is a 24-foot Rainbow Weekender with very austere facilities below. Cooking is done in 1 pot over Sterno—so menus in the past have been limited.

But with the Seal-a-Meal I fix extras of all sorts of things (casseroles, desserts, meat, vegetables) as I cook weeknight meals, seal them in boilable pouches (which takes only minutes) and freeze. On board, boil about 15 minutes—good, easy, hot dinners with hot water left over for coffee and cleaning up—and more time for me to enjoy the evening.

Other items can also be sealed—extra matches, paper products, anything that must stay dry. The bags are extra and easy to find. It's the greatest thing for cruisers since paper plates.

Gale Fretwell

• NO-TREATMENT EGGS

To me, a guy who thoroughly enjoys his 3 scrambled every morning and who doesn't really believe in new-fangled things like cholesterol, the egg is a pretty important item. Encased in its own private package, it amounts to one of the most handy ways to stow protein aboard a cruising boat.

It seems that there are at least as many ways of preserving eggs for an extended cruise as there are ways of making them edible.

There is a school of thought that says, "Buy your eggs FRESH, directly from the hen! Don't let them get too close to a refrigerator! Eggs," says this school, "once refrigerated, then unrefrigerated, lose their keeping power!"

We have used 2 methods successfully to preserve eggs. Once, while provisioning for a trip, we tucked 12 dozen supermarket, Vaseline-coated eggs into *Frosh's* various hidey-holes. About 8 weeks later we cracked the last of the dozen and found it edible.

On another occasion, we stowed 12 dozen, straight from the supermarket cooler, in *Frosh's* various hidey-holes without benefit of Vaseline or vinegar or any other treatment. Ten weeks later, somewhere near Haiti, we cracked number 144. It was still good!

We have concluded, therefore, that the no-treatment treatment is as good as any—and it's easier.

Ray Anderson

• GOOD FOOD AND DRINK

There must be something about *Jester* that encourages good eating and good drinking at sea, perhaps because she demands so little work from her crew that singlehanders need occupational therapy to stave off boredom—what better therapy than eating and drinking well? Both Mike Richey (her present owner) and I share an aversion to canned food and have managed to live very well without it, even when the voyage gets spun out to 50 or more days at sea. The boat has no form of refrigeration, of course.

Out of my own seagoing diet, I would pick four noble ingredients:

York Ham

A well-cured ham, on its bone, will keep indefinitely even in hot weather, *provided it is kept in fresh air all the time*, not in a locker, and wrapped in 1 layer of cotton cheesecloth. Mine used to stand up like a drunken duck, jammed off on top of one of the sideboard lockers. I was eating it all the way from England to the States, and the remains of it were quite unmoved by a sweltering week in Newport Harbor, when I was living ashore and the boat locked up. I finished it on the way home.

You can enjoy eating the lean meat uncooked, but the uncooked fat is not appetizing. Much better, carve off a thick chunk and boil it for a bit with some root vegetables, then get 1 hot meal out of it and 1 or 2 cold ones later. (It will keep only for a few days after cooking.) Its flavor is out of this world.

Salt Beef

It shouldn't be necessary to recommend this historic form of fuel, which played a major part in the exploration of the world, but in fact, I hardly ever find a yachtsman who carries it. It keeps forever. I once knew a professional sailor who claimed to have eaten, as a young man, beef from casks that were marked "Recasked 1903." I *think* he was lying.

I use a 2-gallon polythene jar with screw cap about 3 inches in diameter, and follow, more or less, the instructions given by Eric Hiscock in *Cruising Under Sail*. Dissolve salt in fresh water until a peeled raw potato just floats in it, then add 1 ounce of saltpeter to every 4 gallons of brine. Fill the jar about ¾ full with it. Get fresh meat without bone and as free from fat as possible. Chop it up only as small as is necessary to get into the jar. Cram it in until you have enough, or until no more will go in. Add a bit more salt for good measure and make sure the liquid is within 1 inch of the top. Chuck out any small bits of fat that may float.

When you want meat, fish for it with a bent wire (more therapy). For the first 10 days or so the meat is not very salty and may go straight into a stew provided you don't add extra salt. As weeks grow into months, it becomes progressively saltier and should be soaked for anything up to 24 hours before cooking to get some of it out. If it is vintage stuff, soak in salt water first, then fresh. When cooked, it is delicious.

Brown Rice

Any form of unpolished rice is marvellous at sea and keeps for ever if kept dry. Use a portion of sea water when cooking it, instead of adding salt.

Red Wine

Goes well with strong meaty dishes and should be poured freely into stews while cooking. Buy something young, rough, and cheap. After a double Atlantic crossing in a 5-tonner, it will have gotten a bit sharper than the same wine left at home in a rack, but you won't notice this until you get home. Mike Richey has it in plastic flagons, but I feel more confident with glass bottles chocked off in the bilges.

H. G. "Blondie" Hasler

• WEEVILS! GIT OUTA MY GRITS!

While reprovisioning in Colon, Panama, my wife, Sandy, returned to the boat elated at finding a vendor with Caribbean pigeon peas (i.e., beans) for 5¢ per pound. Upon a closer check of the dried peas, we discovered the usual assortment of rocks—clods—leaves—sticks—twigs and chaff . . . PLUS a healthy herd of weevils. These long-nosed varmints had already eaten up our 5¢ savings and were determined to make a big dent in the remaining peas (they were munching themselves a weevil slum-a-fied apartment complex and carrying on as only weevils can).

Long ago, we had discovered (contrary to popular belief) that cussing, screaming, throwing things and stamping your feet *will not* drive these critters away. They just crowd around to watch the local gringo thrash around and get red in the face—and then go back to their munching when the entertainment has ended.

Outside the U.S., creepy crawlers in the local staples and foodstuffs are quite common and just another facet of provisioning that makes cruising life interesting.

There are numerous methods of ridding yourself of these hungry pests.

Poison 'em

A bay leaf in the food container is supposed to discourage weevils and their starving cousins. This is probably true for the pesticide-weakened and emaciated gringo weevils . . . but the macho grits-munching, long-nosed gluttons we've seen outside the U.S. just grin and wolf the bay leaf first before rumbling on to devour the contents with great relish.

Gas 'em

A piece of dry ice in the bottom of the food container sublimes into heavier than air carbon dioxide, which will not support life (creepy crawlers included?). We haven't tried this method ourselves, as we could never locate dry ice when we had the weevils—or—locate the weevils when we had dry ice. Such is the uncertainty of cruising logistics.

Freeze 'em

We have often wondered if freezing the foodstuffs for several days would be effective against weevils and their eggs. Once, as a joke, we froze a Mexican lisa bug (large, ugly googley-eyed bug) and sent it to a boating friend in the U.S., telling him it was a Mexican No-see-um and that we would have sent him a Mexican cockroach but couldn't afford the postage. It was all a colossal joke until we found out that lisa bugs are venomous. We have yet to hear from our friend, so maybe freezing bugs isn't 100% effective?

Fry 'em

Dry heat is the method we use. We place the beans, rice, peas, noodles, spaghetti, flour, grits, groats, etc., in a pan on top of the stove and simply heat the contents, stirring constantly for approximately 10 minutes or until the food is a constant hot temperature. This dry heat kills the pests and their eggs. We place the heat-treated food into clean, heavy-duty plastic buckets with tight lids. The only side effect we've noticed with the dry heat method is an alteration of the baking properties in flour (the baked goods tend to be heavier in texture).

When bringing new foodstuffs aboard in foreign ports, diligent inspection and treatment procedures should be practiced, as sometimes months later you discover that indeed you did bring varmints (or their eggs) aboard unnoticed—and—not being satisfied with their own paltry food, they have eaten their way out . . . and *into* other more tasty delicacies, such as your last 5 pounds of impossible-to-come-by coarse ground grits.

Dale Stennett

• SUBSTITUTION AT SEA

Even the most organized galley chef occasionally runs out of ingredients—usually in the midst of preparing the dish. However, by blending or substituting ingredients on hand, you should be able to save the meal.

During leisurely weekend cruises, my husband, Davey Jones, spikes his morning tomato juice with a can of beer, commonly called "red beer." When *Gambit*'s supply of tomato juice was depleted he improvised by mixing ½ cup tomato sauce with ½ cup water, then proceeded to blend in the suds. Here are other handy substitutions:

Semi-sweet chocolate: Use 3 tablespoons unsweetened cocoa, 1 tablespoon shortening and 3 teaspoons sugar.

Nuts (for baking): Use oatmeal browned in butter or margarine.

Butter: Use 2 cups evaporated milk slowly beaten then poured into a pan to chill. Equals about 1 pound of butter.

Baking Powder: Use ½ teaspoon cream of tartar plus ½ teaspoon baking soda.

Whipped Cream: Use a few melted marshmallows added to 1 egg white and beaten until stiff, or use ½ cup nonfat dry milk plus ⅓ cup cold water; beat well, then add 2 teaspoons lemon juice, 3 to 4 tablespoons sugar and a dash of vanilla. Beat until mixture peaks.

Sour Cream: Use either 1 cup plain yogurt or evaporated milk, plus 1 table-spoon vinegar (or lemon juice).

Maple Syrup: Use 1 cup brown sugar simmered in ⅓ cup of water, plus a dash of maple flavoring.

Cream (for baking): Use ½ cup butter and ¾ cup milk.

Tomato Sauce: Use ½ cup tomato paste mixed with ½ cup water.

Lynne Orloff-Jones

• VACUUM PACKING

Ask any young man what he missed most after being at sea for several weeks during the Whitbread Round the World Race and the answer will invariably be: "Women and fresh bread!"

Several companies produce special long-life bread, but the experience on most yachts during this race, and *Flyer* in particular, was that this bread found few takers after a week at sea, unless livened up a bit with toasting. It was this dislike that led the French cook aboard *Flyer* to experiment with vacuum packaging (sealing fresh loaves in plastic pouches) during that Dutch yacht's stay in New Zealand.

Results were encouraging; the bread remained edible throughout the 4-week voyage around the Horn to Mar del Plata, a period that could be extended to 6 weeks, we were informed later by experts in London, if the bread is packed soon after leaving the oven and great care is taken over hygiene.

With the help of the Department of Scientific and Industrial Research at Auckland, each of the loaves (which were donated by Hans Klisser Bakeries) was placed in a Cryovac heavy-duty plastic pouch, then set in a vacuum chamber to extract all the air before the gas (nitrogen or CO_2) was injected and the bag sealed.

Even fresh meat merely vacuum-wrapped in a similar manner can be carried on board for 2 weeks or more when stored at a temperature of 7°C (44°F), and this time scale can be doubled if temperatures are re-duced to 4°C (38°F). Many wholesale butchers employ 1 or more of these vacuum chambers, for vacuum-packed cuts of bacon now are common sights on some supermarket shelves. The process is also finding favor with restaurants, for when packaged this way, meat matures more slowly, which improves the taste.

The *Flyer* crew found that the possibilities that this packaging system provides are almost endless. Biscuits, crackers and cookies, for instance, can be protected against the damp, large cheeses can be cut up into more manageable sizes and kept fresh, and bulky items like life jackets, spare sleeping bags or clothing can be reduced down to a fraction of their size when vacuum packed.

Most of the crew on this Whitbread winner took the opportunity to have a spare set of thermal underwear packaged in this way, which then reduced their bulk down to a size small enough to be stowed in a water-tight container along with the flares stored with the life rafts.

Barry Pickthall

• CRUISING JERKY

We lead a simple life and don't care for refrigeration or canned goods. Food is very important to us and seems to be increasingly so as our sons grow. We are always trying new ways of preserving food to keep our costs down.

Did you ever try to find reasonably priced—EDIBLE—canned meats in Mexico? Unable to locate a cruising supply of canned meats, we resorted to making jerky from low-cost biftec (beef steak).

We've never regretted getting involved in that first jerky project. Greater independence is gained in cruising by being able to dry almost anything found along the way. You can actually extend a cruise in interesting, remote areas by drying locally available meats.

Over the years, we've worked at simplifying many of the drying techniques and trying new ideas. Beef, turtle, lobster, crab, fish, turkey, shrimp, conch and shark were dried successfully. (Octopus and sea cucumber dried easily, but weren't worth the effort.)

Sun

Successful meat drying requires clear sun for most of the day. The outdoor temperature isn't that critical. (We've dried meats easily at 45°F with clear sun.)

Pollution

Don't attempt to dry meats in industrial or highly populated areas with air pollution problems.

Soy Sauce

The soy sauce called for in some of the procedures should be a good grade (i.e., fermented, instead of the cheaper, formulated types).

Mini Ovens

Clear plastic Ziploc bags (mini ovens) are used during the final drying stage to remove residual moisture from the meats. The bags are filled halfway with the partially dried meats, then laid on deck with the open ends *held open* into the wind with sticks. After a few minutes, moisture from the meat condenses on the inside of the bags. Shake the bag every 30 minutes or so to rearrange the contents. The meats are considered done when there are no more traces of moisture on the inside of the bags.

Storage

During the drying process, take meats inside each night to keep the night dew off. After the mini-oven treatment, the meats should be dry and cooled to room temperature before placing in storage containers such as double Zip-loc bags, glass jars and plastic galley canisters with tight-fitting lids. Properly dried meats will keep over 1 year if kept dry in adequate storage containers.

Rain

If your jerky project gets rained out, do not despair. With a bit of extra effort, you finish drying the meat on the stove top. Place the meats in a large pot and elevate it above the burner (a wok stand, flame spreader or 2 bricks all work nicely at putting distance between flame and pot). Low flame is used with constant turning of the meat with your hands. If your hand can stand the heat, so can the meats. You want enough heat to dry the meat without cooking it.

PROCEDURES AND TECHNIQUES
Beef and Turtle

Cut meat into manageable slices, no more than ⅜ inch thick. Trim off all traces of fat and soak overnight in soy sauce. Weigh down the meat with a plate or other object to keep it completely submerged in the sauce. Next morning, drain away all excess sauce. Liberally pepper both sides of each piece of meat (it should have a dry look). Arrange meat on plates and set out in direct sun. Two days on plates and 1 day in the mini oven is usually sufficient. (We used to string up the meat with a sail needle and heavy twine but found the plate method more convenient.)

Lobster and Crab

Boil for 10 minutes in seawater. Remove from shell. Shred up with your fingers (this increases the surface area and reduces drying time). Squeeze excess moisture out with your hands. Arrange on plates, no more than ½ inch thick, and place in direct sun. Turn shreds with a fork every 30 minutes. Two days on plates and 1 day in the mini oven is usually sufficient. If you caught your lobster or crab late in the day, you can cover the shredded meat with soy sauce. Weigh it down to keep it completely submerged. Next morning, drain away all soy sauce, squeeze the excess moisture out with your hands and proceed as above.

Fish

Should be a lean variety with a fat content of less than 5%, such as grouper, snapper or flounder. After cleaning and scaling, the fish is steamed until the meat is white and flakes easily. If the fish is caught late in the day, place on a rack in a pressure cooker with enough water for steaming. Bring up to pressure, remove from flame and leave the lid and pressure knob on until next morning. It will not spoil overnight. Proceed as with turkey.

Turkey

Remove the skin and any fat. Pressure steam the meat for 10 minutes. Remove the bones. Knead meat between fingers until it is all "mushed up". (This is vital as turkey and fish can dry in 1 day if the meat is finely divided by mushing it up.) Squeeze out excess moisture and arrange on plates, no more than ½ inch thick. Place in direct sun and turn with a fork every 30 minutes. As the meat dries, break up any clumps with your fingers and roll between your hands. (The turkey will "fuzz up" and the fish will "powder".) The meat will dry rapidly. One day is usually sufficient without using the mini oven. For additional flavor, turkey and fish can be soaked overnight in soy sauce after "mushing up" as with lobster and crab.

Shrimp

Cook 10 minutes in seawater. Head, shell and de-vein. Cut large shrimp in half (down the vein line). Lay on plates (single layer). Place in direct sun, turning every 30 minutes. Two days on plates and 1 day in the mini oven is usually sufficient.

Conch

Clean, skin and cut into manageable chunks. Run through a food grinder or dice finely. Arrange on plates, no more than ½ inch thick. Place in direct sun, turning very 30 minutes. As it dries, pull pieces apart (conch tends to clump up and stick to itself). Three days on plates and 1 day in the mini oven is usually sufficient.

Shark

Due to the shark's very basic excretory system, urea is found in the meat, resulting in that "sharkey smell." With proper preparation, shark meat is very tasty—ask any Costa Rican. Soak fresh fillets in a brine solution of 1 cup salt to 1 gallon seawater. Discard brine and add freshwater until the urea smell no longer persists. Process as with fish. Pay careful attention to "mushing up" and then breaking up of hard chunks. If this is not done thoroughly, you will have difficulty reconstituting the meat.

Drying the Wild Whatzit

Should you find yourself with an abundance of strange meat, the following guidelines can be used: Goat, tapir, wild pig, sea cow and monkey can be dried like beef. Snake, iguana, alligator and wild birds can be dried like turkey. If it crawls, runs, hops, swims or flies, and the locals eat it—then you can dry it.

NOW WHAT DO YOU DO WITH IT? RECONSTITUTION AND REHYDRATION

Add 2 volumes of boiling water to 1 volume of dried meat and let sit 20 minutes.

Beef and Turtle

Eat as jerky or cut up and cook with beans, rice, soups and stews.

Lobster and Crab

Cook with rice, soups and stews, or reconstitute for use in lobster and crab dishes.

Fish, Turkey and Shark

Cook with soups, noodles, rice and stews, or reconstitute for use in instant tunafish or turkey sandwiches.

Shrimp

Cook with rice (or fried rice). Rehydrate for shrimp cocktail and other shrimp dishes.

Conch

Cook with beans. Rehydrate for use in raw conch salad recipes.

The Wild Whatzit?

I'm afraid you're on your own now!

Dale Stennett

• DRYING OUT IN THE TROPICS

Drying food is economical and also increases your storage space because dried foods take 4 to 6 times less space to store than canned foods. No cooking is required in drying, save blanching a few of the harder types of vegetables to insure a longer storage life.

For drying on board, a fiberglass screen can be used, or better yet, cheesecloth stretched over a wire frame. Suspend in a warm area with free-moving air circulating around it. This is ideal for foods that must dry longer than others. In the tropics and using a wind scoop, the area directly below this is perfect since the air is constantly moving.

If you are using a relatively flat awning, fruits and fruit leathers that dry quickly can be placed on a sheet of brown paper on the awning and anchored down somehow to dry in direct sunlight.

Many fruits and vegetables require only a few hours to dry, but remember to turn them over on occasion. Others can take a couple of days depending on weather conditions. Be sure to bring your drying foods inside at night to prevent dew and humidity restoring moisture.

Dehydrating Vegetables

Slice any vegetable—onion, carrot, zucchini, celery, tomato, green pepper, etc., ¼ inch thick. Lay them on the screen, being careful not to overlap (this causes uneven drying time). Zucchini will dry to crispy snacks much like potato chips. Before drying, you can sprinkle the sliced vegetables with salt, seasoning spices, you name it, for a variation in tastes. After drying several different kinds of vegetables, package some

together (i.e. onion, tomato, carrot) for a quick package of soup vegetables.

Your Own Bouillon *(You'll need a blender)*

Purée onion, tomato, chicken and some suitable spices with a little
water, enough to facilitate blending. Then drop spoonfuls of this purée
on to plastic wrap that has been laid on a screen. Make these spoon
drops the size of half-dollars and ¼ inch thick.

When dried, 2 or 3 of these can be dropped into a mug and covered
with boiling water to make a quick, hot, delicious cup of soup.

Dehydrating Fruit

Nearly any fruit can be dried, figs, pineapple, apples, bananas, grapes,
but don't bother with melons or oranges. They're miserable.

Dried apples can be reconstituted in 15–30 minutes to be used for pies
or applesauce, or eat them as is for an easy, on watch, pocket-sized treat.

Plums, peaches and apricots should be pitted and halved or quartered
before drying. It will take less time and they dry more uniformly. As for
grapes, steam momentarily to soften skins before drying.

Fruit Leather *(This stuff is terrific!)*

A blender is pretty necessary, but very soft juicy fruits can be run
through a food mill or sieved—anything to make a purée. If sweetening
is needed, use honey or sugar syrup. Granulated sugar will cause brittle-
ness. Have plastic wrap spread on the screen and tape down the edges.
Pour the purée onto the plastic wrap ¼ inch thick. Set in the sun and
leave it alone for 6–8 hours, depending on thickness. That's it.

Then you roll it up, still on the plastic, and store in an airtight
container in a dark place. Properly prepared and stored, it can last
months (if you don't eat it all first).

Make leather of 1 type of fruit or try mixing flavors. Sprinkle in some
spices you like or add finely chopped nuts before drying. Leather can be
cut or torn off and eaten as it is or soaked in a little liquid to transform
it into jam or sauce.

Using your imagination there is no end to the food you can preserve by drying.

Tina Marie Berntsen

• SMOKING FISH

A smoker is the same as a barbecue except it has a cover and a damper or holes to regulate heat. The fish is cooked more slowly and with less heat. It is succulent and has a delicious smoky flavor. Cooking fish this way is "hot smoking."

Smoking also can be used to preserve fish. Fish are smoked at a lower temperature and for much longer times. This is "cold smoking."

You can buy a small smoker for your boat or you can easily make one from a hibachi or old campstove. The fundamentals of a smoker are: The fire is set on a grate; under the grate is a draft control. About 9 to 12 inches above the fire is the grill for the fish. A foot above the grill is a cover or lid with a hole or vent. The draft control under the fire allows you to control the air—enough to keep the coals going but not to allow flame from drippings.

Whatever kind of smoker you use, you will need a well-calibrated oven thermometer as it takes experience to be able to judge the heat.

A smoker uses charcoal for the initial fire, which is allowed to burn to glowing embers. Then the wood is added for smoking. Hickory is the classic smoking wood, but you can use any hardwood: fruit and nut trees,

maple, beech, alder, oak, willow. Use in the form of chips or sawdust. Do not use conifers or soft woods. They leave a bad taste due to the resin.

Almost all kinds of fish are suitable for smoking. Saltwater types include mackerel, salmon, bonita, tuna, grouper, red snapper, pompano, cod, halibut and sea bass. Freshwater varieties include bass, trout, pike, perch, whitefish, shad and sturgeon.

Small fish are best smoked whole. Large fish need to be split or filleted. Before smoking the fish, there are 2 preliminary steps: Brining and drying.

The fish is first cured in brine. For 1 or 2 pounds fish, use 2½ cups salt and 2 quarts water. The fish is soaked in this mixture for a given period of time.

Brining times:
¼ pound or less....................................30 minutes
½ pound ....45 minutes
1 pound .... 1 hour
2 pounds or more ....2 hours

These times are for lean fish—grouper, halibut, bass, etc. For oily fish, such as mackerel, salmon, trout, cod, increase time by 25%. If the skin is left on, increase by 25% also.

After the brining comes the drying. Remove the fish from the brine and give it a quick rinse in fresh, cold water. Then let dry on a rack, or hanging, preferably in a breezy, shady place. The surface of the fish should be dry and form a pellicle. This will take approximately 3 hours. If the fish is not properly dried, it may soften while smoking.

While smoking, fish should be placed on a wire rack or grid, skin side down and not touching each other. Turn whole fish over once, but do not turn split fish or fillets.

Hot Smoking

First, "cold smoke" for flavor about 30 minutes. This means the smoker should be about 75° to 85°. Then raise the temperature to 125° to 150°. The fish is done when it flakes. If the meat is thick, check with a meat thermometer. It should be 140° in the center. "Hot smoked" fish will keep about 2 weeks in the refrigerator.

Cold Smoking

As with hot smoking, brine and then dry. Smoke at 70° to 85° with a fairly light smoke. Many people just smoke the fish overnight. This way it will keep 1 or 2 weeks in the refrigerator. If you want to preserve fish for longer periods of time, here are the smoking times:

Smoking Time	Keeping Time
24 hours	2 weeks
2 days	4 weeks
3 days	2 months
2 weeks	3 years

It is actually the brining and drying that preserve the fish. Smoking imparts flavor and is essentially a drying process.

Many cooks add spices or marinades between the brining and drying process. This is a spicy recipe for "cold smoked" fish.

Spice-Cured Fish

First brine and drain. Then mix the following ingredients:

4 cups salt
2 cups brown sugar
2 tablespoons saltpeter (this fixes color)
2 tablespoons black pepper

2 tablespoons mace
2 tablespoons cloves
2 tablespoons allspice
2 tablespoons crumbled bay leaves

Rub this on the fish, inside and out. Let stand for 12 hours or overnight; wash off. Dry 3 to 6 hours before "cold smoking."

Here is a spicy marinade for "hot smoking." First, brine 1 pound of fish, cutting brining time by 25%. Drain.

Spicy Marinade

½ cup oil
¼ cup lemon juice
½ cup chopped onion
2 tablespoons catsup
1 tablespoon salt

2 teaspoons sugar
2 tablespoons Worcestershire sauce
2 bay leaves
2 cloves garlic
½ teaspoon pepper

Marinate 1 hour. Allow to dry. Then "hot smoke" at 250° to 275°, until it flakes.

Shellfish also can be smoked. For oysters and clams first steam the shells open. This firms the texture. Then soak in brine mixture, 30 minutes for medium-sized, 45 minutes for large ones.

Rinse, dip in oil and put on foil, then on rack. Smoke at 75° to 80° for 30 minutes, then at 150° for 20 to 30 minutes. Taste to see if they are done. After they are smoked, you can dip them in oil again. Olive oil is especially tasty.

For shrimp, prawns and crayfish, peel while raw; brine 15 to 45 minutes, depending on size; rinse, then dry. Smoke at 85° for 15 minutes, then at 135° for 60 to 90 minutes. They are done when they turn bright orange. They may also be oiled.

Happy smoking!

Cathy Reed

• PICKLING FISH

Contrary to popular opinion, cruising without refrigeration is not a hardship. We chose not to install refrigeration on *Rinaldo,* and we seldom use the icebox for its intended purpose.

However, a problem did arise when we began getting our meals from the sea. Oftentimes we would get a fish that was just too big for the 2 of us to devour in even a couple of meals. We gave away or were forced to throw away the excess, until we discovered pickling.

Pickling requires no extra cooking and is a delicious way to enjoy that oversize fish another day. After reading the recipe you might imagine that you will be eating raw fish. Actually, the acid in the mixture 'cooks' the fish while it marinates.

Conch is also good this way if care is taken to slice it very thinly or beat it well before marinating.

2 cups sliced white fish	2 cloves
1 onion, chopped	1 crushed bay leaf
½ cup vinegar	¼ teaspoon dry mustard
2 tablespoons lemon or lime juice	Pinch of ground ginger, salt and
1 teaspoon sugar	black pepper
Dash of Angostura bitters	Water (to cover)

Slice fish thinly and remove any bloody tissue. Place in a jar or plastic container, mix in remaining ingredients and add water to cover. Cover and let stand in a cool place overnight or longer. Drain and serve.

Sharon Gerl

• CAN YOUR OWN MEAT

As I have never been very domestic (I never baked bread until we were living on the boat), learning the techniques of canning was a little more difficult than learning the simple rules of navigation and basic chart work. But armed with cookbooks, guides from university extension services, and lots of advice from old-timers—I finally made my way through 48 quarts of canned meat.

What started as a trial balloon turned out to be one of the greater successes of our cruising. We actually like the taste of canned meat; in most cases, it tastes equal to or better than fresh.

Now each winter, as we assess the past cruising season and look forward to the next, I begin canning the basics and experimenting with new ideas. The types of meat we have had most success with are roast beef and all the variety of meals one can get from ground beef. Chicken too has been tried, but since it is readily available at reasonable cost, we tend to rely on commercial brands. Attempts with frankfurters and other varieties of meats have not been as successful as hoped.

Our best successes have been with:

Roast beef
Meatballs
Ground beef with seasoning and onion—used for hot dishes
Ground beef patties—to be grilled over charcoal
Plain ground beef—seasoning to be added as required (great for tacos)
Ground beef with salt and pepper, onion, green pepper and tomato paste

It is best to can basic recipes to which specific seasonings and other constituents can be added later. For example, the ground beef and tomato recipe is really a basic recipe for 5 different meals:

Italian Spaghetti

Add mushrooms, garlic, oregano, basil, parsley flakes and 1 can stewed tomatoes. Simmer at least ½ hour, the longer the better. Serve over spaghetti with salad and garlic bread.

Sloppy Joes

Add 1 teaspoon sugar, simmer 30 minutes, serve on bread or hamburger buns.

Chili

Add 1 can kidney beans, 1 can stewed tomatoes and chili powder to taste. Simmer at least 1 hour.

Pizza-Burgers

Add garlic powder, oregano and ½ cup grated Cheddar cheese or 1 can of Cheddar cheese soup. Simmer 20 minutes. Spoon onto half a hamburger bun. Heat in Dutch oven or heavy frying pan 15 minutes. Sometimes we brown the tops with a propane torch.

Goulash

Add 1 package cooked macaroni, 1 cup cubed soft cheese or Cheddar cheese soup—and anything you can get your hands on, such as green beans or kidney beans, garlic and parsley flakes.

The roast beef cans up beautifully and can be used as is, making a delicious gravy to be served over rice or potatoes. It also makes up into a stroganoff that is a gourmet's delight or Beef Burgundy.

As for the canning itself, there are a few points which we have picked up to assure our success. Because the canning process actually tenderizes meat and improves its taste, we do not have to be too fussy about the cuts of meat and can use the less expensive ones.

Basically, in each recipe, the meat is taken off the bone, browned with seasonings, partially cooked, spooned into jars (the quart size works perfectly for our family of 4) and then water or broth is added to cover the meat.

Leave at least 1 inch "breathing space" on top of the liquid. Whenever we have had lids that do not seal, it is because I have cheated on this. Be very careful to wipe the glass rims thoroughly to get rid of any grease or small pieces of meat, add the lids and screw down tightly. Then pressure according to maker's instructions. Our pressure canner is an inexpensive model from Sears Roebuck. It processes 7 quarts at a time.

After canning, cooling and labelling, I pack the jars in their original cases—12 jars to a case. The cases are stored up in the forepeak where the pounding is the greatest—and we have never yet had a jar break.

Bonnie Dahl

• PRESERVING MEAT

Tibor is a beef eater so I was faced with finding a way to keep meat for 3- or 4-week Pacific passages.

I use flank steak as it is versatile and relatively inexpensive. The meat is marinated in a deep plastic container (with a tight-fitting lid) and covered completely (essential or the meat will spoil) with a mixture of oil and vinegar and herbs and spices to taste.

Our refrigeration is not always reliable but tends to keep things fairly cool. I don't know if marinating would work without some kind of icebox.

The ingredients are infinitely variable, but here is the basic marinade:

3 cups oil (olive, peanut, any combination)	Whole peppercorns
1 cup vinegar (or to taste)	Sliced carrots, onions and celery tops (or seed)
Salt	Thyme, parsley, bay leaf

As you get tired of this flavor add a few tablespoons or more of soy sauce, wine, etc.

The meat may be dried and sautéed as is or sliced and cooked with onions, made into stroganoff, Chinese stir-fry, spaghetti sauce . . .

We find the meat stays edible for 3 weeks, as long as it remains covered with the marinade.

Nancy Stefansky

• STORING CANNED HAMS

Canned hams are a staple item on most cruising boats. Through trial and error we've learned which brands we like the best, and they are all stamped "Perishable: Keep Refrigerated."

When stocking up at a large supermarket in Florida, we'd put 3 canned hams in our basket when the butcher walked over and asked, "Will those be stored on a boat?" (Now how did he know? Maybe by our shoes, or our bottom-paint splattered britches!) Then he told us why some are marked "Keep Refrigerated" and some are not. They are all fully cooked, but the "Keep Refrigerated" hams are cooked only *once* prior to canning. The hams that are not marked have been cooked, canned and then cooked *again*. He said we were taking an awful chance if we kept a "Refrigerate" ham unrefrigerated more than a couple of days.

Katy Burke

• WAXING HARD CHEESES

Living on a small boat certainly does teach one to be enterprising. . . .

I used my cheese waxing process on the 20 pounds of cheese that went with me to Mexico aboard *Virago,* and it helped feed 7 ravenous sailors for 1 month with not a speck of mold!

Many things, like cottage and other soft cheese, butter, margarine, eggs, lettuce and vegetables keep for days and days without spoiling when I store them in the bilges or against the hull where it is cool.

On long offshore passages we crave protein other than canned and dried meats or beans, but *Mariposa* has no refrigeration for keeping fresh meats or perishable cheeses. Although some cheeses can be bought pre-waxed, many cannot be purchased in smaller than 10 or 20 pound wheels —once they are opened what do you do with the rest of the cheese? Waxing my own hard cheese at home has been a very easy way to store them for long periods of time.

To wax my own cheese I use:

1. Regular cheesecloth, available at yardage stores and some hardware stores (1 yard, 36 inches wide, will wrap from 10 to 20 pounds of cheese).

2. Apple cider vinegar (to retard the growth of molds).
3. Paraffin wax (about 3 pounds for 10 pounds of cheese).
4. Wax can—a 3 pound coffee can is ideal (with lid, to store unused wax that has already been melted).
5. Double boiler (any large pot that will hold your coffee can and extra water).

I buy 10 or 20 pound chunks of Cheddar, Cassari or other hard cheese (except Swiss), usually from the retail outlet of a cheese factory near our home port (it is cheaper in bulk and usually has no external molds). When possible, I cut it into 2 pound blocks and store it overnight in the bilges to chill—the cold cheese seems to allow the wax to set better. In hot countries where chilling is impossible, a little more wax may be needed.

Each block is wiped lightly with vinegar and wrapped in cheesecloth that has been dipped in vinegar and wrung dry. One layer of cloth is plenty, and try to avoid bulky ends of cloth.

Melt the paraffin in the coffee can set in the larger pot, which should be partially filled with water, as wax flares up rather easily. The large pot also catches drips of wax. (I set my kerosene stove in the cockpit or on the pier to prevent any flare-up from smoking up my wood interior and to eliminate wax odor, as well as lessening chance of fire below.)

Dip each block of wrapped cheese into the melted wax until it is well coated. I set up an assembly line, dipping each block halfway, then setting it on its opposite end, working my way down the row of blocks until there are 5 to 6 coats of wax on each half. Check to be sure the edges and corners are well sealed. Take your time, allowing each coat time to dry before dipping it again. When it appears coated enough, let it cool and recheck again for any cracks or thin spots. If the waxed cheese has oil on the surface, it has thin areas and needs more layers of wax.

I store my cheese in the bilges or against the hull, where it is coolest, packed in Tupperware bread containers, which keep out extra moisture and lessen the chance of breaking corners of wax and spoiling the seal.

Ten pounds of cheese will last 2 of us 4 to 6 weeks; we usually eat it up long before any mold shows but have kept some blocks up to 12 weeks before they were opened—how long we could actually keep it before mold began to grow heavily I have yet to discover . . . although some molds are quite edible. I usually scrape off any bits of mold that I find on older cheeses, just in case.

The whole procedure takes from 1-1½ hours—even in port I wax my cheeses just because of the savings in time and money; and under sail, what could taste better than a heap of good Cassari on spaghetti?

Chris Randall

• BAYER TAKES THE HEADACHE OUT OF PRESERVING KEY LIME JUICE

A recent SSCA bulletin mentioned preserving lime juice with aspirin (2 tablets to 1 quart lime juice). We tried the aspirin method and it works very well, without altering the taste of the lime juice. In our opinion, Bayer's method replaces the Old Sour method that we had been using, as it's easier to make, better tasting and can be used in a wider variety of recipes due to the lack of preserving salt.

Old Sour

To every 2 cups fresh lime juice, add 1 tablespoon salt. Place in sterilized bottle and shake well to dissolve salt. Old Sour ferments and turns dark. Use wherever you would use fresh lime juice. It is supposed to keep for months.

Dale Stennett

CHAPTER 3

SNACKS AND HORS D'OEUVRES

FINGER FOOD

• CHIPS AHOY!

Since you buy tortillas in Mexico by the kilo you will have plenty left to make your own chips.

Cut your leftover tortillas (up to 5 days old) in triangular wedges. Heat 1 inch of oil in a frying pan until it is almost smoking, then lower the heat a bit. Quick-fry the tortilla wedges on each side and dry on paper towels. Add salt. It is an art to make them crispy and not soggy, so just keep practicing.

Soozi Pressley

• SWEET AND SOUR LOBSTER

Teaching school gives me time for long summer cruises, but I like to keep the cooking simple to fit in with my goombay attitude.

I use ingredients that are not difficult to store on a small cruising boat but that make delightful differences in cooking fresh or canned food.

3 or 4 medium lobster tails	1 egg
1 envelope pancake mix	1 jar sweet and sour sauce

Clean and cut up the lobster into bite-sized chunks. Dip in beaten egg, then roll in dry pancake mix with a little pinch of salt and pepper added.

Fry in fresh oil until golden brown. Drain and serve with a small bowl of sweet and sour sauce. Dip and eat. Serves 4.

Howard Olsen

• SUMMER SNACKS

When anchored in our favorite harbor, we like to have snacks which are easy to fix—so we can sample them as soon as possible and enjoy each other's company and the company of our friends—without spending too much time preparing the goodies.

Meat/Olive Puffs

½ cup butter or margarine	Stuffed olives
2 cups grated sharp cheese	Precooked sausage (cut in small
1½ cups flour	pieces)
1 teaspoon paprika	

Cream together cheese and shortening. Work in flour and paprika with your hands. Put dough in a cool place for 15 to 20 minutes for easier handling. Mold ½ teaspoon dough around the olive or small meat piece. Bake at 400° for 10 to 12 minutes.

Dreamy Deviled Eggs

6 hard-cooked eggs
1 cup chopped cheese with chives
3 tablespoons dry sauterne
2 tablespoons mayonnaise

¼ teaspoon Worcestershire sauce
¼ teaspoon prepared mustard
Salt and pepper to taste

Cut eggs in half lengthwise; remove yolks. To yolks add remaining ingredients and blend well. Heap into egg whites; sprinkle with paprika.

Little Pizzas

1 loaf cocktail bread, sliced
Precooked sausage (or other meat)
Tomato sauce (small can)
Grated cheese

Sliced mushrooms
1 package Lipton onion soup
2 eggs

Mix sauce, soup and eggs. Spread on bread. Top with cheese, meat and mushrooms. Bake at 350° for 15 minutes. Serve hot.

Bobbie Steinke

• LITTLE SNACKS

Mix chopped onion, parsley and mayonnaise. Broil some bits of bread, put 1 teaspoon of the mixture on top and cover with Cheddar cheese. Broil for 2 minutes.

Cut frankfurters into 3 pieces. Roll in ketchup and wrap a slice of bacon around each. Bake 5 minutes at 400°.

Remove crusts and flatten slices of bread. Spread with cream cheese, top with a slice of cooked ham and 3 asparagus spears (diagonally). Roll up and fix with toothpicks. Pour melted butter and cheese over the lot and bake 5 to 8 minutes at 400°.

Ginette Villeneuve

• BAKED CLAMS

Dig 6 or more large quahogs (4 to 6 inch) and steam in a large pot with 1 inch water until fully open and tender.

Chop the meat into small pieces and mix with ¼ cup mayonnaise, ¼ cup sour cream, ¼ teaspoon garlic powder, 1 tablespoon chopped scallion greens, 1 teaspoon prepared mustard or horseradish.

Fill the half-shells level and top with breadcrumbs and 1 teaspoon of butter. Cook about 30 minutes at 300° or until tops are brown.

Serve as an hors d'oeuvre or a first course but always make more than you think you can eat—they go fast.

Dulcy Seiffer

• MUNCH

Cruising for 7 to 10 days at a time for a family of 4 plus a dog and a cat takes planning. Everyone pitches in. Jobs are rotated. And everyone respects the others' needs for privacy and to get away at times.

One food we never forget to take, for a quick spin around the river or a 10-day cruise, is our version of "munch." It's filling, nourishing, good and easy to grab.

The ingredients can be varied. I try to avoid salted and flavored seeds and nuts, but if it looks good, I try it.

Just mix together:

1 box chopped dates	2 large cans soy nuts
1 box raisins (white or dark)	2 large cans sunflower seeds
1 large can mixed nuts	2 large cans pumpkin seeds
2 large cans peanuts	

Delicious!

Lucie Alderman

• HUA SENG TAN

Many times in our travels, big ships have offered their help and friendship. They have often provided useful advice, hard-to-find supplies, technical assistance and sometimes a good meal.

The *Kota Melur,* a Singaporean freighter, arrived in Galle Harbor, Sri Lanka, on a 4-month cruise. Her Chinese crew returned our hospitality by throwing a great party where the following recipe from the second cook, Steve, was a smashing success.

2 pounds shelled, raw peanuts
3 whole garlic cloves, crushed
Cooking oil
2 cups sugar

3 cups water
3–4 egg whites, slightly beaten
Flour

Cook the garlic in a small amount of oil for 1 minute. Add the sugar and water and continue cooking sauce over a low flame for 1 hour until thick. Set aside to cool. Pour egg whites over nuts and toss. Add sauce and toss until well coated.

Place 1 cup of flour on a paper towel, then 1 cup nuts. Top with more flour, toss and roll with hands until well coated but not too thick or lumpy. Shake excess off in a strainer; then, toss by hand again. Continue until all nuts are coated.

Heat 1½ inch oil in a large saucepan. Deep fry nuts in 1 cup installments for 5 minutes. After the first minute, stir gently with a slotted spoon. Dry on a paper towel. To keep crisp, store in a tightly sealed container.

Pat Noda

• DEEP-FRIED OYSTERS

Juggernaut's oyster chef d'oeuvre is crumbed and deep-fried oysters. Dip the oysters in a mixture of egg, milk and spices, then roll in dried bread crumbs. To prevent the crumbs from falling off, allow the egg mixture to dry before frying in hot oil. A complete crumb coating mix from a store shelf is the most practical to use on a small cruising yacht.

Patrick Childress

• WINE TOAST

Whenever we eat Italian style we never seem to finish the grinder-size rolls. We came up with a way to use them, not waste them.

Slice the roll into ¼ inch to ½ inch pieces and soak them in white wine for a few minutes. Sauté in butter until they are golden and crispy.

They are really good with fish!

Karen Chase

• BAKED BACKBONE

Fishing is a favorite pastime, and after years of discarding the back-bone we have discovered a delicious snack.

After filleting the fish, rinse the backbone in saltwater. Place on aluminum foil or on a cookie sheet. Dot with butter, season with salt and pepper and bake in a hot oven, 400°, until done (time depends on size). It will be slightly crisp. Cool briefly, then serve as a cocktail snack. Just break pieces off and enjoy!

Karen Huso

• CRISPY FRIED BANANAS

Pour a generous amount of oil in a frying pan. While the oil is heating, peel green bananas with a paring knife and cut into slices lengthwise. Fry for about 15 minutes or until light brown. Drain on paper towels and salt to taste.

Green bananas will make crispy tidbits, but slightly ripened fruit can also be fried if cut in cross sections.

Joan Pease

SPREADS AND DIPS

• LIVER PÂTÉ

1 can liverwurst spread
2 tablespoons onion, finely chopped
2 teaspoons butter or margarine
1 small dill pickle, chopped
¼ teaspoon garlic powder or
    1 clove garlic, crushed

2 teaspoons lemon juice
2 tablespoons mayonnaise
1 hard-cooked egg, finely chopped
Salt and pepper

Crush the liverwurst. Sauté onion in butter until soft, then combine with liverwurst. Blend in remaining ingredients and season to taste.

Serve on crackers with pre-dinner drinks while the main course is cooking.

Norma Lemon

• BRANDIED PÂTÉ

½ pound chicken livers
2 tablespoons butter or margarine
1 small onion
1 small bay leaf
3 rashers bacon
¼ teaspoon ground thyme

1 tablespoon port wine
2 tablespoons brandy
¼ cup mushrooms
½ cup cream
Salt and pepper

Clean and dry chicken livers. Heat butter in a pan, add livers, finely chopped onion, thyme, bay leaf, finely chopped bacon and mushrooms and sauté for 7 minutes.

Remove from heat, discard bay leaf and place ingredients in a blender (including the butter from the pan). Add cream and blend until smooth. Press through a sieve.

Stir in port and brandy, season to taste and refrigerate until cold.

Margot Savage

• CORNED BEEF SPREAD

1 can corned beef	1 teaspoon yellow mustard
2 hard boiled eggs, chopped	¼ teaspoon black pepper
½ green pepper, chopped	Mayonnaise—enough to bind
2 tablespoons pickle relish	

Break up the corned beef with a fork. Stir in the other ingredients and add enough mayonnaise to bind it all together the way you like it for spreading. (Great for regular or open-faced sandwiches.) When you are out of bread at sea, serve it on crackers. It makes a substantial snack to go with your favorite sundowners in the cockpit.

Beth Liggett

• GOOD SPREADS

We prefer eating 4 or 5 small meals or snacks a day rather than the traditional 3 meals. This eating pattern leaves us less lethargic and does provide us with the energy to meet the demands of cruising.

Crab Spread

2 cans crabmeat (1 pound fresh crabmeat if available)	3 heaping tablespoons mayonnaise
	2 tablespoons capers, chopped
Juice and pulp of 1 lemon	Salt and pepper to taste

Combine all ingredients and chill. Serve on crackers.

Cheese Spread

This spread keeps well and is especially good on hard breads.

1 cup cottage cheese	1 cup blue or feta cheese
1 cup cream cheese	Lots of fresh ground pepper

Mix together to form a smooth spread. This can be eaten as is or any of the following can be added:

1 cucumber or	1 small onion, chopped
1 zucchini, finely chopped or	

Marian Saffo-Cogswell

• SHRIMP SPREAD

1 jar frozen shrimp cocktail and
    sauce

8 ounce package cream cheese
Extra chopped shrimp (optional)

Bring frozen cocktail and cream cheese to room temperature and mix.

Joan Young

• SQUID SPREAD

Don't overlook the small squid that arrive on deck from a breaking sea. They make excellent eating. To clean, cut off head, reach inside the hollow fish for the transparent backbone and remove. Clean out all entrails but save a small amount of "ink." Cut the cylindrical squid into tiny donuts, then dip each donut in egg batter and cook in hot olive oil. Brown each side 30 seconds.

Olive oil is the flavor secret when cooking seafood.

If you saved the squid ink you can make a Spanish squid spread.

Combine in a small saucepan 6 to 8 ground squid, ¼ cup onion and ¼ cup green pepper (diced), ¼ cup lemon juice or vinegar, a pinch of salt and pepper and 1 or 2 drops of "ink" for color. Cook for 1 minute, cool, then spread on saltwater bread.

Joan Casanova

• SALMON PARTY LOG

According to the number of guests, simply double or triple the amounts.

1 can salmon (pink preferably),
    drained, boned and skinned
8 ounce package cream cheese,
    softened to room temperature
Juice of ½ lemon
2 tablespoons horseradish

2 teaspoons Dijon-style mustard
Few drops hot sauce
1 cup walnuts, finely chopped
1 bunch fresh parsley, finely
    chopped

Fork the salmon until well flaked, add the cream cheese and mix well. Add lemon juice, horseradish, mustard and hot sauce with a dash of salt and pepper.

Chill for several hours so that molding will be easier. Finely chop the walnuts and wash and chill the parsley before chopping.

Take out the salmon mixture and set on a large piece of waxed paper. Wrap the salmon in the waxed paper and roll out to about 2 inches in thickness. Mix together the walnuts and parsley and sprinkle all over the log.

Chill until the guests arrive, then serve on a platter with an assortment of crackers. Cherry tomatoes or radishes make a nice garnish.

Kathy Russell

• RED CAVIAR AND CREAM CHEESE

Beat 1 pound softened cream cheese until creamy. Beat in the grated rind of 3 lemons. Mound on a serving plate or dish and store in icebox. To serve, make a hole in the center about 1 inch deep and fill the hole with 1 jar (4 ounces) red caviar, letting a little dribble down the sides. Serve with melba toast and quartered pickled eggs.

Joan Young

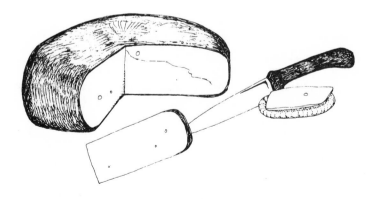

• OTA

Cruising in the tropics taught us to try out local dishes and find ones suitable for the galley of a small yacht. Outside of main cities we often find the local people cook on 1 or 2 burners using kerosene, just like us!

Now we use combinations of fresh local food and old standbys to make a change from our regular fare.

In Mexico this dish is called "ceviche", in French Polynesia, "poisson cru" and in the Samoas, "ota". All start the same. Dice 1 pound fish fillets. Place in a glass bowl. Cover with lime juice and marinate 4 to 5 hours at room temperature.

Now comes the variation.

1 onion, finely chopped	¼ cup olive oil
2 medium tomatoes, chopped	1 tablespoon oregano or parsley
1 jalapeño pepper, finely chopped	Salt and pepper to taste
⅛ teaspoon cumin	

Drain lime juice from fish. Combine fish with ½ cup coconut milk and 1 finely chopped onion. Salt to taste.

Sue McBride

• A MEXICAN HORS D'OEUVRE

Don't tell your friends what this is until they've tried it—then they'll like it. It is a raw fish dish and a delicacy in Mexico. Ceviche is the name, and the fish isn't really raw because it is cooked by chemical action instead of heat. Any delicately flavored white-meat fish can be used. In Mexico sierra is best, then dorado (mahi-mahi), halibut or less expensive kinds will do. Because of my training on small boats cruising far from markets, I know that creativity and imagination are more important than exact ingredients:

1 pound fish fillets	Mexican cilantro (a dozen leaves, if you have them)
1 cup fresh lime or lemon juice	
Tomato (2 should do)	Any other compatible things you have hanging around (avocado, olives, etc.)
1 bell pepper	
Onion (about ½, let your conscience be your guide)	
Celery (2 crunchy stalks)	Spices to taste

Cut and flake fish into dime-sized pieces. Cover with lime juice in bowl for about 3 hours (fish will look cooked when properly marinated). Stir and toss about every 30 minutes. In a separate bowl combine diced tomato, onion, celery, bell pepper, cilantro and whatever. Drain and rinse lime juice from fish. Mix other ingredients with fish (in about equal parts) and let stand in refrigerator several hours. Serve as you would a shrimp cocktail or as a dip with crackers at happy hour . . . Salud!

Dix Brow

• CHEESE BALL

8 ounces packaged cream cheese, softened to room temperature
1–1¼ cup hard Cheddar cheese, shredded
½ cup fresh green pepper, finely chopped

4–5 fresh green onions (bulbs only), finely chopped
2 tablespoons mayonnaise (optional)
Salted sunflower seeds

Combine the 2 cheeses, green pepper, onion and mayonnaise until well blended. Form mixture into 2 balls or logs and roll in the sunflower seeds. Wrap in foil and refrigerate. Allow cheese ball to come to room temperature before serving—this really brings out the flavor. This cheese ball may also be frozen for serving at a later date—great for short cruises!

Susan Andersen

• GOOD SNACKS

Space is limited on our Venture 21, *Reality*, so we use a Sterno Sea-Swing stove. These recipes can be prepared at home ahead of time or on board.

Cheese Ball

8 ounce package cream cheese
5 ounces processed
    sharp cheese spread
2 jars Roquefort cheese spread

1 small onion, chopped
1 clove garlic, mashed
½ cup chopped walnuts

Let cheeses warm, then beat until fluffy and blended. Beat in garlic and onion. Chill a few hours. Roll into ball. Roll cheese ball in chopped walnuts until coated. Keep chilled until firm. Serve with whole wheat crackers.

Pickled Mushrooms

In a saucepan combine:

⅓ cup red wine vinegar
⅓ cup salad oil
1 small onion, thinly sliced and
    separated into rings

1 teaspoon salt
2 teaspoons dried parsley flakes
1 teaspoon prepared mustard
1 tablespoon brown sugar

Bring to a boil. Add 2 6-ounce cans mushroom crowns, drained; simmer 5 to 6 minutes. Chill in covered dish a few hours. Stir occasionally. Drain. Makes 2 cups.

Marinated Artichokes

2 tablespoons lemon juice
2 tablespoons salad oil
Dash of salt
1 teaspoon sugar

¼ teaspoon oregano, crushed
¼ teaspoon tarragon, crushed
15 ounce can artichoke hearts,
    drained

Combine all ingredients and 2 tablespoons of water in a bowl. Cover and chill overnight. Drain and sprinkle with paprika. Serve with cocktail forks. Makes 2 cups.

Lynn M. Dufer

• CURRY DIP

Curry dip for raw vegetables is made from ingredients found in most galleys. I use carrots, cucumbers or whatever is available in the native markets.

Mix together:

⅔ cup mayonnaise   1 tablespoon or more curry powder
⅓ cup ketchup

CHEESE SPREAD

Cheese spread for crackers is complemented by peanuts and cherry tomatoes served with it.

Mix together:

8 ounce package cream cheese   Splash of Worcestershire sauce
1 to 2 tablespoons horseradish   Bit of grated onion

ONION SPREAD

Onion spread is terrific, especially on French bread available in the French islands we've visited.

Mix together:

Mayonnaise and chopped onion and spread on slices of fresh bread. Heat until golden under the broiler.

INDONESIAN FISH PÂTÉ

Mix together:

1 can tuna   1 ounce oatmeal
3 ounces grated cheese   1 tablespoon grated onion
1 egg   Generous splash of pepper, nutmeg,
1 tablespoon butter   curry, paprika, cloves, thyme,
1 tablespoon milk   Tabasco, Maggi seasoning

Grease an 8-inch baking sheet. Add all of above and sprinkle with bread crumbs. Bake at 350° for 45 minutes. Serve sliced in small squares.

Sheryl Krawchuk

• SUNDOWNERS

We often raft up with friends for informal entertaining, so I take along snacks prepared at home and stored in the icebox for lunch or cocktail hour.

Tangy Cheese Spread

Grind together:

½ pound strong cheese   6 to 8 green olives
¼ cup green pepper

Add 1 8-ounce package cream cheese and chives and 1 tablespoon mayonnaise. Mix with a fork and season with salt and pepper. Spreads best at room temperature.

Chili Sauce Dip *(great for cholesterol watchers!)*

12 ounce bottle chili sauce   ¼ cup finely chopped celery
2 tablespoons lemon juice   ¼ teaspoon salt
3 to 4 drops Tabasco sauce   1 tablespoon minced parsley
2 tablespoons horseradish   ⅔ cup low-fat cottage cheese

Blend all ingredients until creamy, then chill. Serve with melba toast or crisp raw vegetables.

Marinated Mushrooms

Marinate a 10-ounce can of button mushrooms in:

⅓ cup wine vinegar   ¼ teaspoon marjoram
⅓ cup olive oil   2 tablespoons chopped parsley or
½ teaspoon onion salt   1 teaspoon parsley flakes
¼ teaspoon celery salt

Cover and chill for at least 4 hours.
These will keep several days if refrigerated.
Swanya Vah! (Gaelic for Good Health!)

Jean Scott

• SPICY STUFF

At the end of the day after sailing, snorkeling or working on the boat, everyone is ready for a drink and a good appetizer. We tend to like spicy foods, and I have developed several dip recipes which can be made quickly with canned goods and cheeses we normally carry aboard.

Mexican Bean Dip

1 can refried beans
1 can jalapeño relish

Pour relish into small saucepan. Place over low heat and stir in beans until well mixed and heated through. For a spicier dip, add a fresh jalapeño pepper chopped finely. For a milder taste, stir in and let melt ½ cup grated Cheddar cheese or sour cream.

Chili Dip

1 can chili   1 medium onion
1 small can green chilies   ½ pound Velveeta cheese

Pour chili into small saucepan. Chop onions and chilies and add to pan. Stir over low heat, gradually adding cheese. Continue stirring until cheese is completely melted.

Suzi DuRant

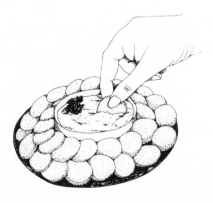

• EASY HOMMOS BI TAHINI *(Chick-pea and sesame dip)*

14 ounce can hommos bi tahini
1 tablespoon salad oil
1 tablespoon lemon juice
1 clove garlic, finely minced, or
⅛ teaspoon garlic powder
(optional)

Salt, to taste
Parsley or mint, finely chopped (if
available)

Mix well and shape into a hollow pie-shape in a shallow bowl or plate. Fill the hollow with a small additional amount of oil and lemon juice and garnish edges with chopped herbs.

Serve as a dip with pita (Middle East pocket bread), French bread, crackers or fresh raw vegetables.

The tasty dip provides a complete protein because of the combination of legume (chick-peas) and seeds and is much lower in cholesterol than cheese dips. It also keeps well without refrigeration. If kept tightly covered, using up most leftovers the next day should not pose any health hazard.

If you prefer to make hommos bi tahini from scratch:

Blend in a food processor or blender:

19 ounce can chick-peas, drained
⅓ cup sesame seed paste (tahini)

⅓ cup lemon juice
Oil to make a smooth (but not
runny) paste

Tahini is readily available in health food stores or Middle East stores, while chick-peas are available in most grocery stores.

Pita, hommos bi tahini and fresh vegetable sticks make an excellent lunch under way, especially if the meal is topped off with fresh fruit.

Anna Patrick

• CURRY VEGETABLE DIP

½ cup sour cream   1 teaspoon curry powder
1 tablespoon mayonnaise

Combine all ingredients, chill. Serve with celery, cucumber, green pepper, carrots, radishes, etc.

Joyan Thompson

• GUACAMOLE OR SOPA DE AGUACATE

This is a no-cooking dish. In Mexico it's used as a dip for crackers or potato chips, in Columbia as a soup or a first course for lunch or as a spread on the good coastal bread.

Press the meat of 1 ripe avocado through a potato ricer. Add 1 tablespoon minced onion, juice of 1 lemon, ¼ teaspoon salt and a pinch of chili powder.

Mix, chill and serve.

Ted Squier

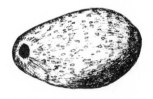

• AVOCADO SMASH

This is refreshing when the sun is a bit too strong and can be varied infinitely to suit individual tastes and avoid repetition. Thoroughly mash 1 avocado with the closest fork. Season with garlic salt and fresh ground pepper. Then fold into a 12-ounce container of cottage cheese. Garnish with chives and chopped black or green olives.

Jack and Pat Tyler

• AVOCADO AND BANANA GUACAMOLE

1 ripe avocado
2 small ripe bananas (or 1 large)
½ medium-sized lime
2 heaping tablespoons mayonnaise

½ teaspoon vegetable salt
⅛ teaspoon black pepper
1 small onion, diced
1 ripe tomato, diced (optional)

Cut the avocado in half, plant the seed on shore, and scoop out the meat into a mixing bowl. Add the bananas and mash with a fork or potato masher. Mix in lime juice and all other ingredients until well blended. Pour into a serving dish and serve with taco chips, potato chips or crackers. This also makes a delicious spread on tostados, topped with shredded lettuce, tomatoes and grated cheese.

Pami Webb

• ROMANIAN SALAD OR DIP

Grill or bake 2 medium eggplants until they are soft. Remove the skin, chop and pulp the flesh, then mix with a few spoonfuls of mayonnaise, salt and pepper and very finely chopped raw onions to taste. This is an excellent dip, or it can be spread thickly on fresh bread at lunchtime.

Gwenda Cornell

CHAPTER **4**

GARNISHES

DRESSINGS

• JAPANESE SALAD DRESSING

½ cup catsup
2 tablespoons mayonnaise
¼ cup soy sauce

¼ cup teriyaki sauce or saki
1 teaspoon powdered ginger
2 teaspoons lemon juice

Combine all ingredients and serve over cabbage or lettuce salad.

Sara Ackley

• SPINACH SALAD DRESSING

Combine:

¼ cup red wine vinegar
¼ cup lemon juice
½ cup salad oil

3 tablespoons Parmesan cheese
¼ teaspoon salt, dash pepper

Joan Young

PRESERVES

• SUNSHINE PRESERVES

My grandmother made this back home on the farm in Indiana. Now my girls enjoy making it aboard *La Donna Ann,* our 27-foot sloop, which we cruise out of Sarnia, Ontario.

3 cups sugar	4 cups fruit (whole berries, sliced
2 tablespoons lemon juice	peaches, etc.)

Mix ingredients together in a pan. Stir very gently, but mix well. Let sit for about an hour. Cook, stirring constantly, until it boils, then let it boil hard for 4 minutes without stirring.

Cool, uncovered, then pour into a plastic container so that it is no more than ¾ inch deep. Cover with clear plastic, leaving a half inch opening. (I use a square Tupperware bread-keeper.)

Set it out on deck in direct sunlight and stir the preserves gently, turning the fruit once every hour. It is done when the fruit is plump and the juice is as thick as corn syrup. It will get thicker when cold.

Put into clean jars and seal with paraffin wax. These preserves have excellent color and texture and make great Christmas gifts.

La Donna Lennington

• MANGO PRESERVES

5 mangoes   1 tablespoon lemon juice
½ cup sugar

Peel and seed the mangoes, then mash. Put in a saucepan with sugar and cook slowly until the desired thickness is reached. Stir in the lemon juice, cool and serve.

Karen Rogers

• FRUITY JAMS

What to do with that huge stalk of bananas all going ripe at once? Banana jam, of course! And when the locals come alongside with a pirogue full of ripe papaya? That's right; golden papaya preserves.

Banana Jam

3 cups bananas, chopped   ¼–⅓ cup lime juice
1 cup orange juice   3½ cups sugar

Mix fruit, juices and sugar together in a heavy pan and bring quickly to a boil. Turn down to a rolling simmer, stirring and scraping sides of pan occasionally. Cook until thickened, about 20 to 30 minutes. Test by placing a spoonful of jam on a saucer. The jam is done when it jells on cooling.

Fill hot sterilized jars with jam. Make sure rims are clear of drips before screwing lids on tightly. Cool away from draft, label and date.

Two variations:

Banana-Rum Jam

After jam is cooked, add 1 tablespoon of dark Caribbean rum for each ½ pint of jam, stir well and continue as above.

Hippo Jam

Add to other ingredients 1 stick of cinnamon for a lovely pink color and spicy flavor. Remove stick after cooking and continue as above.

Yield: Approximately 3 to 4 half-pint jars.

Golden Papaya Preserves

4 cups peeled, seeded and chopped
    papaya
½ cup lime juice
Chopped fresh ginger root, to taste
    (You can experiment with

amounts. I use up to 1 whole
root, as we enjoy the spiciness
of ginger.)
3½ cups sugar

Bring fruit, juice, ginger and sugar to a rolling boil, then turn down to a rolling simmer and cook for 20 to 30 minutes or until set when tested on a saucer as explained above. Put into hot sterilized jars, clean rims and seal.

Yield: Approximately 3 to 4 half-pint jars.

Roxy Darling

• PRICKLY PEARS AND MANGOES

The one thing we miss while living aboard is a garden. So when I feel the urge to fill my jelly jars I comb the seashore for what's available.

Prickly Pear Jelly

While cruising the East Coast and the Florida Keys keep your eyes open for areas that have exposed rocky or sandy beaches. You may find a patch of prickly pear cacti (opuntia humifusa) growing above the tidal zone.

If the time is right (June to August in the north, October to March in Florida) you may find hundreds of plump, dark magenta fruits on the cacti. Do not pick with bare hands; they are covered with tufts of hair-like prickles. If the fruit breaks off easily and is juicy at the break, it is ready for jelly.

The tough outer skin and prickles must be peeled off—keep a pair of tweezers handy to remove prickles that inevitably will stick in your skin, however careful you are!

Put the peeled fruits in a colander and push the fruit through with both hands. You must separate the large seeds from the pulp and juice. It's really quite fun, though you may need a swim once in a while to avoid being permanently stained by the fruit.

For a yield of 4 8-ounce jars or 2 16-ounce jars:

1 cup prickly pear juice and pulp   ⅓ cup lime or lemon juice
1 box powdered pectin

Boil together for 1 minute, then add 3 cups of sugar. Boil hard for 3 full minutes, stirring constantly. Remove from the heat, skim the foam off and pour into sterilized jars. Seal with paraffin or 2-piece screw-band lids. Great for Christmas gifts!

If you are lucky enough to be near an abundant supply of the fantastically delicious mango, try this chutney. The unlucky ones can substitute underripe and very firm apples, peaches or pears.

Mango Chutney

1 seeded and chopped lemon   1½ teaspoons salt
1 skinned and minced clove garlic   ¼ teaspoon Cayenne pepper
2¼ cups brown sugar   2 cups cider vinegar
1½ cups seeded raisins   5–5½ cups peeled and chopped firm
¾ cup cut-up crystallized ginger   and slightly underripe mangoes

Put the lemon in an open kettle (preferably enamel or stainless steel) with sugar, vinegar, garlic, salt and Cayenne pepper. Boil for 30 minutes, stirring frequently. Add the mangoes, raisins and ginger. Boil slowly, stirring to prevent sticking, until the fruit is tender but not mushy and syrup is thick, about 30 minutes more. Ladle boiling chutney into sterilized pint or half-pint jars. Cap immediately with 2-piece screwband lids. Makes 3 pints or 6 half-pints.

For those who are not familiar with canning procedures, please read the directions that accompany jars or refer to the canning section of your favorite cookbook. Canning is not difficult and can be very satisfying, but precautions must be taken to ensure that your results are not spoiled by contaminants. In a boat situation, it will take a little planning and coordinating. Elaborate equipment is not necessary, for I do it with only a 1-burner stove. Just make sure that you make 1 batch at a time, and do not hurry yourself. Homemade goodies are a real treat, so have fun and good luck!

Nancy Hitchins

• CRUISING CHUTNEY

After 14 years of living aboard different boats, from a 50-foot yawl to a 34-foot sloop, back to a 50-footer and finally to our present 27-foot trailerable sailboat, I find galley size makes no difference in what or how I cook, only in the variety of foods we can carry.

Occasionally I try to spice up our canned meats, or fresh meats if we are cruising near shopping areas, with a good complementary sauce. Our Cruising Chutney goes great with a canned ham or pork.

1 pound can applesauce
2 boxes dried mincemeat pie filling
2 tablespoons cornstarch

3 tablespoons to 1 cup vinegar
(according to how tart you
want it to taste)

Cut block of mincemeat into cubes, add to saucepan with applesauce and put on low heat. Combine half the vinegar with the cornstarch. Add slowly to pan, stirring all the while. Turn up heat and stir until the cornstarch is cooked and won't lump. Let simmer for 5 minutes. Taste for tartness and add rest of the vinegar if wanted. Serve hot or cold.

Arliss Newcomb

SAUCES

• FRESH TOMATO SAUCE

Fresh tomato sauce makes a difference. It's excellent with a pasta or in any dish requiring tomato purée.

Chop a suitable quantity of ripe tomatoes, 1 small onion, 1 carrot and 2 cloves garlic. Add salt, pepper, chopped parsley, basil or marjoram and simmer until it makes a purée.

Gwenda Cornell

• HOMEMADE BARBECUE SAUCE

1 medium onion, chopped
2 cloves garlic, minced, or 1
    teaspooon garlic powder
⅓ cup vegetable oil or margarine
2½ cups tomato sauce
¼ cup water
1 cup sugar (brown is best)
2 tablespoons molasses (use less
    with brown sugar)

½ cup prepared mustard
1 teaspoon salt
1 teaspoon allspice
1 tablespoon crushed red pepper
1½ tablespoons dried parsley or 1
    sprig of fresh
1 teaspoon Liquid Smoke
¾ cup lemon juice
1 tablespoon soy sauce

Sauté chopped onion and minced garlic in oil or margarine until onion is clear. A large cast iron Dutch oven is best for this. Add tomato sauce, molasses, water, sugar, mustard, salt, allspice, red pepper and parsley. Bring to a boil, reduce heat and let simmer for 1 hour. Add lemon juice, Liquid Smoke and soy sauce. Cook 10–15 minutes.

Rhonda Harris

• TERIYAKI MARINADE (For 1–1½ pounds of steak)

½ cup soy sauce
2 tablespoons sugar
1 teaspoon dry ginger (½ inch cube
    of fresh, crushed)

1 or 2 cloves garlic, crushed
1 tablespoon vinegar
½ cup sherry or cooking wine
Dash MSG

This is the basic combination, the amounts of ingredients can be altered according to your taste. Sesame oil can be added (2 tablespoons) for an interesting variation. Also, splash in a few drops of Tabasco sauce if you like the hot taste of chilies. Fresh ginger is best if you can find it. Bourbon can be substituted for cooking wine.

To barbecue meat, fish or chicken, cook on 1 side, then dip in marinade before turning. You can continue to dip the meat as it cooks to ensure a delicious juicy coating and use up the good sauce.

Demaris Fredericksen

• SECRET CHINESE MARINADE

4 tablespoons hoisin sauce   3 tablespoons soy sauce
1 clove garlic, crushed   ½ teaspoon grated fresh ginger
¼ cup sherry

Mix and pour over beef or pork.
For fish and fowl, use 4 tablespoons plum sauce in place of hoisin sauce. You will find that barbecued, baked or broiled meat never tasted so good.

Dianna Schwierzke

• SHIPBOARD COTTAGE CHEESE AND SOUR CREAM

Like bread, cottage cheese and sour cream do not keep very well without refrigeration, but they can be made on board with ingredients that keep indefinitely. The finished product does not seem to suffer from all the jostling and temperature changes in the marine environment.

Sour Cream

You need 1 quart milk (reconstituted powdered or diluted evaporated milk) and ½ cup buttermilk (powdered buttermilk is available at supermarkets and health food stores). Mix together and let stand in a place where the temperature will be 75°–80° for 12–15 hours, until the mixture thickens and sets. Where air temperatures are not high enough, warm the milk and pour into a wide-mouthed vacuum bottle, or wrap a tightly covered container in towels or a sleeping bag.

When the mixture has a jelly-like consistency, pour it into a cloth-lined colander set over another pan to drain. Set the whole arrangement in a cool place for 4 to 8 hours until it is quite thick. An occasional stir will speed the process. Save the whey to use as the liquid when making pancakes or bread. Serve the sour cream with fruit or brown sugar or any way you like.

Cottage Cheese

Proceed as for sour cream, but allow mixture to clabber until it is about as stiff as jello. Cut gently into 1 to 2 inch cubes and add 2 cups water. Heat to 100° and hold that heat (more or less) for about 1 hour, stirring occasionally. As the whey is driven from the curds they will settle and become compact. Drain. This whey can also be used for liquid in cooking.

Beth Schwarzman

• GRINGO SOUR CREAM

This recipe presupposes that you do not have access to fresh sour cream and have only canned possibilities. Mix 1 can of chilled Nestlé's Media Crema with 2 tablespoons lemon juice. Add a dash of garlic and salt to taste. Chill again for 1 hour, then re-taste. If not sour enough, add more lemon and chill again.

This can be used as a topping on enchiladas or as the base for your favorite dip . . . the classic being guacamole . . . just add a couple of mashed avocados to this "sour cream" with some chopped onion, cumin, a splash of hot sauce and salt to taste.

Soozi Pressley

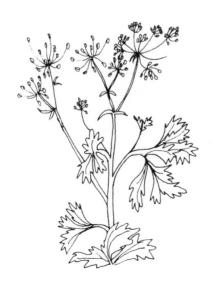

• COCONUT MILK

Philippine cooking, like most South Pacific cooking, calls for the use of coconut milk in many recipes. Today, in any ordinary supermarket, you can find packaged dessicated coconut or tinned coconut milk. For those cruising in the tropics, finding fresh coconuts should be no problem. Here are 2 ways of making coconut milk:

Using Fresh Coconut

Pierce the eyes of the coconut and discard liquid. Crack coconut in half and grate the meat. Soak coconut flesh in 2 cups water and leave for 15 to 20 minutes to soften. Squeeze out liquid with cheesecloth or strainer. (The proportion used is always 2 cups water to 1 cup grated coconut.) Do not use young coconuts.

Using Desiccated Coconut

Use 1½ cups water or water-and-milk mixture to every cup of desiccated coconut. Pour desiccated coconut in a bowl and add water or water-milk mixture. Stir well. Let stand for 15 minutes. Squeeze out liquid with cheesecloth or strainer.

Shirley Young-Shannon

• ANOTHER METHOD FOR COCONUT MILK

To make coconut milk, first shake the nut. If you hear liquid inside, it's ready for milking. Remove the husk (store-bought nuts usually have been husked), puncture the eyes of the nut and drain the water into a pan. Reserve.

Crack the shell and remove the white meat. Grate finely into a bowl. Add enough water to the coconut water to make 2 cups, heat to a boil then pour over the grated meat. Mash with a potato masher.

When cool enough, use your hands and work all the juices out of the meat. Strain through cheesecloth, squeezing well. You should have about 4 cups milk.

Nancy Hitchins

STUFFING

• FARUSHUI STUFFING

Slice any type of bread thinly (stale is best). Pop into a very hot oven for 15 minutes or until done. This makes great stuffing. It also goes great with wine and cheese or is a good midnight watch nibbly.

Farushui or bread crumbs	Celery (if available)
Small onion	Sage
Melted butter and water	Salt and pepper to taste

Smash farushui (in a plastic bag) with a wooden mallet or make fine bread crumbs. Add the diced onion. In a pan heat together 3 parts water to 1 part butter and pour over the bread and onion until it is the consistency of a wet sponge.

Add chopped celery, sage, salt and pepper and mix thoroughly.

Stuff a chicken with it, or bake covered with foil in a loaf pan at high heat until brown on top, about 30 minutes.

Robert Kohlman

CHAPTER 5

SALADS, SIDE DISHES, AND SOUPS

SALADS

• SPROUTING ACROSS THE PACIFIC

We love fresh green salads and, because lettuce lasts only a few days, we've discovered some delicious alternatives.

Sprouts are our favorite. When you grow your own you can have a fresh crisp vegetable even on the last day of a passage. Almost any bean will sprout: Alfalfa, lima, lentil and soy are a few.

We use a sprouting tube, but a big jar with a screen wrapped tight around the top will work just as well. All you do is soak 2 rounded tablespoons of seeds for 24 hours then pour off the water and rinse them twice a day. In 4 to 5 days—Voilà! Healthy, crunchy sprouts.

Two tablespoons makes 1 quart. They are full of protein and are a good source of vitamins A, B and C. In the tropics these salads are especially refreshing.

Mid-Pacific Salad

1 quart sprouts (alfalfa is good in
    this one)
¼ cup fresh chopped onion (or 2
    tablespoons dried)
2 tablespoons lemon juice

1 can chopped olives
1 can garbanzo beans
1 can flaked tuna
¼ cup Parmesan cheese
Italian or oil and vinegar dressing

Combine all ingredients except cheese and dressing, toss. Add cheese
and dressing, toss slightly. Serve immediately. Yields 4 servings.

In Port Salad

1 quart mixed sprouts
2 small ripe tomatoes (sliced)
3 long green onions (chopped)

3 tablespoons zucchini (grated)
1 cup croutons
Your favorite dressing

Combine all ingredients in order, toss and serve.
Another vegetable that can be used instead of lettuce is cabbage.
Wrapped in a damp towel, it has a shelf life of 4 weeks.

Sweet and Sour Salad

⅓ medium cabbage (shredded)
1½ cups mung bean sprouts
½ small onion (chopped)
1 can water chestnuts (sliced)

1 can bamboo shoots
¾ cup almonds
¾ cup sweet and sour sauce

Combine all ingredients and mix thoroughly. If you add a can of whole
cooked shrimp or crab, this recipe will make a light meal for 4 people.

Kathleen Decker

• OVERNIGHT TOSSED SALAD

6 cups chopped lettuce (or spinach)
½ teaspoon salt
Dash of pepper
½ teaspoon sugar
6 hard-cooked eggs, sliced
10 ounce package frozen peas,
    thawed

½ pound bacon, cooked and
    crumbled
½ cup sliced green onions
2 cups shredded Swiss cheese
1¼ cups mayonnaise

Put ½ lettuce in an unbreakable serving bowl. Sprinkle with salt, pepper and sugar. Top with the eggs, then the bacon, then the peas. Add rest of the lettuce, the onion and cheese. Spread the mayonnaise thinly over the top to cover. Cover the bowl and refrigerate overnight. Toss to serve.

Variations: Add sliced mushrooms, water chestnuts and/or chopped celery.

Joan Young

• PERPETUAL SALAD

Finely chop any or all of the following vegetables: Carrots, green peppers, cabbage, onions, celery, seeded cucumbers, seeded tomatoes (seeding prolongs the life and increases the firmness).

Mix with instant or bottled Italian dressing and serve. The beauty of this one is that you can keep adding vegetables as they become available and the salad goes on and on. . . .

Cindy Putt

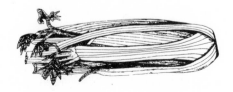

• SPARKY SALADS

We carry vegetables that stay fresh without ice and find lettuce is not necessary for a good salad. But a good dressing is and here's our basic recipe.

Combine: 3 parts oil, 1 part cider vinegar, salt and pepper. Then add: Dry mustard, oregano, garlic powder.

Slice cucumbers, green peppers, carrots, radishes, tomatoes and, of course, onions. (Do drain the soppy tomatoes.) Toss them into the sparky dressing and presto! A fresh relish, good with anything, and easily assembled for 2 or a crowd.

When you're on the hook and far from food stores dredge up 3 cans of beans—red kidney, cut green and yellow or wax. Drain, rinse and shake dry. Add sliced onions, of course, and pimento, perhaps?

Then add that old-style dressing. Simply boil together: 2 parts oil, 2 parts cider vinegar and 1 part white sugar.

Stir, cool and pour over the beans, which will then have that whizzy zip needed to perk up canned fare on board.

James Beck

• SALAD DAYS

In addition to their many other qualities, salads help satisfy one's creative urge. It seems unbelievable, but almost any combination of edible foods (excluding peanut butter and jam) makes a great salad. The possibilities are endless.

Two of our favorite salads are Rice Twice and Vegetable Mix.

Rice Twice

This delicious goodie starts out as last night's vegetable course. First of all, cook at least twice as much rice as you need for the evening meal. Then add some cooked (or canned) vegetables such as peas, cubed carrots or chopped beans. Add a little parsley and butter, and serve with your main course. Refrigerate the leftovers. Next day, add any other leftovers or perhaps 1 can of salmon, 2 or 3 tablespoons of vinaigrette sauce or other salad dressing and voilà—lunch!

Vegetable Mix

This is where you can really let your imagination run wild. A fairly conservative version is:

1 cup cooked macaroni	1 tablespoon chopped pimentos
1 can corn	1 tablespoon chopped green pepper
1 can peas	Mayonnaise to moisten
1 can mushrooms	Salt and pepper

Mix it all together and serve with buttered brown bread to 3 hungry or 4 normal adults. An interesting way to dress this up for company is to serve on a large platter covered with halved hard-boiled eggs. The eggs are turned yolk side down, then spread with a mixture of thin white sauce and mayonnaise to taste.

Carolyn Ross

• SEAFARERS' CHINESE SALAD

19 ounce can bean sprouts, drained	1 tablespoon chopped pimento
1 can mushroom slices, drained	2 tablespoons soy sauce
½ cup bamboo shoots, drained	1 teaspoon lemon juice
½ cup sliced water chestnuts, drained	1 teaspoon salad oil
1 tablespoon sesame seeds	Pepper to taste

To bean sprouts add mushrooms, bamboo shoots, sliced water chestnuts and sesame seeds. Pimento adds color and flavor and should be added at this time if available. Remaining ingredients may be added while tossing or mixed together and poured over vegetables prior to tossing.

Marinate at least 1 hour (the longer the better), stirring often.

This nourishing and tasty salad is made entirely from canned ingredients and yet tastes very fresh and crisp.

Any ingredients may be deleted, increased or decreased, according to taste and supply, and leftovers can be heated for a Chinese vegetable the following day.

Serves 4–6.

Anna Patrick

• LENTIL SALAD

Cooking aboard while cruising can be an odd combination of careful planning, making do, desperation and pure accident.

After adding water to lentils in preparation for making that old standby soup, we were invited aboard another boat for more festive fare. It wasn't until the next morning that I came across the soaked lentils and absentmindedly popped a few in my mouth—a delightful, peppery crunch, not at all hard.

With experimentation, I found that 4 hours was minimum soaking time for an edible texture if you haven't planned further ahead. The next step is to drain the water and add a liberal marinade of oil and vinegar dressing. Sometimes a few dollops of ketchup were mixed in too. The rest of the ingredients depended on availability, which in Central America usually included chopped onions, tomatoes, green peppers and cucumbers. Bacon bits can be tossed in too, and the flavor is certainly enhanced by leaving everything to marinate together as long as possible before serving. Even without refrigeration in the tropics, this was no problem.

It was such a delight not to have to light the stove or to have something prepared ahead of impending bad weather that we found ourselves enjoying this refreshing, nutritious dish frequently.

Katie Dickerson

• MEXICAN SALAD

1 head lettuce	1 package taco seasoning
2 medium tomatoes	1 bag taco-flavored corn chips
1 bell pepper	1 can chili-flavored kidney beans
1 onion	(drained)
1 cucumber	1 cup Cheddar cheese (shredded)
1 pound ground beef	Thousand Island dressing

Chop and mix first 5 ingredients and set aside. Fry ground beef with taco seasoning mix as directed on package. Just before serving toss salad mix with ground beef, corn chips, beans and cheese. Add Thousand Island dressing to taste. Serves 6 hungry people very well. This is our favorite when we have company.

Jill Gaither

• SAUERKRAUT SALAD

Mix together:

1 large can sauerkraut, washed and
   drained

1 cup minced onion
1 cup minced green pepper

Boil together 2 cups sugar and ½ cup of vinegar and pour over the mix. Chill for 24 hours.

Kept chilled, sauerkraut salad will last indefinitely. We use it as a salad and on hot dogs.

Pamela Hanlin

• ANTIPASTO FOR A RAFT-UP PARTY

1¼ cup ketchup
1 cup chili sauce
1 can solid tuna, drained
1 small can sliced mushrooms,
   drained
½ cup each diced carrots and
   celery, cooked in salted
   water 6 minutes

½ cup each sweet mixed pickled
   and stuffed olives, drained and
   chopped
4 tablespoons salad oil
1 teaspoon garlic salt
Salt and pepper to taste

Mix and store in icebox. Serve with crackers.

Joan Young

• SEA SALADS

Sardine-Pea Salad

1 can chick peas or black-eyed peas,
   drained
1 can sardines, chopped
1 hard-boiled egg, chopped
   (optional)
1 tablespoon creamy salad
   dressing mix

1 tablespoon milk (or 2 teaspoons
   dry milk solids)
1 teaspoon lemon juice
2–3 tablespoons mayonnaise to
   taste

Mix all ingredients together. Serve on lettuce if available.

Tuna Vegetable Salad

1 can tuna, drained and chopped
1 can mixed vegetables, drained
1 hard-boiled egg, chopped
  (optional)
1 small onion, chopped fine
  (optional)

1 tablespoon Green Goddess salad
  dressing mix
1 tablespoon milk (or 2 teaspoons
  dry milk solids)
1 teaspoon lemon juice
2–3 tablespoons mayonnaise
  to taste

Mix all ingredients together. Serve.

Gladys Paulin

• SPROUT AND COTTAGE CHEESE SALAD

Mix cottage cheese with mayonnaise (about ¾ cup mayo to 1 container cottage cheese). Dish out individual servings and put alfalfa sprouts atop each serving. Cover this lightly with Italian salad dressing. Excellent flavor and very nutritious.

Nancy Schoellkopf

• BAHAMIAN COLE SLAW

Before leaving the U.S. we stored canned and dried staples in every space available and hoped to round out our menus with whatever local fresh produce we could find.

While cruising in the Abacos during the autumn months we noticed a decided lack of fresh green vegetables. There was, however, a profusion of cabbage and an occasional green pepper and cucumber.

After much experimenting and some luck we came up with a cole slaw that pleased everyone.

For 4 large servings, combine and toss the following:

½ head cabbage, shredded
½ green pepper, diced
½ cucumber, diced
1 small onion, diced
½ cup salted peanuts

¼ cup mayonnaise
¼ cup sour cream
½ teaspoon celery seed
2 tablespoons vinegar
1 tablespoon sugar

Even our ever-discriminating 3-year-old crew member, Morgan, asks for seconds!

Bonita Agnew

• COLOMBIAN COLE SLAW

We like salad and this cole slaw will keep well and satisfy a longing for salad for weeks after lettuce runs out. It will keep for a month in the refrigerator or icebox and for 2 or 3 weeks without artificial cooling, depending on the climate. Since a head of raw cabbage will keep for several weeks, this recipe provides a lot of flexibility for both long and short cruises.

Combine:

3 pounds green cabbage, chopped	2 onions, chopped
1 green pepper	1 cup sugar

Mix and bring to a boil:

1 cup cooking oil	2 tablespoons celery seed
1 cup vinegar	1 tablespoon salt

Pour over the cabbage and stir until well mixed. Store in a refrigerator or in a cool place in an airtight container. Let stand for at least 3 days.

Priscilla Squier

• CHINESE STYLE CABBAGE SLAW

Making the dressing up a day ahead is advantageous. Use 6 or 7 parts sesame seed oil and 1 part white wine vinegar. The sesame seed oil is difficult to find except in the best supermarkets or health food stores, but absolutely essential.

Add about ½ part soy sauce and some hot sauce such as Tabasco. The dressing should be spicy-hot. A touch of garlic can be added if desired.

A couple of hours before serving, take a head of cabbage and shred it as you would for cole slaw. Put in a large bowl and add a couple of tablespoons of salt. Toss the cabbage to mix the salt around and let stand for 1–2 hours.

Then rinse the salt out of the cabbage, add the dressing and let stand for an hour or so before serving. It is great eaten alone or as a side dish with a meal—hamburgers, stew or almost anything—except possibly cheesecake or ice cream.

Jay Stuart Haft

• MAUI POTATO SALAD

5 large potatoes	3 tablespoons sweet pickle relish
5 hard-cooked eggs	2 carrots, grated
1½ teaspoons salt	½ cup cooked frozen peas
1 large onion, chopped	1½ cups mayonnaise
¼ teaspoon MSG	

Wash the potatoes and boil unpeeled until tender. Cool, peel and dice into ½-inch cubes. Add other ingredients, mix thoroughly with the mayonnaise. Chill overnight and keep on ice. Absolutely unbeatable after a good day of sailing.

Variations: Add cooked lobster or crabmeat for a super taste treat. If you can't afford lobster or crab, and the divers haven't had any luck, a can of well-drained and rinsed tuna isn't a bad substitute. Use 3 potatoes and 3 cups of cooked macaroni and the same other ingredients for a slightly different taste. As we say in Hawaii—ONO!

Demaris Fredericksen

• POTATO SALAD

5 potatoes, diced	½ cup sour cream
3 eggs, hard-cooked, diced	1 tablespoon mayonnaise
1 stalk celery, diced	2 tablespoons red wine vinegar
1 onion, medium, diced	½ teaspoon sugar
½ green pepper, diced	1 teaspoon curry powder

Combine all ingredients. Chill.

Joyan Thompson

• LOBSTER-GRAPEFRUIT SALAD

We discovered this recipe quite by accident one day, when Gary speared a huge lobster—the tail alone must have weighed 2 pounds. We ate all we could that night and still had half left for morning. Since we had several grapefruit on board, it was clear that breakfast would be an experiment. The lobster and grapefruit turned out to be a heavenly combination. The flavors are more appreciated, we found, if it is served cool rather than ice-cold.

1 pound cooked lobster, cut into bite-sized pieces
1 cup grapefruit sections, cut in half
6–8 maraschino cherries cut into quarters (not essential, but they add color if you have them)
½ cup sour cream or yogurt
½ cup mayonnaise

Stir gently all together. The mayonnaise I use is sweet and tangy and needs no refrigeration. It is: 1 can sweetened condensed milk, ½ cup brown cider vinegar, ¼ cup water, 1 teaspoon salt and 1 teaspoon dry mustard. Stir together until clabbered.

Sour cream can be faked by adding 1 teaspoon vinegar to ½ cup milk with extra milk powder added. Or, the sour cream can be replaced with another ½ cup mayonnaise.

After discovering this salad, we came across a lobster salad recipe that was essentially the same but called for 1 cup green grapes (cut in half) instead of the grapefruit. This, too, is refreshing.

As you can see, the recipe is flexible. Have fun!

Diane Taylor

• BREADFRUIT SALAD

Quarter, peel and core 1 breadfruit and cook in salted water until tender. Cool, dice into a salad bowl and add 1 medium onion, chopped, 2 or 3 spring onions (scallions), chopped, 2 tablespoons oil and vinegar dressing and enough mayonnaise to make it moist.

Garnish with parsley and serve with fried chicken, cold plates, sandwiches, etc.

This is ideal in the Caribbean where potatoes are scarce and breadfruit almost always is in season.

Sonya Elliot

• CAESAR SALAD

If you have a quantity of salad greens aboard, Caesar Salad is a great luncheon. First, make up a quantity of croutons. Figure on 2 slices of bread per crew member. Cut into little squares. Heat the skillet with some cooking oil or olive oil. Squeeze a large clove of garlic (peeled) through the press into the oil, simmer for 5 to 10 minutes to allow the garlic to permeate the oil. The amount of oil used depends on the amount of bread.

Place the bread cubes in the oil and stir around so that all of the cubes get some oil. Stir carefully to let the bread brown, but not burn. When done, put the croutons aside—hide them from the crew and yourself or they'll all be gone before the salad is served.

Make a salad dressing of 1 part vinegar (white wine is best, red wine second choice, cider vinegar third) to 3 parts oil (olive oil is best). Dip a fork into some Dijon mustard then stir the dressing with it vigorously. This adds a bit of flavor to the dressing and helps emulsify the oil. A pinch of basil leaves will add a new taste to the dressing.

Wash the salad greens in the folding colander and tear (not cut) them into small pieces. Put the greens into the salad bowl, add the dressing and break a raw egg on top. Toss well. (Some prefer a coddled egg rather than raw. I like 'em raw.) As you toss the salad, add some cut up anchovies and capers if you have them. Then sprinkle on some grated Parmesan cheese, toss again, add the croutons and toss for the last time. Serve at once.

Jay Stuart Haft

• CHICKEN SALAD

We got fabulous avocados in the Bahamas and stuffed the peeled halves with this salad in place of the Pacific shrimp we used at home in Canada.

Mix in a salad bowl:

1 small can chicken, flaked, with juice

¼ to ⅓ cup finely chopped onions

¼ to ⅓ cup sliced pitted black olives

½ to ⅔ cup fresh alfalfa sprouts

Dress with: ⅓ cup oil, 2 tablespoons wine vinegar, 2 tablespoons lemon juice, parsley flakes, garlic powder, pepper and salt to taste. Sprinkle some dressing on the avocado halves, then stuff with the salad.

Marg Desfosses

• CONCH SALAD

Any number of conch (sliced very thin)

Onions (sliced)

Carrots (sliced)

Celery (sliced)

Green pepper

Combine any of the above ingredients available with enough mayonnaise-type salad dressing to moisten. Add salt and pepper to taste. Serve at once.

Janet Harbach

• MIDDLE EASTERN SALADS

We enjoy gourmet food, so it has become our challenge to find interesting, tasty meals that are simply and easily prepared.

Two Middle Eastern dishes, Couscous and Tabbouleh, fit our requirements and are adaptable to any galley or imagination. Their whole grains provide nourishing and sustaining fare, and they require little or no cooking, making perfect hot-weather dishes.

Couscous

Sauté half a large onion, chopped, in 2 tablespoons butter or oil. Add:

2 cups water or broth
1 or 2 cans chicken, or any other
    meat or fish available (amount
    depends on how many other
    ingredients are included)

1 small can vegetables
1 can mushrooms (use drained
    liquid of mushrooms and
    vegetables as part of basic
    liquid measure above)

Salt and pepper to taste, add any other spices which taste good. Bring to a boil. Cook just long enough to heat ingredients.

Stir in 1 cup couscous (cracked wheat, available in natural food stores). Remove from heat and let stand 10–15 minutes. Fluff with a fork and serve. Makes 4 generous servings and is even better the next day, served either at room temperature or reheated.

Tabbouleh

Classic ingredients are bulghur (crushed wheat, available in natural food stores), tomatoes, parsley, onions and mint. But as with couscous, practically anything on hand can be substituted.

½ cup fine bulghur
2 large, ripe tomatoes, chopped
1 onion, finely chopped (mix in
    chopped green onions also if
    available)
¾ cup parsley, finely chopped (less
    if dried)
½ cucumber, seeded and chopped

⅓ cup fresh lemon juice (or
    vinegar, but use less)
1 teaspoon salt
⅓ cup olive oil (vegetable oil can
    be substituted, but the
    characteristic flavor is lost)
Crumbled dried mint to taste
    (double the amount if fresh)

Cover the bulghur with cold water and soak for 10–15 minutes. Drain in dampened cheesecloth. Wrap the bulghur in the cheesecloth and squeeze it until completely dry.

Place in a bowl, add all other ingredients except olive oil and mint and toss thoroughly but gently. Add olive oil and mint just before serving.

If you are lucky enough to have fresh lettuce, serve it on a large leaf and garnish it with anything that strikes your fancy. Serves 4.

Jacqueline Davis

• LONG-DISTANCE SALADS

Most of our cruising has been near the Equator, with some very long passages, so special thought had to be given to the choice of fresh produce.

I try to have a vegetable salad at lunchtime, either as the main course or an addition to cheese and crisp bread. I make it right after breakfast to give it time to cool and mellow in taste and free me to stand my watches.

Pickled Cucumber Salad

1 fresh cucumber
½ cup white vinegar
2 tablespoons water
¼ teaspoon salt

Few grains white pepper
3 tablespoons sugar
2 tablespoons minced parsley

Slice cucumber very thinly without peeling. Mix together vinegar, salt, pepper and sugar, pour this over cucumbers. Sprinkle with parsley. Let stand 2 hours before serving. Serves 6–8.

Rice Salad

2 cups cooked rice (Add 1 teaspoon
    tumeric powder to rice water
    for flavor and color)
1 can mixed vegetables, drained
1 minced onion

Vinegar and oil dressing (½ cup
    salad oil, ¼ cup vinegar, salt,
    pepper, dry mustard and
    paprika to taste)

As you have them, vary the taste by adding minced hard-boiled eggs, shredded carrots, 1 can tuna or 1 green pepper, minced. Mix the ingredients together and serve.

Long-Distance Salad

2 cups shredded raw pumpkin or
  similar squash
1 minced onion
1 can peas (or vegetable of choice)

Vinegar and oil dressing (½ cup
  salad oil, ¼ cup vinegar, salt,
  pepper, basil and oregano to
  taste)

Pare pumpkin and shred raw into bowl. Add remaining ingredients and mix well. If peas are omitted, increase shredded pumpkin by 1 cup. Season to taste and enjoy.

Most pumpkins or squash will keep for at least 2 months uncut. After cutting, the unused portions will keep for one week if sealed. I use a slice per day, varying the additional vegetables and seasonings.

Beverly Larson

• MACARONI SALAD WITH BACON

4 cups cooked macaroni
½ cup mayonnaise
3 tablespoons vinegar
¼ cup pickle relish
Small jar chopped pimento

Few drops of Tabasco
8 slices bacon, fried crisp and
  crumbled
Salt and pepper to taste

Mix all ingredients, preferably a few hours before serving so that the full flavor has time to develop. Boneless canned chicken, flaked tunafish, cubed ham or Spam or cooked, diced lobster may be added in addition to, or in place of, the bacon.

If fresh green peppers or tomatoes are available, finely chop some and add to the salad for some extra flavor and color. If you really want to be fancy, garnish the salad with sliced hard-boiled egg and sprinkle your creation with paprika.

Linda Turner

• MANY-FLAVORED SALAD

We spent 5 months in the Bahamas and as we had to be careful with our food funds we found eating "vegetarian style" helped. The correct combination of grains, legumes, milk and seeds provides good nutrition.

I missed fresh salads so put together this protein-rich vegetable/macaroni salad using stores that keep on a boat without refrigeration.

Basic Salad

1½ cups cold, cooked macaroni
    (preferably whole wheat)
¼ cup cold, cooked split peas or 1
    small can peas, drained

½–1 cup chopped cabbage
1 grated carrot
1 small onion, chopped

Optional extras: sunflower seeds, peanuts, walnuts, olives, peppers, parsley, spinach, celery, scallions, sprouts, chopped or grated cheese, purple cabbage, chopped tomatoes, wheat germ, raw bran, chopped hard-boiled eggs.

Dressing

Mix together:

2 tablespoons mayonnaise
1 teaspoon mustard
Garlic salt

Pepper
Lemon juice

I really would like to have ice on my next boat!

Judith Sugg

SIDE DISHES

• POTATOES À LA BEACH FIRE

For 6 people allow about 4 or 5 potatoes. Wash them, leave the skins intact and cut into slices about ¹⁄₁₆ inch thick. The beach fire should be reduced to hot glowing coals, not flames.

Half-fill the frying pan with vegetable oil and heat; put 1 layer of potatoes in at a time and fry, turning potato slices over so that they brown evenly. Lift out with spatula and sprinkle with salt.

This recipe is guaranteed to keep the frying pan tender so busy that he doesn't have time to eat. The pan is later cleaned at the water's edge with a little sand and salt water.

Patty Slingluff

• SEASICK MASHED POTATOES

When you get seasick, the last thing you want is to eat, but the best way to get over being under the weather on board is to eat something, get busy doing anything and stay topside. Now the food that works the best must be colorless and pretty free from high seasoning but should have good food value such as carbohydrates and proteins. Seasick mashed potatoes fill this bill.

Use instant potatoes or fresh, it doesn't make any difference, but whatever, set up the portions and cook with a little extra water so that the mess will be a bit sloppy. After the potatoes have been cooked, add 1 beaten egg per serving, salt and pepper, and jam the mess down the poor person's throat.

The flavor isn't all that bad and can be eaten under severe conditions. I have used seasick mashed potatoes many times, and the results have been exceptional for restoring friends back to health. Of course, my idea of a good breakfast on board would be a bowl of chili and a Pepsi, but I had good training; I was in the Air Force in World War II and now have cast iron insides.

David von Döerfler

• EASY POTATOES AU GRATIN

Mix 1 can Campbell's Cheddar cheese soup and ¼ cup milk. Slice 4 potatoes thinly. Put layers of potatoes and cheese mixture in a greased casserole dish.

Put on a trivet in a preheated Dutch oven and cook over medium heat for 1 hour, or cook 1 hour in an oven at 350°.

Beverly Salkin

• BIANDA WITH BACALAO

"Bianda" means many kinds of edible tubers of the potato family. Some grow under the ground, such as malanga, apios, yautia, ñame, and batata blanca (a variety of sweet potato with a purple skin).

Others grow on trees, such as avocado, panapenes, plantains, challote and panas de pepita.

Many of these grow wild in the tropics or can be bought very cheaply. You do not need all of them to make a meal, 1 or 2 will make a fine dinner. Do not cook the avocado. Keep this for the salad.

Simply skin or peel the bianda and cut into medium/large pieces. Put into a pot of boiling water with some salt and cook until tender.

Boil about 1 pound bacalao (salt cod) at the same time as the bianda. Boneless bacalao is best, but if it hasn't been boned you must pick out the bones after cooking.

Separate the bacalao into pieces with your fingers, put into a ditta or bowl, add sliced onions, diced avocado and olive oil and mix gently.

You simply take a piece of bianda in your fingers, scoop up the salad and eat! This food keeps well in hot and humid climates.

Try the white batatas with black coffee in the morning—superb!

José Acevedo

• MACARONI AND CHEESE

2 cups uncooked macaroni
2 tablespoons butter, margarine,
    shortening or oil
1½ cups cubed or grated Cheddar
    cheese
½ teaspoon salt
Mustard to taste (½ teaspoon dry or
    1 tablespoon prepared)

2 eggs, beaten
2 cups milk
½ cup stale bread crumbs mixed
    with 2 tablespoons melted
    butter, margarine, shortening
    or oil (optional)

Combine and mix well all ingredients except crumbs. Put in greased 1½-quart baking dish. Sprinkle with buttered crumbs. Bake, covered, at 350° for 40–50 minutes. Let stand 5–10 minutes to thicken liquid in casserole.

For variety:

Add any or all of the following:

2 tablespoons chopped, canned chillies (or fresh equivalent), 1–2 chopped green peppers, small head of cauliflower, broken into florets, 1–2 cups chopped broccoli, leftover ham, sausage, or chicken, etc. Instead of all milk, use 1½ cups milk and ½ cup white wine or 1¾ cups milk and ¼ cup rum (but not with chillies!).

If using powdered or canned milk, make it 1½ times normal strength for added richness and protein power. Though canned or pasteurized cheese doesn't melt well, it's acceptable in this recipe if it's grated instead of cubed. Or use ⅓–½ cups powdered cheese.

Dried eggs work fine and don't have to be reconstituted. Just add the water with the other liquid.

Letting the mixture sit for 40 minutes before baking will cut the cooking time by 10–15 minutes. But with some macaroni this trick will produce a chewy product.

Joanne Sandstrom

• CURRIED RICE

Wash 1 cup rice 3 times with saltwater. Cover with 1¾ cups fresh water. Add:

1 tablespoon butter or margarine   2 tablespoons curry powder
1 teaspoon salt

Cook over medium heat, stirring occasionally, until water disappears. Cover and simmer over a very low flame for 10 minutes, then let it steam off the fire for 10 more minutes and you will have a deliciously fluffy rice.

Marilee McAlpine

• SOUTHERN SPOONBREAD

We are "home-baked goodie" freaks and I really enjoy having time to cook and bake when we cruise.

Southern spoonbread is super-nutritious and made from easily stored provisions.

4 cups milk (I use 2½–3 cups   1 teaspoon salt
    evaporated with 1–1½ cups   2 teaspoons baking powder
    water)   1 tablespoon soft butter or
1½ cups yellow cornmeal   margarine
3 eggs, separated

Heat milk to boiling. Add cornmeal very slowly, stirring constantly until smooth. Cool. Stir in well-beaten egg yolks, salt, baking powder and butter. Beat egg whites until stiff then fold into mixture.

Pour into a well-buttered 2-quart baking dish or casserole and bake at 375° for 45–50 minutes. Makes 8 servings.

Spoon out, put a pat of butter on top and eat with the main course.

Leftover spoonbread will keep overnight without refrigeration and is delicious for breakfast.

Make a sauce with some butter, a handful of raisins, a bit of honey, some cinnamon and allspice. Let it get gooey and pour over warmed-up spoonbread—a great cruising breakfast!

Lulu Behrmann

• MIGHTY MATZO

I always keep a couple of boxes of matzo meal on board. You can make a great teatime pancake with it or make a batch of matzo balls and drop them into any chicken soup mix.

Matzo meal can be used with egg for breading fish or meat, for thickening sauces or for adding to meat loaf or hamburger meat.

Matzo Balls

1 cup matzo meal
½ cup water
4 eggs

⅓ cup melted shortening
1 teaspoon salt
Dash pepper

Add water, melted shortening, salt and pepper to the beaten eggs. Mix well. Add matzo meal and stir thoroughly. Allow to thicken for 1 hour. (For thicker matzo balls add approximately ¼ cup more meal—this will lessen thickening time.)

Form into balls and drop into soup or into 1½ quarts boiling water to which 1 tablespoon salt has been added.

Cook for 20 minutes. When no soup is available cook in water and serve as a side dish.

Matzo Pancakes

½ cup matzo meal
3 eggs

½ cup water or milk
½ teaspoon salt

Beat yolks and blend with water, salt and matzo meal. Fold in beaten whites and drop teaspoonfuls of the mixture onto a greased griddle. Brown on both sides. Serve with sugar, jelly or jam.

Sarah Dworkin

• CORNMEAL DUFF

I'm a singlehander with a single-burner stove and like simple fare that I can whip up in a few minutes.

One of my favorite hot side dishes is cornmeal duff made with raisins and oil.

Cookbooks mostly agree the meal should be sprinkled gradually into boiling water and stirred for 20 to 40 minutes. That's a bore; it is apt to go lumpy and spits hot plops on the hands.

As a lad I wondered why it took so long to make mush, whereas flapjacks required only a few minutes. Digging into the subject, I found scientists admit cereal is "done" after 2 or 3 minutes of cooking when it has absorbed all of the boiling water it can. Hence my quick and low-calorie recipe.

Bit less than ½ cup yellow cornmeal	2 heaping teaspoons raisins
Pinch of salt	Generous dollop oil
1½ cups cold water	

Use a small pan about as wide as tall. Put in the meal, salt and cold water. Stir occasionally while bringing to a boil and then stir constantly for 3 minutes.

The mixture should thicken and start to spit plops, then turn down the fire or use a flame tamer. Continue to stir until the bubbles cease and steam hisses up through the ex-bubble holes.

Remove from the fire and fold in the raisins and oil. Then set aside to rest for a couple of minutes. Eat while hot. It makes 3 moderate servings, just enough for a hungry sailor.

Dried raisins are improved if sprinkled with rum and stored in a closed jar. Try ⅓ jigger for 1 cup raisins. This cornmeal duff has a nutty flavor that can be controlled by the amount of moisture, i.e., the drier, the nuttier.

To add voltage the raisins can be replaced or supplemented by a tiny can of spaghetti cause, beef ragôut or tunafish.

Frank Williams

• YORKSHIRE PUDDING

The basis of this dish is a good batter.

Put ½ cup all-purpose flour and 1 teaspoon salt into a bowl. Make a well in the center. To 1 egg add enough milk to make 1½ cups liquid and mix. Pour liquid slowly into the flour, mixing in gradually with a fork until all flour is absorbed. *Do not beat.*

Let stand for 15 minutes. Meanwhile, heat oven to 425° and melt 1 tablespoon beef dripping or other shortening (bacon fat is good) in an 8-inch pie pan. Stir the mixture thoroughly and pour into pan.

Bake for 30 to 40 minutes, reducing heat to 350° if cooking too quickly. It should rise and be a delicious golden brown. It is usually served with roast beef and fat from the roast adds a special flavor.

Do not overcook! If you cook too quickly or too long the pudding will collapse and have the flavor and consistency of an old suede shoe.

Barbara Davis

• PEAS INDIENNE

When the fresh vegetables, and finally the cole slaw, run out, this recipe serves 4 if used as a vegetable course or 2 when eaten as a light, vegetarian dinner.

2 tablespoons butter
½ teaspoon curry

½ cup salted peanuts, chopped
1 can peas

Melt the butter and mix in the curry. Add peanuts, sauté for 2 minutes. Add drained peas. Mix with fork until peas are hot. Don't gobble.

Priscilla Squier

• PEAS 'N RICE

Cook brown short grain rice (1 cup rice to 2 cups water, baked or simmered). Sauté in safflower oil: celery, onion, green pepper and any other vegetables you like.

Add cooked rice and 1 can of pigeon peas. Add hot sauce to taste. If you like, add ¾ cup of raisins and some coconut.

Linda Bosley

• HERB-GRILLED CORN

With 2 or more boats rafted together there are usually several grills, so fire up 1 to use for this vegetable that everyone loves.

½ cup soft butter	½ teaspoon salt
2 tablespoons parsley	Dash pepper
2 tablespoons chopped chives	8 ears of corn, husks removed

Blend the butter and spices together. The morning of the raft-up, spread 1 heaping tablespoon on each ear and wrap in heavy foil. Grill over medium coals 15 to 20 minutes, turning occasionally.

Joan Young

• SUCCOTASH

Fry up a few strips of bacon in a saucepan. Add 1 can each of creamed corn, drained whole kernel corn and drained lima beans. When warm, stir in ½ to 1 cup dry non-dairy creamer or powered milk. Add garlic salt and pepper to taste and it's ready in minutes!

Dian Jacobs

• SWEET-SOUR BEANS

1 pound can cut green beans, drained	3 tablespoons sugar
3 strips bacon (canned or fresh)	1⅓ tablespoons vinegar

Fry out bacon, remove and set aside, leaving drippings in pan. Add beans, sugar and vinegar. Cover and simmer for 30 minutes. Just before serving toss crumbled bacon in with the beans. If bacon is not available, use margarine or cooking oil and add imitation bacon bits (available in jars at most supermarkets).

Binnie Bowman

• GLAZED CARROTS

6–7 carrots   Peel from ½ orange

Glaze:

6 tablespoons butter or margarine   ½ teaspoon ground ginger
4 tablespoons brown sugar   6 tablespoons rum

Scrape and julienne-cut the carrots. Boil in salted water with orange peel until tender. Do not overcook! Heat glaze ingredients in a skillet, drain carrots and place in skillet. Stir until completely glazed.

Wanda Parker

• MARINATED CARROTS

This recipe can be used as a vegetable or mixed with other vegetables as a salad.

Peel and thinly slice 2 pounds carrots and cook in salty water until done but not mushy. Boil 1 can tomato soup, ½ cup oil, ¾ cup vinegar, ½ cup sugar, 1 teaspoon dry mustard, 1 chopped green pepper and 1 onion.

Quickly pour over the cooked and drained carrots and refrigerate. These will keep for up to 2 weeks without refrigeration and even longer in the fridge.

Peg Brinck

• CARROTS—ALL-WEATHER VEGETABLE

Fresh carrots are the cook's best bet for variety and nutrition. They're sturdy little things and seem to survive quite well on the bottom of the icebox with a 2-week's supply of food on top of them!

To prepare, just lop off both ends and rinse them, under cold water. No scraping necessary and no tin cans to bother with.

My favorite way to cook carrots is to slice them diagonally into thin pieces, steaming them in a metal steamer until just tender enough to pierce with a fork. One bag of 6–7 medium sized carrots will feed about 5 people.

After steaming, they may be served in a variety of ways. Here are a few:

To a bowl of freshly steamed carrots, add 1 tablespoon butter and 1 tablespoon honey. Toss until carrots have a shiny glazed look.

Add the juice of ½ orange to hot carrots and toss.

Add ½ cup of pineapple bits (fresh or canned) to carrots during the last few minutes of steaming, or just long enough to warm up the pineapple.

Sprinkle ¼ teaspoon cinammon or ¼ teaspoon nutmeg and 1 tablespoon butter on steamed carrots. Spicy and good after a brisk sail.

Add ⅓ cup shredded coconut, ¼ cup chopped peanuts, a dash of curry powder and a dab of butter to steamed carrots. Mix lightly for a zesty, Indian curry flavor.

Patt Hildebrandt

• ISLAND TREATS

One of the nice things about cruising in the islands is being able to shop in local markets and buy fresh, locally grown produce.

Breadfruit and christophenes are cheap, easy to prepare and a big hit with my crew. They are almost unheard of in the U.S.

Breadfruit

Peel, core and cube. Steam until soft. Serve with salt, pepper and butter or gravy.

Or mash them with butter, salt and pepper and grated onions, then make into patties and fry until golden on both sides.

Christophenes

These are very prickly on the outside, so be careful.

Peel, core, cube and steam for 20 minutes. Drain, toss with grated cheese and serve.

Peg Nelson

• FRIED GREEN BANANAS

6–8 hard green bananas
3 tablespoons butter or margarine
½ teaspoon celery salt or plain salt

¼ teaspoon black pepper
1 medium onion, chopped

With a sharp knife, peel the green skin off the banana, then slice into ¼ inch circles. Melt butter in a skillet (preferably cast iron), add the bananas, seasonings and onions. Stir to mix, then cover and cook over medium/low heat, stirring occasionally until the bananas are cooked through and soft, about 10 minutes.

Pami Webb

SEAFOOD CHOWDERS AND BISQUES

• BAHAMIAN CLAM CHOWDER

One of our favorite retreats in the Bahamas is Conception Island, a small, unpopulated, unpolluted plot of paradise 15 miles northeast of the northern tip of Long Island.

One rainy evening last summer we were safely anchored in 20 feet of water on the northwest side of the island, talking on the ham radio to some of our friends anchored 400 miles away, near Sebastian Inlet, Florida. They were telling us about the fat, succulent clams they had just dug from the shallow waters of the Intracoastal Waterway. Immediately our mouths started watering; what a perfect night to brew some steamy clam chowder!

Unfortunately, we have never found clams among the smorgasbord of seafood delights in the Bahamas. However, being even more resourceful than hungry, we began an all-out search through our food lockers, and in less than 30 minutes served up a delicious hot soup made from nearly all canned ingredients.

1 large onion, chopped
4 tablespoons bacon drippings
1 pound can tomatoes (stewed or
    whole)
1 pound can mixed vegetables
8 ounce can tomato sauce

8 ounce can minced clams
8 ounce bottle clam juice
Salt and pepper to taste
Tabasco (more or less according to
    the tolerance of your stomach)

Sauté the onion in the bacon drippings until soft and lightly browned. Add the rest of the ingredients and cover the pot. As soon as the chowder comes to a boil, turn down the heat, tune up your radio for some rare DX, and be prepared to defend your galley from impatient, ravenous members of the crew. After the soup has simmered for about 20 minutes, it is ready to be served.

If the day's snorkeling expedition has been successful, you may substitute diced, cooked lobster in the place of or in addition to the clams. When preparing the lobster, it is a good idea to lock your ship's cat in the head, for the aroma of fresh lobster meat will drive most normal, red-blooded felines to the point of attacking both meal and cook.

Linda Turner

• BERMUDA CHOWDER

On a cruise to Bermuda we enjoyed this chowder made with the locally caught fish. Laced with dark rum and sherry peppers, it was one of the tastiest chowders we had sampled in a long time.

Simmer at least 1 pound of white fish fillets in 4 quarts water with salt, pepper, bay leaf, thyme, peppercorns and a pinch of ground cloves.

In another large pan, sauté 3 large onions (preferably Bermudian) chopped finely, 8 celery stalks, 2 green peppers and 1 clove garlic—also chopped finely—until the onion is clear. Add 1 large can of tomatoes and 1 can of chicken or beef consommé and simmer for at least 30 minutes. Add the mixture to the fish when done. Add 1 cup catsup, ¼ cup chopped parsley, Worcestershire sauce to taste, 2 tablespoons lemon juice, 2 pounds finely chopped potatoes and ½ pound shredded carrots.

Add a good dose of dark rum and sherry peppers to taste. Cook slowly for at least 4 hours. Serve with fresh bread and more rum and sherry peppers to serve 6 people. If serving only 2 people, there will be enough left over to can about 6 pints.

Lee Griffin

• NO KA OE (*Clam Chowder—Samoan Style*)

I believe that Americans miss a lot by not including good homemade soup in their cruise menus. Soup is the most important meal for most Europeans and Orientals. To all Polynesians it is No Ka Oe (the greatest). This recipe came through my crew, Randy Grounds—a guard for U.C.L.A.—who got it from an even bigger Samoan guard on the team. It certainly bears no resemblance to anemic canned soup or soup-mix concoctions and can be made from canned or fresh stores.

Into 4 cups of water, mix about ½ cup dried milk, then add ½ cup dried onions and about 3 cups dried hash-brown potatoes (or grated raw potatoes). Simmer until the potatoes are soft then add 1 can mixed vegetables and 1 can chopped clams, salt and pepper, and stir until hot. Serve in a deep bowl with a BIG glob of butter on top and crackers on the side. It is important not to cook the butter as this destroys the food value. Add it at the end and you will have a very tasteful, complete meal.

Don La Terre

• SEAFARING CHOWDER

By accident, I discovered the versatility of my fondue pot (with lid). First, it fits perfectly snug in our Sea Swing stove. Second, because of its concave top and lid, the liquid doesn't spill over when heeling under sail. Third, when it's not being used for cooking, it makes an attractive mixing and serving bowl for fresh fruit and green salads, marinated vegetables, snacks, etc.

Out of necessity, this recipe came into being one Friday when it was decided at high noon to sail to the Channel Islands for the weekend. I had all these ingredients in my cupboard so I threw them together, put it in the oven to bake, and went back to work hoping for the best.

When we got home 4½ hours later, I poured ½ of it in the fondue pot, froze the other half in another pot for the following weekend, and off we went. It turned out to be the best sailing and camping recipe I've got.

For extended cruising, you can keep adding to the diminishing pot and use fresh caught, cleaned and cubed fish, which cooks through within 30 minutes.

Mix together 1 can each:

Cream of shrimp soup
Cream of mushroom soup
Cheddar cheese soup
Tomato soup
New England style clam chowder

Sliced new potatoes with juice
Kernel corn with juice
Minced clams with juice
Shrimp with juice
2–3 cans water

Stir in:

1 cup Minute Rice, Lawry's
seasoned salt, pepper, dill,
basil, tarragon, Tabasco
(optional)

Bake in a 200° oven for 4–5 hours. Divide into 2 3-quart cooking containers and freeze. Add a pinch of gumbo filé (powdered sassafras leaves) to each bowl at serving time, if desired.

Lynn Knuth

• QUICK CONCH CHOWDER

Conch is a favorite and plentiful seafood in the Bahamas. There are many methods of preparing it for lunch or dinner—like most cruising families we've made conch fritters, cracked conch, conch salad, etc., but our favorite has been conch chowder.

I tried several recipes (each needing 2 to 3 hours' preparation and cooking time), and every one required fresh vegetables. Vegetables are not only hard to come by when you've been away from port for awhile, but also are best saved for a crisp, crunchy salad rather than being cooked.

One day after our conch were cleaned and ready for chowder making, I decided to try the following method, which turned out to be quick and easy—and the tastiest chowder of all.

5–6 medium conch
16 ounce can mixed vegetables,
    drained
16 ounce can tomatoes

Salt, pepper, garlic, oregano—to
    taste
Dash of hot sauce

Put conch through food grinder. Then combine ground conch and all other ingredients in a pot. Cook over medium heat for about 15 minutes or until chowder is steaming and seasonings well blended.

Served with crusty, homemade bread this makes a delicious and nourishing meal.

Jean Carter

• DELECTABLE CONCH CHOWDER

Conch must have wide flaring lips before they are old enough to harvest. Cleaning conch can seem a formidable task to the uninitiated

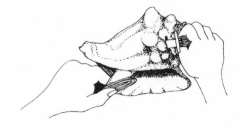

(as we were), but with a little help from Paul and Mavis Hill's excellent book, "The Edible Sea", we did the job admirably.

First, you must cut through the shell about 4 or 5 spirals from the tip with a heavy diving knife or a large screwdriver. Loosen the animal by slipping the knife through the hole, then pull it out. Remove the soft viscera and use the white meat.

Many people recommend pounding the meat to tenderize it before cooking, but we felt that this was unnecessary and that the chewy texture was interesting.

½ pound salt pork, diced
2 medium potatoes, diced
1 large onion, diced
1 stalk celery, diced
½ green pepper, diced
19 ounce can tomatoes
1 quart boiling water
1 bay leaf

1 clove garlic, smashed (or 1
     teaspoon garlic powder)
½ teaspoon herb seasoning
     (preferably thyme or oregano)
1 or 2 drops Tabasco
Salt and pepper to taste
Meat from 1 conch, diced (may be
     cooked or raw)

Brown salt pork and remove from pan. Brown onion, potatoes and celery in the salt pork fat. Reserve half the potatoes to add later. Add all remaining ingredients except the conch and the reserved potatoes. If you are using raw conch, add it at this point as well.

Simmer for 30 minutes or longer. Add the cooked conch and remaining potatoes and simmer for at least a further 30 minutes before serving.

This chowder was so good that we decided it should become our traditional hot-weather Christmas Eve dinner. Don't save it only for special occasions, though, it is much too practical for that.

Anna Patrick

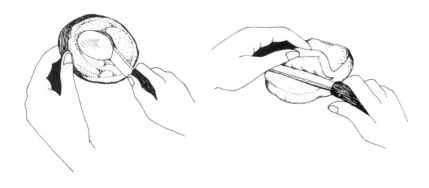

• SEAFOOD CHOWDER

This can be prepared in advance of a cruise and can be frozen. It also seems to keep well just being refrigerated.

1 cup small shell macaroni
½ cup chopped onion
1 clove garlic, minced
½ cup chopped celery
8 ounce can minced clams (reserve liquid)
4 ounce can tiny shrimp (reserve liquid)
6 oysters or 10 ounce can oysters (reserve liquid)
⅓ cup dry white wine
¼ cup butter
1 teaspoon chicken bouillon powder
½ teaspoon each thyme, nutmeg, pepper
1 teaspoon salt
1 bay leaf
5 tablespoons flour
1 pound cod fillets, cubed
½ cup diced green pepper
8 ounce can evaporated milk *
¼ cup each chopped parsley and pimento

Cook macaroni about 8 minutes until tender. Drain and set aside. In a large saucepan with high sides sauté onions, celery and garlic in butter for 5 minutes.

Combine reserved liquids, adding water to make 3 cups. Pour into saucepan, add wine, chicken bouillon powder, salt, thyme, nutmeg, pepper and bay leaf. Cover and simmer for 15 minutes.

Mix flour and ⅓ cup cold water to a smooth paste. Add to saucepan, stirring constantly, and cook until thickened. Add cod, green pepper and oysters.

Simmer uncovered for 15 minutes. Remove bay leaf, stir in macaroni, milk, clams, shrimp, parsley and pimento. Heat to simmering and serve. Makes 2 quarts.

* This makes a very thick chowder. Additional evaporated milk may be added for a thinner soup.

Debbie Bertland

• OYSTER OR CLAM STEW

Boil 2 potatoes in water to barely cover. On another burner slowly sauté a large sliced onion in a stick of butter until golden brown, then add onions and butter to potatoes. Add enough water to feed everyone. Cook gently for 10 minutes.

When everyone is at the table, add chopped oysters or clams and heat until just cooked.

Isobel Crittenden

• LOBSTER BISQUE

This recipe produces the finest lobster bisque available anywhere. Don't leave out the sherry—it pulls the dish together. Serves 2.

½ pound lobster meat
1 can condensed cream of
   asparagus soup
1 can condensed cream of
   mushroom soup

Few grains of Cayenne pepper
1 cup light cream
2 tablespoons chopped chives
2 tablespoons sherry

In a saucepan stir together soups, cream and Cayenne. Bring to simmering. Add lobster meat and chives, reserving some chives for garnish. Reheat, stirring occasionally, to simmering. Add sherry when hot. Serve into preheated tureen or bowls. Serves 2.

Lobster meat may be augmented or substituted by cod, crab, scrod or white meat of bluefish. Interesting flavor treats arise using oysters, clams and mussels in varying combinations, alone or with fish. Well-drained and rinsed canned fish may be used without serious degradation of flavor.

R.I. Marine Services
in Snug Harbor

• QUICK SHELLFISH BISQUE

This is a filling soup and good for the crew on damp and nasty days.

1 can tomato soup	1 cup canned crabmeat, lobster or
1 can pea soup	shrimp
2 cans beef consommé	Chopped freeze-dried chives
	Sherry to taste

Put all soups in a pot and mix well (with a rotary beater if possible). Warm slowly. Add the seafood and heat thoroughly. Just before serving add the sherry and chopped chives.

Serve with a loaf of fresh bread. It is even more delicious if fresh seafood is available.

Dori Dolce

• BLUE CRAB DELIGHT

I'm the world's worst cook. However, whenever I prepare a meal on board, rave notices are the rule. I like to combine natural seafoods with canned staples to provide tasty freshness and simplicity.

Blue-claw crabs are usually very plentiful in our area but have little meat and lots of work. Here's a recipe that extends a few blue-claws into an excellent dinner.

6–12 blue-claw crabs
1 can Campbell's cream of
  shrimp soup

Empty the soup into a saucepan and add meat from 6 to 12 crabs. Heat, and serve over a piece of toast for each person. Season to taste. This makes a delicious dinner for 2 to 4 people.

Don Launer

• FRESH CRAB SOUP

After a hard day of sailing along our breezy Gulf coast, we often anchor *Dancing Girl* in the lee of one of the barrier islands for the night. Everyone is tired but as hungry as sharks. Over we go for a swim and a walk ashore, taking along a crabnet, bucket, sack and castnet so as not to pass up any largesse the sea may offer.

This soup uses fresh crabmeat, but everything else will be found in the galley of any well-found cruising yacht.

1 can cream of mushroom soup	1 tablespoon parsley flakes
1 can golden mushroom soup	1 heaping tablespoon dried onions
1 can mushroom pieces (reserve liquid)	(or fresh)
	½ teaspoon tarragon leaves
1 pound picked crabmeat	¼ cup dry sherry
1 tablespoon dried celery flakes (½ cup of fresh)	1–2 cups water

Get these ingredients together, then mix yourself a shooter.

Mix together all ingredients except the sherry and crabmeat, using mushroom juice for part of water needed to dilute soup. Bring to a boil and simmer on low heat for at least 1 hour.

Mix yourself another shooter and one each for all hands. Then let them pick out the crabmeat.

After an hour or so, bring soup to a brisk boil, reduce to simmer and add crabmeat. This is hot work, so you will need another shooter. Enjoy it and when it's finished, turn off heat under soup, add sherry, cover and let stand 5 minutes.

The result is so elegant and delicious the crew will think you spent all that time over a hot stove and never realize you sneaked three drinks to their one.

You could, of course, use canned crabmeat, in which case you'll have to find something else to keep the crew busy so they don't have time to watch you.

Warren Norville

• SAVANNAH CRAB SOUP

The sailing season starts early on the Chesapeake Bay, and the spring days can be bitter cold. After a morning in the cockpit a hot lunch is a must.

At noon, cooking is a definite pain. What's needed is a quick, hearty, 1-burner lunch, simple to make but a bit more memorable for any guests aboard than canned beans. The answer—Savannah Crab Soup, the sailor's friend.

The recipe was given to me in a Savannah, Georgia, shipyard some years ago. We finished an all-night ship inspection at about 4 a.m. The owner of a fine Savannah restaurant had stopped by after closing to watch and offer constructive criticism. In spite of the efforts of the whole crew, he refused to return to his restaurant to get us a pot of his famous crab soup.

However, he said that he had most of the fixings for a pretty good substitute in his car, if we could find some milk among the beer in the refrigerator. He returned with a stack of cans and in a few minutes produced a meal fit for a tired shipyard crew—or for cold springtime sailors.

1 can condensed cream of celery soup	1 can crabmeat
1 can condensed cream of mushroom soup	Milk

Place the condensed soups in a pan. Add 1–1½ soup cans of milk, depending on how thick you like your soup. Add the crabmeat. Heat, but don't boil. Season to taste. Serves 4.

Dick Brooks

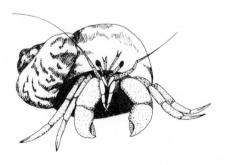

• TUNA CHOWDER

Sauté 1 chopped or sliced onion in oil, then add:

1 pound can tomato sauce or stewed tomatoes	1 can vacuum-packed corn
	1 can tuna

I usually cook this for at least 20 minutes, but in rough weather you could just warm it up. I sometimes add fresh seafood, vegetables, leftovers, wine, etc. For seasoning, I like pepper and oregano.

We've made many hearty soups by mixing various canned foods, but this was our greatest success.

Sue Thompson

• MUSSEL BISQUE

In a large pot, place:

½ cup sherry	2 cloves garlic
½ onion	Salt and pepper
Handful of parsley	3 quarts mussels
1 teaspoon paprika	

In a separate pot, heat 1 can cream of mushroom soup. Steam the mussels until they open. Remove the mussels with a slotted spoon and keep warm. Strain the mussel broth and whisk it into the mushroom soup. Place the mussels, still in shells, in large soup bowls, and pour the broth over the mussels. Serve with garlic toast.

Cathy Reed

• CLAM BISQUE

1 can chunky vegetable soup	2 inch slice of Velveeta cheese (or
1 can clams	½ cup grated mild Cheddar)
1 can evaporated milk	Pinch of curry powder
1 cup water	

Blend all ingredients and simmer for 20 minutes. Be sure the melted cheese is well blended into the soup.

Dianna Schwierzke

• GOLDEN OYSTER-MUSHROOM BISQUE

The ingredients for this soup are easily stored on board. We are proud of our Chesapeake Bay oysters and make this on cold days.

1 pint shucked standard oysters
    with liquor
¼ cup margarine or butter
1 tablespoon flour
1 quart milk

1 can condensed golden
    mushroom soup
¼ teaspoon instant minced onion
Salt and pepper to taste

Put oysters and liquor in a small pan, bring to a boil and remove from heat.

In a large pan, melt margarine or butter, blend in flour and slowly stir in milk. Cook over medium heat, stirring constantly until mixture just reaches boiling point. Reduce heat and blend in soup. Add onions, oysters with liquor, salt and pepper.

Heat but do not boil. Makes 6 1-cup servings.

Harry Wolf

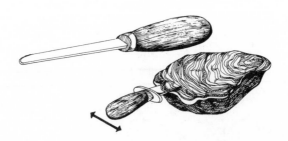

• PERUVIAN FISH SOUP

When we were in the quiet little Bay of Ancón, a few miles north of Lima, we got this recipe from Señora Phyllis Chesterton, whose charming house overlooked our anchorage. The bare desert hills of the brown landscape climbed above the peaceful blue of the tropical Pacific and usually the only sound was the putt-putt of a small fishing boat or the shouts of fishermen as they put out their nets or hooks for the jejerrey, the lenguada or the corvina.

Fillet any white-fleshed fish, large or small. Set aside the fillets. Put the head and backbone in a pressure cooker and cover with water. Season with a little salt and pepper. Cook under high pressure for 10 minutes. Strain the stock and throw away the bones. Return the stock to the pressure cooker.

Chop a medium-sized onion and a clove of garlic. Put them in a frying pan (with a little oil) together with 2 sliced tomatoes (without skin). Fry on low heat for a few minutes until the onions begin to soften. Add the contents of the frying pan to the stock in the pressure cooker.

Add 1 pound cubed pumpkin, 1 pound cubed yellow or white potatoes, 2 tablespoons rice and 1 red pepper (without seeds). Boil the soup mixture slowly until the potatoes and rice are cooked. Add 1 can drained peas and the raw fish fillets. Boil for 2 minutes.

Just before serving, add 1 small can evaporated milk to a well-beaten egg. Pour the hot soup *slowly* over the mixture of milk and egg (if you pour too fast the milk will curdle).

Substitutions: Instead of fresh tomatoes you can use canned whole tomatoes. If you don't have pumpkin add more potatoes. A few drops of Tabasco sauce can take the place of the red pepper.

With an 18-inch fish, this thick and delicious soup makes 6 generous servings. The soup will keep a day or so if you don't add the milk until just before serving.

Hal and Margaret Roth

• SALMON POTATO SOUP

As a farewell surprise, our friends gave us a "Provisioning Party". Each family brought a recipe that used canned goods or dried foods as the main ingredients. They also brought all the canned stores or packaged foods for the dish.

Here is one we especially enjoyed on our cruise through the San Juan Islands.

1 can potato soup	1 small can peas
1 can salmon	1 tablespoon butter
2 cups milk	1 cup shredded Cheddar cheese

Heat and stir ingredients until piping hot.

Nan Hollis

MEAT SOUPS

• MINESTRONE

4–8 slices bacon (canned bacon; use the remainder for breakfast next morning)
1 large onion, chopped
1 cup each diced carrots and celery
2 cans beef broth (10½ ounces each)
1 quart water

1 cup ditalini (or any small soup macaroni)
1 can chick-peas (undrained)
1 can peas (drained)
1 can green beans (drained)
1 jar Ragu cooking sauce
Salt and pepper

Fry bacon in large pot. Add and sauté onion. Add celery and carrots. Cook 5 minutes, then add water and broth. Bring to boil, cover and simmer 20 minutes. In a separate pan, cook ditalini until firm (do not overcook). Add sauce, chick-peas, salt, pepper to soup and simmer 20 more minutes. Add peas and green beans. Cook 5 more minutes.

We found it best to cook the ditalini separately, put in the bowl at the table and spoon hot soup on top. This way if there is any soup left over all you have to do is heat it up and the macaroni will not overcook.

Chris Lantis

• WARMER-UPPER

This is filling and warming in cool weather. It originated at sports car races in spring and fall but is easy to prepare on board as it requires only boiling water.

In each cup put ½ to ⅔ cup of instant rice and 1 beef or chicken bouillon cube. Add boiling water and let stand until the rice is fluffy.

Alice Hidy

• LENTIL BEEF SOUP

This recipe is vegetarian, but adding a little leftover roast and gravy is flavorful if you're meat-eaters.

½ cup lentils (soak overnight)
2–3 tablespoons cooking oil
1 clove garlic
1 large yellow onion, chopped
1 green pepper, chopped
1 can tomatoes
Any other vegetables you have
(carrots, celery, potatoes, etc.), chopped or sliced
Salt and pepper
2 bay leaves
½ teaspoon celery seed
1 teaspoon basil
⅓–½ cup rice

Sauté minced garlic in oil; then onion, celery and green pepper. Add tomatoes and other vegetables, as well as lentils. Add spices and enough water to make soup.

Bring to a boil and simmer as long as you can, adding water if necessary. Add meat at the simmering stage if you've got leftovers. Thirty minutes or so before eating, add rice, which makes this a hearty meal.

Carol Moorhead

• SLOOP SOUP

2 cups dried lentils
5 cups water
1 carrot, sliced
1 potato, peeled and sliced
2 small onions, chopped
1 celery stalk (with leaves) chopped
1 bouillon cube
1 teaspoon bacon bits (imitation)
1 tablespoon catsup
1 pinch garlic powder, poultry seasoning, oregano
Salt and pepper

You can pour boiling water over the lentils and let them soak for 50 minutes, then cook the soup for 2 hours. I've made good soup with no soaking at all, but the best soup is made when the lentils have soaked for 24 hours. Then the soup needs only 30 minutes' cooking time.

Wendy Kimball

• SHIVER ME TIMBERS SOUPS

Nothing beats a steaming mug of rich, hearty broth for restoring good humor and quelling that all-over-damp feeling being out on the water can sometimes induce. Soups are perfect on-board meals because they're so simple to prepare—just pile the fixings into a good-sized pot, simmer and voilà! Soup. They can even be put together ahead of time and brought aboard in plastic containers for heating and eating.

Each of these recipes serves a *hungry* crew of 4.

Spicy Sausage Soup

Any spicy, precooked sausage can be used in this recipe, which will keep without refrigeration for quite awhile.

1 package chourico or linguica or kielbasa or other spicy cooked sausage
1 can spinach, drained

1 pound can Campbell's baked beans in tomato sauce
½ small head cabbage, shredded
2 cups water (or more depending on how thick you like your broth)

Slice sausage into bite-sized chunks and place it in the bottom of a large soup pot. Add beans (make sure you get beans in tomato sauce; this is what makes the broth). Place drained spinach and shredded cabbage on top. Add water to cover. Stir ingredients, cover pot. Simmer for about 1 hour or until broth picks up spicy, tomatoey flavor. Delicious with a loaf of sweet bread or corn muffins.

Escarole and Bean Soup

2 cans Progresso escarole in chicken broth
2 cans Progresso cannellini beans

3 or 4 large cloves garlic
2 tablespoons cooking oil
Salt and pepper to taste

Crush garlic or mince into tiny pieces. In a large soup pot, sauté garlic in oil, pressing lightly to extract flavor. Add escarole in chicken broth and undrained cannellini beans. If the broth is too thick, add a little water. Cover and simmer until broth absorbs escarole and garlic flavors (about 30 minutes). Add salt and pepper to taste. Great served with crusty French or Italian bread. (Even bread that's lightly stale will do with this recipe; just soak it in the broth to soften it.)

Nutty Chicken Curry Soup

2 cans Campbell's cream of
   chicken soup
1 cup nuts (cashews and peanuts
   are best)

1 cup raisins
1 can unsweetened evaporated milk
1 soup can water
1 or 2 tablespoons curry powder

Empty cans of soup into large pot. Add milk and water. (Again, more water can be added to thin consistency.) Sprinkle in curry powder. Add nuts, raisins and stir until heated through.

Lynda Morris

• TASTER'S BEAN SOUP

I'm a great taster. I generally start with an idea of how something should taste and just keep adding and tasting until it's right. The big danger with my method is that when it's time to eat, I'm too full.

My Newfoundland grandmother, another great taster, used to make the best bean soup I've ever tasted and while I've never hit it exactly right, I've come close lots of times. The recipe which follows is for 2 and good only for tasters. The measurers will have to use a cookbook.

½ pound pea beans
¼ pound salt pork or a ham bone if
   you have one
1 large onion or more
Carrot
Celery
Potato

1 clove garlic or more
Tomatoes, fresh or canned
   (optional)
Bay leaf
Pepper
Savory

Wash the beans and soak overnight. Put beans and soaking liquid in a large pot. Add either the tomato liquid, if you are using canned tomatoes, or water to cover well, and bring to a boil. Cut the salt pork in ¼ inch slices, then cut across the rind into ½ inch pieces and add to the pot. Coarsely dice the onion and add to the beans. Smash the garlic between the flat of a knife and the cutting board and add it, along with the savory and bay leaf. Taste a lot, guessing at what's missing and adding as you see fit. When the beans are fairly soft, add the cubed carrot, potato and tomatoes. Add pepper to taste.

You now have to decide whether the soup you want is to be thick or thin. Estimate the amount of water and add. Simmer until the beans are soft, tasting and adding until you are satisfied.

Chuck Patrick

• MANY BEAN SOUP

To prepare Many Bean Soup, you need at least 10 different kinds of dried beans and peas. They usually come in 1 pound bags. Mix them all together and store in tins or doubled Zip-Loc bags. (I use the bags. They seal well and store in small places.)

1½ cups dried mixed beans	1 clove garlic, minced
1 large onion, sliced	6–8 slices bacon (canned or fresh)
2 medium tomatoes chopped or 1 pound can whole tomatoes with liquid	2 tablespoons bacon fat
	Dash or 2 of red pepper
	Juice of ½ lemon
2 bay leaves	

Wash the beans and place in a large saucepan. Add 3 cups water and 2 teaspoons salt and bring to a boil. Boil for 2 minutes, then remove from heat. Let stand covered for 1 hour. This method of soaking is the easiest, especially at sea.

While beans are soaking, brown the bacon and save 2 tablespoons of the fat.

Place the beans back on the burner and add 2 more cups water. Next add the bacon, fat, onion, tomatoes, garlic and bay leaf. Simmer covered for about 2½ hours or until beans are tender. Add the lemon juice, red pepper and salt to taste. Serves 4.

Excellent when served with freshly baked bread!

Laurel Warburton

• PORTUGUESE BEAN SOUP

3 ham shanks	6 to 8 ounces linguica (Portuguese
2 beef soup bones	sausage)
	2 cups red beans

Cover the bones and shanks with about 4 quarts water. Dice the linguica into ½-inch cubes and add to the broth. After 1 hour or so, add the beans. Simmer until beans are done (1 to 2 hours). Take out the cooked bones and add:

8 ounce can tomato sauce	2 teaspoons salt
1 large onion, diced	2 teaspoons Portuguese allspice (2
1 or 2 carrots, sliced	parts ground anise, 1 part
3 tablespoons minced parsley	cinnamon, 1 part black pepper,
2 large potatoes, diced (macaroni	1 part ground cloves)
can also be used)	

Continue to cook until the vegetables are done. A slow-cooker is ideal for this, after the beans are cooked. The longer it simmers, the better it tastes! Chill thoroughly and keep on ice until ready to heat and serve.

Demaris Fredericksen

• SIMPLE GAZPACHO

Early spring sailing days on Lake Champlain call for a special warmer-upper on return to the mooring. We pack an extra Thermos of cream of tomato soup and as the mugs are passed around, we add 1 ounce of sherry and stir.

As summer brings beautiful sailing days, with the bluish Adirondacks on one side of the lake and Vermont mountains and meadows on the other, we have a favorite cooler soup for the luncheon anchorage.

1 pint tomato juice	½ cup mixture of chives, parsley,
1 pint beef broth (2 packages MBT	basil, thyme, tarragon, chervil,
and hot water)	crushed garlic or garlic powder
1 pint chicken broth (2 packets	1 pepper, chopped
MBT and hot water)	1 onion, chopped
Juice of 2 lemons	1 cucumber, chopped
3 tablespoons oil	1 tomato, chopped

We blend and chill it at home and transport it in a vacuum bottle, but it could be chopped and put together on board, then iced. Stir in desired amount of vodka and serve.

Andrena Huntsman

VEGETABLE SOUPS

• CREAM OF VEGETABLE SOUP

¾ cup instant potatoes
¾ cup hot water
1 tablespoon butter
1½ cups milk

1 bouillon cube
½ teaspoon onion powder
1 small can mixed vegetables

Dissolve bouillon cube in hot water, mix with potatoes, blend in butter and milk. Drain vegetables and add to mixture. Heat and eat.

Marguerite Allen

• QUICKIE ORIENTAL SOUP

1 can Chinese vegetables
¼ cup noodles
2 bouillon cubes

1 can water
2 to 3 teaspoons soy sauce (to taste)

Place all ingredients in a large saucepan. Bring to a boil, then reduce to simmer until noodles are done.

Howard Olsen

• MADEIRA TOMATO SOUP

In the summer of 1977 five of us went to Málaga to help a friend bring his boat back to Britain, via Madeira and the Azores.

In Madeira tomatoes were very plentiful and we concocted a rather interesting soup.

1½ pounds tomatoes	⅛ bottle gin
2 tablespoons olive oil	¼ to ½ pint water
1 onion	1 teaspoon curry powder
¼ cup mushrooms	Salt, pepper and Cayenne pepper
1 clove garlic	Cream
¼ cup butter	

Skin tomatoes and rub through a sieve. Mix olive oil, water, curry powder and seasonings into the juice.

In a deep pan, fry finely sliced onions, mushrooms and crushed garlic clove in butter until onions are soft but not brown. Add tomato mixture and bring to a boil.

Heat gin in a large ladle. Set it alight and pour, flaming, into the pan of soup. When the flame dies add the cream and serve immediately.

These quantities will serve 6. To double the amount, use twice the ingredients except garlic and curry powder.

David Cowper

• MISO SOUP

We get most of our protein from nuts, brown rice, sprouts and soybean products. Miso (fermented soybeans) is a brown paste. A 30-pound keg cost us $30 and lasted more than a year, though we eat it regularly.

Miso is also made from rice or barley and varies in saltiness. It contains all the essential amino acids, and we believe it protects us from the effects of smoking and pollution. We usually eat it as miso soup. Boil enough water for the bowls you need. Pour into the bowls and add to each the following ingredients, mixing with a spoon: 1 tablespoon miso, 1 tablespoon brewers' yeast (high in vitamin B), ¼ teaspoon Cayenne pepper (natural stimulant), ½ teaspoon powdered kelp (high in calcium) and 1 tablespoon coldpressed oil (wheatgerm, avocado, etc.).

Optional ingredients: Sautéed tofu (soybean curd) cut into cubes, fresh raw peas, grated carrots, any kind of sprouts.

Miso can also be used to make sauces, dips or spreads.

Ann Segal

• QUICK ONION SOUP

Melt 1 stick margarine and lightly brown 4 to 6 sliced onions. Add 1 quart boiling water and simmer for 15 minutes. Add 1 package onion soup mix, 1 tablespoon Gravy Master, 2 beef bouillon cubes and pepper to taste. Simmer for 20 minutes.

Toast a slice of bread, cut in quarters and top each piece with a slice of cheese. Melt cheese under broiler, put soup in bowls and float the cheese toast on top. Crackers can be used in place of toast if you are out of bread.

Dian Jacobs

• ONION SOUP AU GRATIN

3 cups water	8 crackers
1 cup dry red wine	1 big onion, chopped
1 envelope dehydrated onion soup	Savory, thyme, oregano,
4 slices processed Cheddar cheese	rosemary, parsley
Sliced Emmenthal cheese	French bread

Bring 3 cups of water to a boil, add onion and onion soup. Cook over medium heat for about 3 minutes, then add spices, wine and Cheddar cheese and stir well. Add broken crackers and mix. Cook for about 10 minutes, stirring occasionally.

If the liquid reduces, add more water or wine. When the onion is tender, reduce heat and keep warm.

Broil 8 slices French bread. Pour the soup into 4 bowls, put 2 slices bread on top of each, cover with Emmenthal cheese and sprinkle with parsley.

Put in the oven to melt the cheese, then broil for 3–5 minutes.

Do not serve a heavy meal afterwards—this soup is very nourishing by itself.

Ginette Villeneuve

• PIGEON PEA SOUP

Pigeon peas are found all over the West Indies, fresh and canned. For this recipe, either may be used, but fresh will need at least twice as much cooking time. Dried peas are equally good but also require more cooking, so allow 3 or 4 times longer than for canned ones. This dish is very high in protein and a complete meal when served with salad and bread. Enough for 4 as a main dish, 6 as a starter.

Small chunk salt pork or 2 slices bacon
1–2 onions, chopped
1–2 cloves garlic, pressed or finely chopped
1 cup diced cooked ham
2 cups cooked West Indian pumpkin (optional)

2 medium tomatoes, or 1 cup drained canned tomatoes
1 quart chicken or vegetable broth
1 pound pigeon peas, fresh or canned

Sauté salt pork or bacon in a large, heavy casserole, until crisp and brown. Remove, add garlic and onions to fat, stirring frequently, and cook for 5 minutes until soft. Add ham, tomatoes and pumpkin, bring to a boil, then lower heat and allow to simmer for 15 minutes, until somewhat thick. Add pigeon peas and broth and cook until peas are soft. Season with salt and pepper, and serve hot.

Allison McGeary

• CREAM OF SUMMER SOUP

Finely chop or shred into a large kettle:

1 large carrot
½ head cabbage
4 small yellow summer squashes

1 stalk celery with leaves
1 small bunch parsley

Add 4 chicken bouillon cubes, ⅛ teaspoon pepper and 5 cups water. Cook until the vegetables are very tender, then mash to blend. Add ¼ pound Velveeta cheese cut into small cubes. Simmer over very low heat just until cheese melts. Taste, correct seasonings, if necessary.
Serve hot or chilled with bread sticks.

Barbary Chaapel

• WEST INDIAN SOUP

This is one of our favorite soups aboard *Chrysalis*, our Alberg 37. We found pumpkins available throughout the West Indies, Netherlands Antilles, Panama, French Polynesia and the Samoas.

A pressure cooker is invaluable on a cruising boat, especially for homemade soup.

1 pumpkin (about 5 pounds)	1 teaspoon salt
2 onions, sliced in rings	½ teaspoon black pepper
2 cloves garlic, crushed	2–3 dashes Tabasco sauce
1 tablespoon brown sugar	3 cups water
1 teaspoon ground thyme	

Cut pumpkin in pieces, peel and remove seeds. Pressure-cook with ½ cup water for 10 minutes. Mash pumpkin in pressure cooker. Add remaining ingredients and simmer until onions are cooked, about 30 minutes.

A variation of this soup is to leave out all the ingredients except the pumpkin, water, salt and pepper and add ½ cup evaporated milk just before serving to make Cream of Pumpkin Soup.

Sue McBride

CHAPTER 6

BREAKFASTS

CEREALS

• VANILLA GRANOLA

With prices as they are and with horrible fishing luck, we use lots of grains and nuts. Having no oven, we became adept at baking over a burner.

This was a lifesaver during the many gales we rode out.

Mix together:

4 cups rolled oats	¼ cup coconut
1 cup sunflower seeds	½ cup wheat germ
½ cup sliced almonds	2 tablespoons non-fat dried milk
½ cup cashew pieces	

Mix together, very well:

½ cup oil	1 tablespoon vanilla
¼ cup honey	

Then mix this into the dry ingredients, as thoroughly as possible. Add ½ to 1 cup brown sugar and any desired dried fruits. Put into a large ungreased skillet over low flame. Brown on 1 side *slowly*, then flip and brown the other side *slowly*. Store in tightly sealed containers.

Marni Suttle

124 •

• VERSATILE GRANOLA MIX

This recipe is delicious and requires no baking. In fact I like it better than baked granola. Try your own variations of ingredients.

2 cups Quick Quaker Oats
½ cup wheat germ, bran, peanuts or nuts
½ cup brown sugar or honey

¼ cup margarine
½ cup coconut
½ cup raisins or other dried fruit
½ teaspoon cinnamon

Combine everything in a skillet. Mix well. Cook over medium heat, stirring constantly, for 10 minutes. Spread on a plate to cool, then store in a tightly covered container.

It keeps well, but you'll find it won't be around long. It's too good.

Serve as a topping. Eat it as a snack. Use in place of nuts and serve with milk as a cereal.

We miss fresh milk, but here's a substitute we find almost as good:

Put a tablespoon of non-dairy creamer and a scoop of nonfat dry milk in a glass. Add 2 tablespoons of almost boiling water and stir until dissolved. Fill the glass with cold water and let sit.

We use it on our cereal. If we have ice we chill the milk, which tastes even better.

Colleen Seyer

• HOT SHREDDED WHEAT

Large Shredded Wheat biscuits
Very salty water

Butter or margarine

Fill a shallow bowl 1 inch deep with water (seawater is O.K., if clear and clean). Stir in a rounded tablespoon of salt. The salt will dissolve better if the water's hot. Dip each biscuit in the salted water. Turn them over only once and handle them carefully as they tend to get soggy and fall apart. Arrange them round-side up in a greased skillet. Dot the tops with 2 or more pats of butter or margarine (tinned butter, if you can find it, is quite good). Cover tightly and cook on medium heat until the butter melts and the bottoms get toasty and begin to crisp. Serve with scrambled eggs or in place of potatoes with any meal.

Annie Graves

• OFF-WATCH REJUVENATOR

My favorite rejuvenator after a cold night watch is a mug of oatmeal and milk sweetened with hot buttered rum mix and braced with ½ jigger of rum. The mix consists of 1 pound butter, 2 pounds dark brown sugar and 2 teaspoons each of ground nutmeg, cinnamon and cloves. Adjust spices to suit your taste. Barely melt the butter to facilitate mixing.

Ernie Copp

EGGS

• BUILT-IN EGGS

This requires bread, preferably galley-baked, but store-bought will do. You "build in" the eggs by first whipping up, in a large bowl, as many eggs as you have slices of bread. Just eggs—no milk, sugar, spices or seasoning except a little salt.

When the eggs have become a pale yellow froth, dip a slice of bread in them and let it absorb as much of the froth as it wants. Then drop it into the pan of fat that you've had heating since you began this operation.

The fat doesn't have to be any deeper than ½ inch in a pan large enough to accommodate 1 slice of bread. When it has turned a golden brown on both sides, fork it out of the fat and smear with butter or honey or peanut butter or maple syrup or strawberry jam or whatever your little heart desires. For best results, eat it as hot as you can stand it.

Built-in eggs are full of calories and cholesterol and all sorts of things that folks ain't supposed to eat. But they sure do taste good!

Ray Anderson

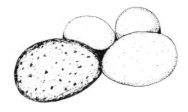

• BREAKFAST SANDWICH

Coping with breakfast while under way can be especially taxing. But Bill and I are breakfast eaters and seldom skip this meal. Therefore, when we up anchor early, we make breakfast a sandwich. This is convenient, as the helmsman can eat with one hand and steer with the other. Also, if you serve the sandwiches on paper plates or napkins, you only have one pan to wash.

Per sandwich:

2 slices of bread
1 or 2 eggs
Thinly sliced cheese to cover 1 slice
    of bread (optional)

Salt and pepper to taste
Mayonnaise, margarine or butter

Toast bread on griddle. Remove, apply spread, then put cheese on 1 slice. Lightly coat griddle with oil and fry eggs your favorite way (we prefer them over-easy). Salt and pepper eggs and place on top of the cheese. Cover with second slice. The heat of the eggs will partially melt the cheese.

Alma Russell

• SAILOR'S EGGS

1 packet potato pancake mix
2 packets scrambled egg mix

2 cups water

Stir until blended, let stand 10 minutes. Add 1½ tablespoons melted butter and cook until set.

Optional additions: Ham, Spam, mushrooms, peppers, cheese.

Nan Hollis

• MORNING-AFTER EGGS

This takes only 1 skillet, but 2 people to fix. One person shakes, then opens, a large can of tomato juice, adds a very generous dash of Tabasco, several drops of Worcestershire sauce, a dash of salt and pepper and a squeeze of lemon, pours ½ cup juice into mugs and laces them with vodka. While the helper passes the juice up the hatch—the cook (me) gets busy!

Dice franks, 1 per person, and brown in greased skillet. Beat eggs, 2 per person, using the leftover bloody mary mix with the eggs as you would usually use milk as liquid. Add eggs to skillet, over the franks, slowly stirring until the eggs are set.

The cook then mixes himself another cup of juice to catch up with the others, and everyone relaxes to a *quick* breakfast that really starts a "morning after" just right.

Ed Rhodes

• TAKE TWO FRIGATE EGGS AND ONE SPROUTED COCONUT

Take a large brown coconut that has sprouted a green shoot approximately 12 inches high and has roots that are just penetrating the soil. With a very swift whack of a machete or an axe lengthwise across the nut, the coconut will split conveniently into 2 halves. At this stage of growth the interior white meat has changed into a moist white fibrous matter, filling the whole inner cavity.

Scoop this fiber into a bowl and shred with your fingers. Mix 2 frigate eggs, flour, a little sugar, salt, pepper and water to form a thick consistency similar to ordinary pancake batter. Cook the same way as any other pancake.

For variation, bits of shredded coconut can be added, which will change the flavor and consistency of the pancake. Cooked and diced lobster tail is also a succulent addition.

The frigate eggs came from a "bird island." Being a low flat island void of trees, the frigates, terns and boobies take their turn to nest on ground free of predators.

Test the eggs in question to determine their state of incubation or decay by dropping the egg in a bucket of seawater. If the egg falls like a rock to the bottom and stays there, then it is newly laid and fresh. If the egg drops to the bottom of the bucket then tends to turn one end up or shows the slightest sign of buoyancy, replace the egg on the nest; it is either beginning to rot or is in the beginning stages of incubation.

The yolk of the frigate egg is red and tends to give the pancakes a pink color. When used in cooking, the slightly different flavor of the frigate egg is undetectable. If scrambled by themselves the eggs are extremely palatable, but the whites will tend to gain a rubbery consistency.

Patrick Childress

• PITA EGGS

4 pita rounds, halved	Chopped and sautéed bacon, ham
8 thin slices Cheddar cheese	or sausage
8 eggs	Sautéed peppers, onions and
	chopped mushrooms

Scramble the eggs with a little milk and mix in the sautéed ingredients. You can brown the pitas in the oven if you like. Place 1 slice cheese inside each pita half and the eggs inside the cheese (which will soon melt).

These are very tasty and easy to eat while under way. Serve with whole fruit.

EGGS IN CROISSANTS

When cruising in French islands, buy fresh croissants and scoop out the middle. Fill with scrambled eggs, top with a little black caviar and garnish with curls of smoked salmon. Serve with mimosas.

Geri Carlbom

• BAHAMA BREAKFASTS

We start each day on *Shohola* with a hearty breakfast, and these are 2 of our favorite dishes.

Poached Eggs

Spread 1 English muffin (½ per person) with Underwood deviled ham and top with a tomato slice. Toast the muffins under a broiler. Place a poached egg on top of each and serve. Fried eggs could be substituted for poached eggs.

Hashbrown Omelette

This recipe can be stretched to feed from 2 to 8 people. Fry 4 to 6 slices bacon; drain and crumble. Prepare a box of dehydrated hashbrown potatoes with onions according to the package directions. Half a box is plenty for 2 to 3 people. While they brown, whip 1 to 2 eggs per person with seasoned salt, pepper and a teaspoon of parsley flakes. When the hashbrowns are almost done, gently press them to form a layer on the bottom of the pan and pour the egg mixture on top of them. Lay several slices of processed cheese on top of the eggs and sprinkle with crumbled bacon. Cover and cook over medium heat until the eggs are set. Slice in wedges to serve.

Vienna Moore

• OVERINDULGERS' BRUNCH

Having served as guest-crew-menial on a number of sailing ventures, I've found even the most genteel crews are given to occasional overindulgence—usually on a festive night ashore or tied up to the dock.

The symptoms are classic: An inclination to double vision, queasiness, leather tongue, spastic confusion and loss of appetite. Obviously, if things are ever going to get better the crew must first eat. This fact of the sea resulted in the evolution of the following recipe, which seems to have a very real restorative effect beyond just jacking up jaded appetites.

Assemble:

2 4-ounce cans chopped green
    chilies
1 pound canned tomatoes
¼ large Spanish onion, minced
1 tablespoon oregano (or to taste)
1 tablespoon lemon juice

Cayenne pepper (just a pinch)
3–4 slices (per serving) of lightly
    toasted whole wheat bread
3–4 eggs per serving
Tabasco sauce

Dump the tomatoes, minced onion and 1 can of chilies into a mixing bowl. Add the lemon juice, oregano, Cayenne pepper and a pinch of salt and lace the ingredients liberally (this sauce must be "hot" to be good) with Tabasco. Mash the ingredients vigorously by hand until they are well broken up and blended. Simmer for a few minutes in a saucepan over low heat. Cool and mix in the second can of chilies, but do not mash or blend.

Arrange the toast on each plate and top off with eggs that have been fried (basted) in butter, pouring the residual butter over the eggs and toast. Finally, spoon the prepared sauce copiously over the whole. The sauce recipe is adequate for 6–8 servings and may be stored.

A few minutes before serving the brunch, place a tin cup containing about ¾ cup of dark fortified wine before each crew member, retaining possession of the bottle. Tin cups are suggested because they are stable ashore or at sea and have sufficient volume. Follow with the brunch.

Though the sauce may sound like a digestive nightmare, it really is not. When eaten with the bland toast and eggs it provides a truly zestful brunch dish for sickish appetites and "sets" well.

Bloody marys may be substituted for the wine, though we believe the wine actually has the greater restorative power and goes better with the meal. It also is less conducive to further excess.

Distressed or not, the eggs topped by the tangy sauce are a real brunch treat—particularly on crisp autumn mornings!

Larry Williams

• BREAKFAST SOUFFLÉ

My breakfast soufflé is definitely not for those on a stringent diet. Use 2 eggs per crew member and whip with a whisk in a mixing bowl. Dice some Cheddar cheese—about ½ cup per crew member. Add 2 heaping tablespoons cottage cheese and a like amount of sour cream per crew member. Mix the whole lot thoroughly.

Coat the skillet with cooking oil, pour in the mixture and cook over a low flame for about 15 minutes. It is most important to have the skillet covered and to cook slowly. Then it will rise nicely and forms a great foundation to prepare for whatever vicissitudes are to be faced when hitting the deck to greet the new morn.

Jay Stuart Haft

• BREAKFAST PUFFS

These dishes can be cooked in the oven along with a coffee cake and make a nice change from scrambled eggs.

Cheese Egg Puffs *(each serving)*

2 eggs
1 tablespoon milk
Salt, pepper

½ cup Swiss or
    Monterey Jack cheese

Optional:

1 tablespoon mild green chilies
1 tablespoon chopped parsley

1 tablespoon chopped ham
    or shrimp
1 teaspoon chopped onion

Butter individual soufflé or custard cups. Beat eggs, add seasonings, milk and any desired options; sprinkle with cheese. Place dishes on a baking tray in a 350° oven for 20 to 30 minutes until puffy, browned and set.

Chili-Cheese Puff *(for 6)*

½ cup butter
8 eggs
½ cup flour
1 teaspoon baking powder
Salt, pepper (½ teaspoon)

1 can mild green chilies, chopped
1 pint cottage cheese
¾ pound grated Monterey
    Jack cheese

In 400° oven melt ½ cup butter in 1½-quart soufflé dish. Beat eggs, add flour, baking powder, salt and pepper. Mix in chilies, cottage cheese and most of the Monterey Jack cheese. Pour in the butter, return the mixture to the soufflé dish, sprinkle with remaining cheese. Bake at 400° for 15 minutes, then at 350° for 30 to 40 minutes until brown and the center appears firm.

Robyne Holt

• CAPE MAY OMELET

This recipe was born during a layover in Cape May waiting out a blow.

Allow, per person:

1 egg (plus 1 for the pot)
1 tablespoon milk
1 tablespoon instant
    shredded potato
1 teaspoon dehydrated onion

1 tablespoon dehydrated mushrooms
1 tablespoon dehydrated ham bits
Salt and pepper, savory and Tabasco
    to taste
Oil for frying

Reconstitute potato, onion, mushrooms and ham bits. Fry in oil until lightly browned. Beat the eggs and mix in the milk, salt, pepper, savory and Tabasco. Pour over meat and vegetables and cook, covered, over low heat, tipping occasionally to allow the uncooked mixture to run underneath and cook.

This allows a generous-sized serving for brunch.

Anna Patrick

PANCAKES

• SOUR MILK PANCAKES

We have trouble keeping milk fresh, but my mother taught me a good recipe using soured milk, preferably soured for more than 1 day.

Sift or stir thoroughly together:

1½ cups flour	2 teaspoons baking soda
1 tablespoon sugar	½ teaspoon salt

Add:

1 cup or more sour milk	1–2 tablespoons oil
1 egg	

Stir lightly until the batter is mixed but still somewhat lumpy. Cook the batter on a lightly oiled frying pan. The sour milk and baking soda react to one another to create a beautifully fluffy pancake.

Kristin Porter-Saunders

• BARBADOS GIANTS

This recipe evolved from the famous "Bermuda Giants," a pancake invented by an obscure sailor-cook faced with feeding a gang of hungry sailors each morning while the boat stood on her ear and the crew got their heads bashed during that biennial gear-busting insanity, the Newport to Bermuda Race. I have only made it more palatable as a food treat and a morning eye-opener. It's great for either cold-weather sailing or as a tropical breakfast treat.

2 cups pancake mix	2 tablespoons melted shortening
1–1½ cups milk (dried or fresh)	½ cup or more Mount Gay Rum
2 eggs	½ large can peaches (reserve liquid)

Into the pancake mix, add the beaten eggs, shortening, and enough milk to make a thick, not runny batter. Stir, do not beat. Add the peaches, which have been chopped into small chunks, along with a little juice from the can. (Save the other half of the can for the next day's command performance encore.) Stir in the rum. Ladle enough batter to almost cover the bottom of a hot, well-greased 10 inch skillet. Cook slowly as per any pancake recipe: Until bubbles rise on the surface. Flip and cook the other side only until browned.

Serve swimming in butter and molasses or syrup and, if you are lucky to have weather calm enough, the usual ham, bacon or sausages alongside will make this a heavenly dish. The recipe will provide enough 8 inch cakes to seduce 6 or 7 starving sailors with 1 serving each.

James E. Mitchell

• BREAKFAST CAKES

When we moved aboard *Chrysalis*, I was given my first cookbook and it had an extensive baking section. Our first cruise in a remote area, where there was no reliable supply of fresh fruits and vegetables, taught us to appreciate baked goods. A hot loaf of bread or some cookies really taste good and can provide some of the necessary nutrients we all need.

I have found whole wheat flour, honey, wheat germ, milk powder and nuts available in main cities throughout the areas of the South Pacific we have cruised. This recipe is simple and a favorite for breakfast under way, especially with the next island in sight.

1 cup whole wheat flour	¼ cup honey
3 teaspoons baking powder	¾ cup milk
1 teaspoon salt	2 tablespoons vegetable oil
2 tablespoons milk powder	2 eggs
1 cup wheat germ	½ cup raisins

Mix first 4 ingredients in a bowl. Add and mix well the rest of the ingredients. Butter cupcake tins or an 8 inch square baking pan. Bake at 375° for 15 to 20 minutes. Great hot from the oven with butter and jam!

Sue McBride

• WHOLESOME FOOD

We carry whole grains on board rather than pre-ground flours and cereals because they cost less, last longer and taste better, too. They are easy to store and keep well. Any galley with a counter can have a place to clamp on a grinder, and it can be stored away when not in use.

Our grinding mill is the type readily available in many natural food stores and has steel grinding plates.

Whole Wheat Pancakes

These can be heavy, but we have worked out a recipe using beaten egg whites to give the pancakes a texture better than white-flour pancakes.

First, grind a hopper-full of wheat. This takes about 3 minutes and produces 2 cups. Add ½ teaspoon baking soda, a bit of salt, 1 cup instant milk powder and mix. Add 2 or 3 tablespoons vegetable oil and 2 or 3 egg yolks.

Add water until the right consistency is reached. Whole wheat flour absorbs water more slowly than white flour, so the batter will continue to thicken for several minutes and more water may be needed. Beat the egg whites until stiff and fold into the batter.

Cook the pancakes in a hot, lightly oiled skillet until golden brown on both sides and devour with butter and maple syrup. The light fluffy texture and the nutty flavor of the freshly ground whole wheat flour makes this meal much more satisfying than plain white-flour pancakes.

Soy Grits

We also use our grinder to make soy grits from soybeans. On a loose setting, the grinder just breaks each bean into a few pieces, so that when mixed with brown rice both cook in equal time without pre-soaking.

A mixture of ¼ cup brown rice to ¾ cup soybeans can be eaten like rice or mixed into soups or fried with vegetables or eggs.

The grinder also allows us to make our own oatmeal and cracked-wheat cereals. Freshly ground whole grains are a welcome addition to the diet of any sailor who appreciates wholesome, down-to-earth food.

Gary Lepak

• HEALTH FOOD PANCAKES

Keeping health foods on board is not difficult. I always store them in paper or cloth bags, never plastic. We find that bugs hatch out if the foods are packed in a vacuum. Our health foods keep for weeks without refrigeration.

We find these pancakes very good in cold weather or when it's rough and especially during the Round Britain race with just the 2 of us as crew —very warming and leaving a nice feeling in our stomachs!

2 cups whole wheat flour	1 egg
2 dessert spoons soybean flour	A little sea salt
1 cup fine oatmeal	Pure honey
½ cup bran	

Stir all the ingredients in a bowl. Add enough milk or water to make a thick batter.

Over medium heat brown some butter in a fry pan. Pour in ½ the batter (for the skipper's pancake) and cook for a few minutes until the top dries. Turn the pancake, add a little more butter and cook a few more minutes.

Spoon some honey on top of the pancake and fold it over. Add some extra honey and serve with a glass of grape juice.

Nancy Roemers

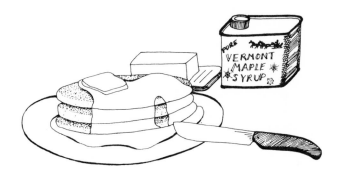

• CRISPY BACON PANCAKES

Aboard *Moon Shadow* we value bacon equally with staples such as flour and sugar mainly because, purchased in 1 pound cans, it can be stored in a dry place almost indefinitely.

Having cruised for six summers in the Bahamas, many times without refrigeration, we have found many ways bacon can perk up a sometimes drab diet.

1 egg
1¼ cups flour
2 tablespoons salad oil
½ teaspoon salt

1¼ cups milk (fresh or made from evaporated or powdered milk)
1 teaspoon sugar
2 teaspoons baking powder
16 slices bacon (approximately)

Mix the first 7 ingredients to form a smooth batter or use your favorite pancake mix following package directions. For each pancake cut 1 strip of bacon in 2 pieces, lay the slices side by side in the skillet, and fry until about ¾ done. Pour a small amount of batter over each pair of bacon strips; cook until the pancakes bubble on the surface. Turn over and fry until the other side is nicely browned.

Not only does this method produce the pancakes and bacon both piping hot at the same time, but the fat from prefrying the bacon is just the right amount to give each pancake a delightful, crispy texture.

Linda Turner

• BANANA PANCAKES

2½ cups flour
½ teaspoon salt
1¼ teaspoons soda
2 cups sour milk

2 tablespoons oil or melted butter
1 egg
1 teaspoon cinnamon

Mix dry ingredients, add milk, shortening and egg—mix well. Thinly slice 1 or 2 bananas and add to mixture. Drop by spoonfuls onto hot griddle and brown on both sides.

Marguerite Allen

• GERMAN APPLE PANCAKES

3 eggs   ½ teaspoon salt
¾ cup flour   ¾ cup milk

In bowl beat eggs; add milk, flour and salt. Stir until batter is smooth.
Melt butter or oil in a heavy skillet, then pour in batter. Cook with lid on, over medium heat.
Pancake may produce bubbles while cooking which should be poked down with a fork (takes about 10 to 15 minutes).
While pancake is cooking, sauté 3 to 4 sliced apples in another skillet in ¼ cup of melted butter; add ¼ cup sugar and cinnamon and nutmeg to taste. Cook until tender.
After both are cooked, pour apples over pancake and sprinkle with powdered sugar. Cut in wedges and dig in.

Lynne Orloff-Jones

• FLAPJACKS

When my mother was a small girl her family always made flapjacks at home. Now we find it an ideal bread for cruising.
We think they taste better than store-bought bread, and they are very easy to make, as the dough does not need to rise.

4 cups flour   1½ tablespoons vegetable oil
1½ tablespoons sugar   1½ cups water (or half water/
1 package dry yeast   half milk)

Heat water until lukewarm. Pour in yeast and stir until dissolved. Add milk, sugar and oil. Mix together, then add 1 cup flour at a time, stirring until smooth after each addition.
After 3 cups of flour, start kneading, adding the last cup and any extra to get a good workable dough. The longer the bread is kneaded, the better it gets.
Heat a fry pan with just enough oil to grease the bottom. Break off pieces of dough, flatten and fry, covered, on both sides until brown.
Even with the limited space in my galley I have room to make a double batch and store half in the cooler for fresh flapjacks the next day.

Tammy Elliott

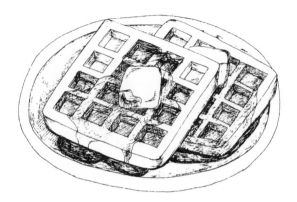

• WAFFLES AT SEA

It is possible to dine on waffles in the middle of the ocean or at a remote anchorage, thanks to a non-electrical waffle iron called the Belgian Waffler. This appliance resembles the type of waffle-maker grandma used on the coal stove—one that contains no heating element.

The Waffler is placed directly on the stove burner (even works on an electric burner) to preheat. The temperature is indicated on outside gauges on either side of the appliance—ranging "cold-bake-hot". After the batter is poured into the Waffler, it only takes several minutes to cook. First one side is cooked, then the iron is flipped over so the other side can be cooked. The Waffler is Teflon coated to prevent sticking, but play it safe and brush on extra oil.

I prefer whole grain waffles and always whip up a large batch of mix and store it in plastic containers.

Homemade Waffle Mix I

3 cups whole wheat flour
2 cups unbleached white flour
½ cup yellow cornmeal
⅓ cup sugar

2 tablespoons baking powder
2½ teaspoons salt
½ teaspoon baking soda

Homemade Waffle Mix II

3 cups whole wheat flour
2 cups unbleached white flour
1½ cups instant nonfat dry milk

⅓ cup sugar
2 tablespoons baking powder
1 tablespoon salt

With a whisk, thoroughly mix all the above ingredients in a large bowl. Store in airtight containers. Should last up to 6 months.

Waffles

2 to 3 eggs
1¼ cups milk
2½ tablespoons melted butter
    or vegetable oil

1¾ cups waffle mix
Optional—1 cup fresh strawberries
    (or freeze-dried, reconstituted)

With a whisk, beat all the above ingredients. Don't worry about lumps, there will be a few. Bake the waffles in the preheated Waffler using about ¾ cup of batter per batch. Follow manufacturer's recommendations. Serve with real maple syrup!

Lynne Orloff-Jones

• COLLISION MATS

Aboard *Piper*, my Alberg 35, it has always been my practice to cook breakfast for the crew. After all, a good breakfast is the reward one gets for having survived the night. One of my crew's favorites is Collision Mats. This is not your normal run-of-the-mill collision mat, but a special version of the old standby with French toast.

Into a large bowl, break 6 eggs. Add 1½ cups milk (whole or powdered) ± ¼ cup and season with salt and pepper as you would scrambled eggs. Beat well—I use a wire whisk.

Now add 1 ounce Mount Gay rum, a good dash or 2 or 3 of cinnamon and a light dash of nutmeg. Again, beat well. Soak bread in mixture and cook on a hot griddle (aluminum ones are great, but a frying pan will work just as well). Cook until brown, then turn and brown other side. If you are having bacon, add some of the drippings to the batter. It's an added plus.

Serve with maple syrup—the real thing if you have it, or imitation if not. Sugar or jam can be substituted, but be careful not to smother the rum flavor or all is lost . . .

Gordon MacKenzie

POTPOURRIS

• BREAKFAST AND GO

While singlehanding, it's nice to get up at first light and get under way promptly but unhurriedly. The next harbor seems closer if an early start is made, even if it means using the steam plant for an hour or two until the breeze makes up.

With such intentions, breakfast can't be a full dress affair. Here then is my recipe.

Open one eye.
If barely light, rise.
Set tea kettle to work, using little water to speed boiling.
Exercise toothbrush.
Check weather (if inclement, belay all that here follows and take leisurely
    eggs-or-porridge approach)
Open 1 can sardines, kippers, or, on special occasions, something exotic like
    smoked oysters, turkey or octopus. Do not remove from can.
Prepare a dozen crackers, which means just get them out.
With trusty pocket knife, quarter 1 crisp, cold apple and salt lightly.
Break off a hunk of rat-trap cheese.
Pour boiling water in mug containing instant tea, the lemon-and-sugar-
    included variety will do.
Place all on paper plate and shove out the companionway.
Now roll and stow sleeping bag.
Adjourn to cockpit to dine in the first warm rays.

This entire recipe takes almost less time than is required to get into a safety harness. It permits departure—liberally and functionally proteined, vitamined, sugared and roughaged—in about 20 minutes.

Dale Nouse

• SKILLET CORN BREAD AND BACON

This yummy recipe has bacon baked right in the batter. For those without the luxury of an oven, the skillet may be covered and placed on top of the stove over a low flame until the corn bread is done.

2 eggs
1 cup milk
¼ cup bacon drippings
1 cup corn meal
1 teaspoon salt

2 tablespoons sugar
1 cup flour
3 teaspoons baking powder
4 slices bacon

Fry bacon in heavy medium-sized skillet until absolutely dry and crisp. Drain and crumble bacon, set aside and reserve ¼ cup drippings. Beat eggs well, add milk and bacon drippings, then add dry ingredients, which have been thoroughly mixed in another bowl. Add the crumbled bacon, mix well. Pour into the original skillet. Bake in a 400° oven for 25 minutes.

You may prefer to use a packaged mix. Muffin tins may be used for baking, but be sure to grease them well or use muffin cups and reduce the baking time by 5 minutes.

Linda Turner

• ONE-PAN BREAKFASTS

We are basically lazy sailors who like to eat well but detest galley chores.

To ease the trauma of scullery duty, we have developed the habit of making a meal in 1 pan whenever possible and using paper plates and cups for serving.

Red Beret With Daisies

Whenever we have corned beef at home, we buy a large brisket and make hash with the leftovers. This is stored frozen in heat-sealed plastic bags. These defrost slowly in the ice chest and can be kept aboard for 4 or 5 days.

For breakfast, break open the bag and level the hash over the bottom of a heavy skillet, adding such seasonings or chopped onions as desired. Press wells into the top with the back of a spoon to accommodate the number of eggs needed. Break eggs into the wells, cover the pan and begin heating over a low flame.

Continue heating until the eggs are poached; we prefer the yolks soft. Meanwhile, serve juice or fruit while the coffee brews and break out the pastries. When the hash is done, serve hot and season to individual taste. My daughters love this with a dollop of "bottom paint" (catsup).

Pan-Fried Cabin Carpet

Using a heavy skillet, fry bacon or sausage patties while chopping 1 small or medium onion as the coffee works. Set the meat aside in a warm place, retaining about half the fat in the pan.

Sauté the onions lightly and then break the eggs into the skillet, breaking the yolks. Stir the entire mess together and season immediately with salt and pepper. When fried completely solid, serve hot, on toast if you wish, with the meat. Again, for an added taste or color thrill, spill "bottom paint" on the "carpet."

Curried Beach Pebbles With Eggs

While stocking for an outing, we always include a quantity of partially boiled potatoes as this cuts cooking time about in half. Dice several of these into the trusty heavy skillet containing the rest of the melted fat from yesterday's breakfast and brown them over a medium high flame, stirring regularly.

For additional flavor, add chopped green pepper and/or celery when you start the potatoes. Midway through the browning, add chopped onion and season to taste with salt and pepper, along with your choice of garlic (chopped, minced or powdered), celery seed, salt or whatever appeals to you. Cook for a few minutes, then add cut-up mushrooms.

Reduce the heat to low, break in the eggs (about 1 per person) and sprinkle with curry powder. Continue stirring frequently until the eggs are cooked, then serve. The curry flavor is delightful, so this time refrain from daubing with bottom paint.

This is also good Italian style. Here you simply omit the curry, use more garlic and add oregano, anise and/or cumin.

Flat Rocks With Shivering Tams

Once more, break out the heavy skillet (no, this is not the only pan I own). Fry more bacon or the other half of the roll of bulk sausage and set aside. This time, using all of the fat, brown potato patties formed from leftover mashed potatoes and precoated with flour, seasoning each side with salt and pepper. When browned on both sides, add to the waiting meat.

Now fry 1 egg for each potato patty, seasoning to taste. We like them sunny side up with the yolks shivering. Serve with the routine fruit or juice and coffee, with the tam (egg) on the flat rock (patty) and the meat on the side. Hold the bottom paint.

All of these recipes can weather a great deal of variations to suit the cook—the crew has no say in the matter.

William Doty

• SHIPBOARD YOGURT

In Martinique, we were drawn into a competition with other cruising boats to make good yogurt in the most casual manner possible. The result was a process of mixing up extra-rich full cream powdered milk, adding starter and putting the mix in a warm place, where the bacteria flourishes and the yogurt sets in 6 to 8 hours to a consistency thick enough to support a spoon.

The warmth, which must be enough to nourish the culture but not to kill it, is the necessary, critical element. Technically, the temperature should be between 90° and 105°; in practice, that is about body temperature—warm, but not hot to the hand. The simplest method is to use a widemouthed flask.

My own system involves using the equipment I have on board. I mix the yogurt in a ½ liter glass canning jar, place the jar inside a 1 gallon drink cooler and pour warm water around the jar. The cooler holds the temperature; the bacteria does the work.

Mix the desired amount of full-cream powdered milk double-strength (using twice the amount of milk powder called for) in warm water. Shake vigorously. Skim milk powder produces yogurt, but not the thick, jello-like solidity we prefer.

Add 1 or 2 tablespoons yogurt starter when the milk has cooled to the approximate temperature. The starter can be your own yogurt, a neighbor's, or commercially prepared yogurt, plain or flavored. Again, shake vigorously. Set the mixture in a warm place. In 6 to 8 hours, the yogurt should be solid and ready to eat. It will continue to "ripen" like some cheeses, but storing in the refrigerator or icebox will slow the process. If, like *Rebel,* your boat has no means of refrigeration, it is best to make the yogurt in amounts that can be enjoyed before it goes off.

Old yogurt which has separated can be made into a cream cheese by squeezing the liquid out through a cloth. The addition of pickle or onion or what-have-you makes a sandwich spread. I discovered by accident that yogurt reaches a particular stage of ripeness, then goes no further. We were once away from *Rebel* for a week, and on our return I found that I had forgotten a container of yogurt in the Thermos. I expected an incredible stench when I opened the jar, but the yogurt was quite like any which had been left unrefrigerated for a day or so. I squeezed it and made cream cheese as usual. But it may have been a fluke!

Ann Glenn

• CODFISH CAKES

Bermudians traditionally enjoy fishcakes for supper. These are made of leftover fish, potatoes, a little freshly ground pepper, parsley or thyme, Bermuda onions and an egg all mixed together then shaped into cakes, rolled in flour and fried. They are just as good for breakfast.

Penny Voegeli

• SUPER PORRIDGE

It was dark by the time Tzu Hang was on her way to Borkum, West Germany, from Terschelling Island along the Dutch coast. The low flat land was part of the dark horizon, but the Terschelling light kept in touch with us as it had with departing sailors for so many years. We had the wind abeam and the motion was easy as we headed for the Nemedri channel, the swept channel which, 6 years after the war, was still used by all shipping along the coast. *Tzu Hang,* being built of wood and under sail, did not have to worry about old and unswept mines.

We crossed the channel and beat up on the north side against a fresh head wind and into a steep short sea. The wind seemed suddenly to blow stronger and the decks were soon wet, while an occasional cold splash of spray whipped our faces and made us catch our breath. Beryl and I soon began to feel seasick. A week in the Ijssel River had disposed of any benefit that we might have gained from the short North Sea crossing. In those days we thought that seasickness was something that one had to suffer and get over and never thought of taking a pill.

Kevin O'Riordan, who was with us, ate a hearty supper, but Beryl and I toyed with ours and lost what we ate during the night watches. Early in the morning the mainsail appeared to be behaving rather strangely and daylight revealed that the main boom gooseneck had broken.

"Only one thing to do," said Kevin. "Put back into Terschelling and get it repaired. Anyway," he added, "I've got to get back to England as I'm due on another yacht next week." Kevin was a very experienced sailor and we readily agreed.

We put *Tzu Hang* about. The rough motion eased, the east wind that had seemed so harsh and cold caressed us and *Tzu Hang* slipped easily along in front of a following sea. Ameland Island was to port. Low and brown it looked, and the sea and sky dull grey. Our seasickness vanished and suddenly we felt a heightening of the spirits and an all consuming hunger. "I'll get breakfast," said Beryl as she disappeared below.

I have never forgotten how I enjoyed that breakfast, nor do I think that I have ever had a breakfast that I enjoyed so much. And what did this marvelous meal consist of? Quaker oats cooked in milk, covered with brown sugar and laced with evaporated milk. It was followed up with oeufs au plat. I can remember how I scraped the bottom of the dish to get the last scrap off. Looking back over a lifetime of breakfasts in many parts of the world, on mountains, in the jungle, in the desert and at sea, that breakfast surpassed all others for pure enjoyment. When hungry and empty there is no need for a recherché meal and as for the porridge, it could only be described as super porridge.

Super Porridge

2 cups milk	Pinch salt
1 cup Quaker oats	

Cook in a double saucepan over boiling water for about 5 minutes. Serve with brown sugar and evaporated milk.

Miles Smeeton

CHAPTER 7

LIGHT MEALS

BEANS

• BEANS, BEANS, BEANS

Dry beans and grains make perfect cruising staples. They're not only easy to store for long periods of time but also are high in protein and can be used with great variation.

Dry beans require soaking or sprouting before cooking. A quick way to do this is to bring some water to a boil, add beans, cover and remove from stove. Let sit for 1 hour, then cook by the method of your choice.

Don't add any salt or spices until beans are cooked through. Another tip is to add 1 or 2 tablespoons vegetable oil after the beans are soft to lighten the texture a bit.

Lentils, pintos, soybeans and limas make delicious and satisfying soups, stews and casseroles. Kidney beans and garbanzos (chick-peas) make a great cold salad or top-off for a fresh green salad. Pea beans with maple syrup are an old favorite—Boston baked beans.

There are a hundred different ways to serve beans. Never underestimate the potential of 1 cup of dry beans.

Lentil-Tomato Loaf

1 pound lentils (cooked)
2 cups tomato purée or tomato soup
½ cup onions, sautéed
½ cup celery, sautéed
2 teaspoons salt

1 clove garlic, minced
½ teaspoon thyme
4 slices bread, crumbled
2 tablespoons vegetable oil

Mix bread with tomato purée or soup. Add lentils (cooked almost dry) and rest of ingredients. Mix well and bake in loaf pan at 350° until set, about 1 hour.

Baked Beans

Soak and cook until tender 2 cups beans (pea beans or soybeans). Then add:

⅓ cup sorghum (or ¼ cup molasses, honey or maple syrup)
1 onion, chopped
1 cup tomatoes, fresh or stewed
1 tablespoon salt

1 teaspoon dry mustard or 2 teaspoons prepared
¼ teaspoon garlic powder
4 tablespoons oil

Mix well. Bake in a covered dish for 3 hours at low heat in the oven. Uncover for last hour.

Black Beans and Rice

1 cup cooked black beans
¾ cup dry brown rice, cooked
1 minced onion

Cumin, chili powder, garlic powder, salt and pepper, to taste
Dash of Tabasco or hot sauce
½ cup grated cheese

Cook beans and rice separately. After beans are tender, spice with onion and seasonings. Serve a scoop of hot rice, topped with hot bean mixture, topped with cheese, with homemade bread and butter.

Barbecued Soybean Burgers

2 cups cooked soybeans (1 cup dry)
2–3 tablespoons barbecue sauce
1½ cups dry bread crumbs
1 tablespoon sea salt; pepper to taste
Onion slices

Sliced cheese (mozzarella,
    Provolone)
Bread rolls
¼ cup vegetable oil

Mash soybeans with potato masher, fork or blender. Mix mashed beans with bread crumbs, barbecue sauce, salt and pepper. Form into patties, placing an onion slice in the middle of each patty.

Heat oil in skillet and fry patties until brown on both sides. Place cheese slices on patties and cover pan until cheese melts. Grill buns. Serve with sliced tomato and lettuce. Store extras in aluminum foil for later.

Rhonda Harris

• UGLY BEANS

Black beans are probably the ugliest concoction you can prepare in your galley. There are few foods that are so dark in color, but these beans, which are widely eaten in southern Florida and the Keys, are an excellent variation for a cruising diet. They are also called black turtle beans.

12 ounce package dried
    black beans
1 can tomatoes
2 bay leaves
1 clove garlic diced or ⅛ teaspoon
    garlic powder

2 onions, diced (or equivalent dried
    onions)
2 tablespoons vinegar
Salt and pepper to taste

Optional:

1 stalk celery, diced

1 bell pepper, diced

Pick over and examine beans thoroughly. Throw out all rocks and other suspicious-looking debris. Wash beans several times. Soak at least 8 hours.

Combine all ingredients in pressure cooker and cover with water. Bring up to pressure and cook 30 minutes. Serves 8 hungry sailors. This is an excellent side dish.

Serve the beans over brown or white rice as a main dish. To make a meat dish, add canned or already cooked chicken or ham to the beans before cooking.

Alma Russell

• NO-BAKE BAKED BEANS

The secret to this recipe lies in the dry mustard which so well complements the sweetness of the brown sugar. (If your boat is equipped with a good oven, you can make the dish even more attractive by pouring the beans and bacon into a shallow pan, adding several more slices of bacon, then baking for 25 to 30 minutes or until the beans are bubbling and the bacon is crisp).

6 slices of bacon cut into 1 inch squares 1 medium onion, chopped	1–2 teaspoons dry mustard ¼ cup brown sugar 1 can pork and beans

Sauté the bacon and onion together in a small saucepan until the onion is soft. Add the beans, mustard and brown sugar and simmer covered for 10 minutes, then serve. It's a good idea to double the recipe as this dish makes an excellent cold accompaniment for sandwiches for the next day's lunch.

Linda Turner

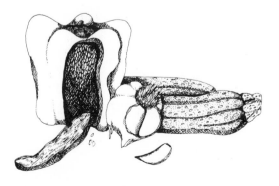

• MARINATED MEAT MEDLEY

This recipe is a delicious hot-weather meal that can be prepared in the morning and allowed to marinate in the cooler until lunch or, even better, until supper at anchor.

1 steak	5 scallions, sliced
1 can chick-peas, drained	1 cup Italian salad dressing

Cook steak in pressure cooker for 1 minute. Let cool. Combine all ingredients and let sit in cooler.

Serve with a loaf of crusty Italian bread, a bottle of red wine and enjoy!

Kathy Rizzo

• BEGGAR'S BOWL

When a small, light boat starts getting really thrown around as a gale builds at sea, there may come a stage when just avoiding injury becomes difficult, and cooking has to be ruled out altogether. Just before reaching this stage, try a Beggar's Bowl.

Use a small pressure cooker with lid on, but the valve open. This is the only cooking container that can roll all over the cabin without loss of your dinner or your equanimity. Gently boil brown rice in it with the exact quantity of water that (experience has told you) it will absorb. Five minutes before the rice is cooked, while there is still some water left, chuck in chopped-up ham, bacon, salt beef, onions, currants, nuts, or any other damn thing that comes to hand.

By this time it is done you may have to put on oilskin trousers, hold the hot pan between your knees and eat it straight out of the pan with a spoon, holding on to the ship with the other hand. Your red wine can be allowed to swill around in the bottom of a pint mug in a secure fiddle. Soon the gale will seem a good deal less frightening, but remember to lay off the vino before your Superman syndrome develops.

H. G. "Blondie" Hasler

EGG-BASED

• OEUFS À L'HURRICANE

It had started out so well. There was me and my crew (two strong young men), a boat groaning with food, a favorable wind and the hopes of a fast and fair passage from Newport to Bermuda.

And there we were, a day and a half later, in the most unwelcome embraces of a storm of hurricane force (take the tail of Hurricane Gilda, one early winter storm, no warning and mix well). Caught in the middle of the Gulf Stream, the waves did their usual thing and became unpleasantly large.

Things were not too rosy aboard the good yacht *Gulliver G.* We were miserable, wet and frightened. We also were hungry. I use the word 'we' in the collective sense: I had not the slightest desire to eat due to a nasty knot in my stomach. But my crew was absolutely convinced they were about to die from lack of nourishment before they drowned, which they were sure was imminent.

When the first cry for food was heard over the screeching of the wind, I did what any skipper would—I ignored it. But then the cry rose again, from two mouths. I grabbed a jar of honey and a spoon and ladled some down their throats as they lay moaning in their bunks.

"I need protein," said the health food fanatic in the crew.

"Rubbish!" I replied firmly, "you need energy," then forced some more honey down his throat. "And if you think I can cook in this, you're mad."

At last, the wind moderated a little and, realizing that they were going to survive to eat three full meals a day, the boys began to send up a cry for food that would not be ignored.

"Still too rough to cook," I pointed out.

"Er, I could try my egg thing if you like," suggested one of the boys.

"If I like? Oh, I like very much!" I cried, overcome with relief at the thought of someone else cooking. "You just go right ahead."

Ten minutes later we were tasting, then positively pigging the most delicious concoction we had ever tasted. Later, when I tried my hand at the dish, I found it to be virtually ejection-proof. Even on a gimballed stove most food will do its best to slide, slither or shoot out of a pan in really bad weather; not hurricane eggs. Best of all, it can be eaten in the hands. The "watch" need not be called in to eat; you just shout at him to open the hatch and pass out his meal, hand to hand.

It is really nothing more than egg cooked in bread, but it really hits the spot. (I am assuming that, if you do not have store-bought bread, you bake your own.)

1 egg	Butter, margarine or oil
1 slice bread	Salt and pepper

Put fat into a deep pan and heat. Cut a hole in the middle of the bread. (Obviously it's difficult to cut a neat hole in a gale. Use your fingers.) Keep the center. Put the bread and the center into the pan and break the egg into the bread. Sprinkle with salt and pepper. When the egg starts to set flip the whole thing over to cook the other side (you may need to add a little more fat). When the yolk is more or less set, fold over and hand to hungry crew or, if you're being civilized, put in a bowl with the center of the bread sitting on top of the egg like a hat.

Warning: Your crew will want at least 2 each.

Clare Francis

• EGGS BENEDICT

I have two recurring "wish fulfillment" dreams. One is that Room Service will arrive with Eggs Benedict on Sunday morning. The other is Haagen Dazs chocolate ice cream that doesn't require a freezer!

While I've yet to encounter Room Service knocking on the hull in a quiet anchorage, I occasionally am inspired to fix Eggs Benedict myself. It takes no more skill or precision than rounding a mark or setting a chute, is just as impressive and never fails to please the crew and amaze guests.

Timing is the essence of success or failure, but even a novice cook can try it.

For vegetarians, a slice of cheese can be substituted for the meat.

Per person:

2 eggs	⅛ pound bacon, sausage, ham
2 English muffins or 4 slices toast	or cheese

Top with Hollandaise sauce (2–4 portions):

6 egg yolks

1 stick butter or margarine

⅓ cup lemon or lime juice

Dash garlic powder, Dijon mustard, curry powder, salt, Cayenne pepper

Garnish:

Parsley, watercress, capers, truffles or Cayenne pepper

Muffins or toast: Melt a small amount of butter in a frying pan and brown the bread or halved muffins until warm. Wrap in foil and keep warm. (Two pillows make a good warming oven.)

Meat: Cook the meat in the frying pan, wrap and keep warm with the muffins. Wash the frying pan, rinse and fill to 1½ inches with water. Add 2 tablespoons vinegar and bring to a boil.

Hollandaise sauce: Melt butter in the top of the double boiler over boiling water. Lower heat. Beat the egg yolks in a small bowl; add lemon juice and seasonings. Slowly add this mixture to the melted butter, beating constantly until the sauce thickens. Then remove from heat immediately. Let cool slightly, adjust seasonings, cover and set the entire double boiler aside.

At this point prepare the assembly line: plates, muffins, meat, sauce and garnish. Call the crew to the table and open the champagne.

Parboil the eggs for 30 seconds (in the shell) then remove with a slotted spoon. Carefully break two eggs into the water and poach till the white is firm. As you remove and drain the first two eggs, add the next two. Assemble the first plate with meat, egg, sauce and garnish on two muffin halves with the two extra halves on the side. Serve, with instructions to begin immediately. Repeat process until everyone is served.

Alexis Strickland

• ZUCCHINI OMELET

For each omelet:

3 eggs	½ small zucchini, finely chopped
1 tablespoon water	2 thin slices processed Swiss cheese
½ small onion, finely chopped	1 tablespoon butter or margarine

Chop onions and zucchini and sauté in pan with a little butter. (You can do this step for all your omelets at once.) Remove from pan. Beat eggs with water and pour into buttered skillet. Cook until set. Place zucchini, onions and cheese on ½ the omelet mixture. Fold and turn. Cook until cheese melts. Serve immediately.

This is a great way to use up bits and pieces of raw vegetables.

Cindy Putt

• CHINESE OMELET

This recipe, inspired by egg foo yung, was developed from provisions that were on board at the end of a long day's sail by 4 hungry sailors.

½ pound bacon, diced	8 eggs, beaten with fork
2 medium onions, diced	½ cup milk
19 ounce can bean sprouts, well drained	½ teaspoon each Worcestershire sauce, salt and pepper
1 small can mushrooms, drained	Accent, if desired

Fry bacon in skillet until crisp, remove and drain. Fry onions in bacon fat. Add bean sprouts and mushrooms and brown lightly. Sprinkle bacon over vegetables.

Mix eggs, milk, sauce, salt, pepper and Accent with a fork and gently pour over mixture in skillet. Cover, cook over low heat, occasionally lifting edge of omelet to allow liquid to run underneath.

If you use imitation bacon bits and dehydrated onions, use oil, butter or margarine for cooking.

Serve with soy sauce for a Chinese flavor.

Anna Patrick

• VERMONT CHEESE PIE

I'd been at sea for nearly a year when I sailed into Auckland, New Zealand. I'd rattled around the Pacific basin like a marble, stopping in the Galapagos, Marquesas, Tahiti, the Cooks and Kermadecks, and once again on dry land I was definitely looking for a solid situation.

Rosie had been out larking as well, though I didn't know it. She'd left her New Zealand home to work and wander in Europe, finding her way onto a Rhine riverboat as deckhand, into a camel driver's hut in Cairo, under a tycoon's shade tree in Cyprus, and had just returned to her South Pacific homeland when we first met, starry-eyed, on a pier in Auckland.

She said she was looking for someone solid, but settled for me. That was how we discovered each other; how we came on the recipe for Vermont Cheese Pie is another story.

Cover the bottom of an unbaked piecrust shell with a layer of sautéed onions, then cover with a layer of sliced tomatoes. Fill the shell with grated Cheddar cheese.

Beat together ½ cup milk and ½ cup cream, 3 eggs, salt and pepper. Pour this over the cheese, then bake at moderate heat for 45 minutes to 1 hour.

George Day

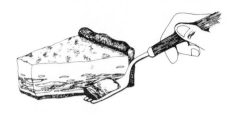

• CRUISING QUICHE

Quiches are simple to prepare, can be made with a variety of ingredients and are simply delicious to eat! They are great for entertaining, served with a green salad and a bowl of fruit.

Preheat oven to 425°.

1 piecrust stick (available in most markets)
2 tablespoons soft butter or margarine
4 eggs
2 cups canned evaporated milk
½ pound grated Swiss cheese
6 pieces bacon

½ pound fresh mushrooms (or canned)
1 small onion, chopped
¼ teaspoon salt
½ teaspoon sugar
¼ teaspoon nutmeg
⅛ teaspoon Cayenne pepper

Prepare piecrust according to package directions, but do not roll out with a rolling pin. Using your fingers, press the dough out to fit a deep 9 inch pie plate. Rub crust generously with soft butter.

In a skillet, fry bacon, drain. In bacon fat, sauté mushrooms (if fresh) and onion. In a medium-sized bowl, beat together eggs, milk and spices.

Crumble bacon in bottom of piecrust, adding mushrooms and onion on top. Sprinkle grated cheese over and pour egg/milk mixture over the top. Bake at 425° for 15 minutes. Reduce heat to 350° and continue to bake 30–40 minutes or until a knife inserted in center comes out clean.

The real secret to this is the nutmeg and the Cayenne. In fact, you can add either one or both of these spices to eggs for an interesting change.

Quiche can be made with almost any combination of cooked meat and cooked vegetable: Ham, chicken, turkey, broccoli, spinach, asparagus. Just make sure all vegetables are well drained or they will make the quiche soggy. It can also be made using half Cheddar cheese and half Jack with chillies added to give it some zip. Serves 4.

Linda McIntosh

• BLINTZES

For the blintz skins (pancakes):

4 eggs, well beaten
½ teaspoon salt

¼ cup water (this can be whey)
3 tablespoons flour

Mix together, trying (it's impossible) to smash all the lumps. Cook over low heat, using a small amount of batter at a time. Swirl the pan to spread the batter over the bottom of the pan, pour excess back.

For the filling:

1 cup cottage cheese
½ teaspoon salt

2 tablespoons sugar
1 egg

Mix together and place 1 to 2 tablespoons on each blintz skin (depending on the size). Fold in 2 opposite edges, then roll up and fry lightly over low heat until filling sets.

Serve with sour cream, and fruit if you desire. Serves 4–6.

Beth Schwarzman

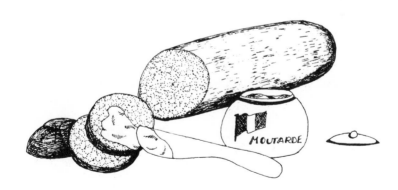

• CRUISING CRÊPES

Prepare very thin pancakes. This can be accomplished for 2 people by using all the suggested dry ingredients in your favorite pancake recipe and adding only half the milk or water. Set the crêpes aside but keep them warm while preparing the important part, the fillings.

These suggested fillings should be mixed together and warmed in a saucepan.

Spinach

I can cream of chicken or cream of mushroom soup (undiluted)
1 can spinach, drained

1 small can sliced mushrooms, drained (optional)

Chicken With Mushroons

1 can cream of chicken or cream of mushroom soup (undiluted)

1 can deboned chicken pieces
1 can sliced mushrooms, drained

Ham and Asparagus

1 can cream of mushroom or cream of celery soup

1 can asparagus, drained
1 can ham pieces

Spread filling on crêpe, roll up and top with Parmesan cheese and parsley.

Sheryl Krawchuk

MEXICAN

• HALCYON TACOS

I pre-freeze meats before a cruise, using each as it thaws to provide a variety of meals. This is a favorite for our second night out and will serve 4 people 3 tacos each.

2 pounds lean ground round
1 dozen corn tortillas
1 medium onion
Salt, pepper, garlic powder

1 head lettuce
Tomatoes
Grated Parmesan cheese

Break up the meat and cook over medium heat. Add ¼ cup chopped onion, salt, pepper and garlic powder to taste. Stir frequently. Reduce to low heat when cooked.

Mix thinly sliced lettuce in a bowl with chopped onion and tomato.

Deep fry each tortilla in enough vegetable oil to cover the bottom of a pan. Fry for 1 minute on first side. Then turn over, fold in half and cook to desired crispness. Turn with tongs and add oil as necessary. Drain on paper towels.

Serve tacos, meat and salad stuffing separately for each crewmember to help himself. Fill the taco shells with a layer of meat first, then salad stuffing and garnish with grated Parmesan cheese.

To make the meal even more delectable, serve a side dish of canned refried beans garnished with thin slices of Jack cheese, and another side dish of avocado slices. The final touch—chilled ale or a red wine to make a meal that even "Mamacita" would be proud of!

Joanne Chavez

• HUEVOS RANCHEROS

To anyone who has cruised the west coast of Mexico, no Sunday is complete without huevos rancheros. If the preceding Saturday night has included an overabundance of tequila, huevos rancheros often serve to clear the head, open up the sinuses, get the heart started and take the red out of the eyes.

Before settling down to the actual preparation of the dish, I always serve a round of bloody marys liberally spiced with Tabasco sauce to put my guests in the proper state of mind and condition the palate for things to come.

At the proper moment I open 2 medium-sized cans of chili salsa (ranchero sauce will do) and heat the sauce in a large frying pan. When the sauce is very hot, add 8 eggs, one at a time, until they are all looking up at you and frying in the sauce.

Cover the eggs with a liberal amount of grated Jack cheese, cover the pan, and lower the temperature to allow the mixture to simmer until the eggs are cooked to suit your taste.

Divide the mixture into 4 portions and serve with hot flour tortillas, butter, Mexican refried beans and either coffee or beer, depending on the time of day.

Dorie Bradley

• HUEVOS ENCHILADAS

This is another dish that needs lots of chili sauce. Just mash up with water fresh Rio Grande chilies or canned El Paso brand hot chilies. Heat.

You will need tortillas, too. Make them yourself, with corn flour and water mixed, then pressed between sheets of wax paper. Instant tortilla! If you're not up to making your own, buy El Paso brand canned tortillas.

Tortillas
Shredded lettuce
Shredded beef, pork or chicken (browned in chili sauce)
Pinto beans (heated in chili sauce)
Jack cheese or sharp Cheddar (shredded)
Chili sauce
Beer

Heat a tortilla in a hot skillet, remove to a plate and put a large dollop of meat (cooked in chili) on top. Add a dollop of pinto beans over it, a layer of lettuce, a layer of cheese and a dollop of chili sauce.

A second tortilla is added on top, followed by meat, beans, lettuce, cheese and chili sauce. Top it off with a sunny-side up egg and serve—with lots of beer.

Joe Bossom

• NO-PLATE MEXICAN LUNCHES

Our galley has a Sea Swing and a one-burner alcohol stove, so I look for recipes that are filling, tasty, use a minimum of pots and pans and preferably no dishes!

A great standby is a #1 can of ham. By slicing half of it and dicing the other we have 2 light meals that fit my requirements.

Burritos

1 package defrosted	Grated Jack and/or Cheddar cheese
Potatoes O'Brien	Flour tortillas, lightly sprinkled with
½ pound diced ham	water and wrapped in foil
1 large carton egg substitute	Margarine

Sauté the ham in margarine, add potatoes and cook over medium/low heat, stirring periodically. (Use the foil-wrapped tortillas as a lid and you'll be heating them through at the same time. Flip over each time you stir the contents of pan to heat both sides.)

When the potatoes are cooked, add eggs and cheeses and keep stirring until set. Divide among tortillas, add Tabasco if desired, roll up and serve in a napkin.

Huevos Ran-Pitas

1 small can refried beans	Jack and Cheddar cheeses, grated
Thin ham slices	Margarine
Pita bread	Salsa
Eggs or egg substitute	Avocado slices (optional)

Heat beans until bubbling hot in a non-stick pan. Spread inside pita bread pockets. Wipe out bean residue from pan and sauté ham in margarine. Put on top of beans. Cook eggs as desired adding cheeses just before they are done. When cheeses have melted, put eggs on top of ham and beans, sprinkle with salsa and top with avocado slices.

Serve on napkins and pass the bloody marys!

Lynn Canute

RICE

• SCHOONER RICE

This recipe requires only ingredients that store easily on a cruising boat.

3 tablespoons margarine (keeps up to 3 months)	¼ teaspoon pepper
1 medium onion, chopped	1 teaspoon salt
1¼ cups uncooked rice	Dash of Tabasco
8 ounce can tomato sauce	12 ounce can smoked sausage or ½ pound can bacon or 2 small cans Vienna sausage
1 pound can stewed tomatoes	
1 tablespoon minced dried parsley	2 cups water
2 teaspoons Worcestershire sauce	

Sauté onion in margarine, add remaining ingredients. Bring to a boil, cover, reduce heat and simmer 30 minutes or until all the liquid is absorbed.

Sally Graham

• RED BEANS AND RICE

¾ cup dried red kidney beans
¾ pound smoked sausage (we prefer
  it hot)
1 or 2 stalks celery
1 small onion, chopped

2 cloves of garlic, chopped
1 bay leaf
1 tablespoon parsley
Salt to taste
Rice

Early in the day, I rinse and pick through the red beans, cover with water and set to soak, as this shortens the cooking time. I use my pressure cooker for this because the gasket-lined lid fits securely, and I don't have to worry about spills underway.

The dried beans more than double in volume, so be careful not to overdo it—a few beans go a long way, which is why they're so good as a cruising staple. They're high in protein, too.

About 1 hour before dinnertime, I temporarily transfer the beans and their water into a plastic container with a lid.

Then the sausage, celery, onion and garlic are cut up and browned in the cooker. A very small amount of oil can be used, if necessary. Then the beans are returned to the pot with the bay leaf, parsley, salt and enough water to barely cover, and cooked under pressure for 30 minutes.

If you have only 1 burner, remove the cooker from the heat early and start your rice; the beans will continue to cook in the sealed pot. If you don't use a pressure cooker, you will have to simmer the beans for 1½ to 2 hours, and it would be best to soak them overnight.

To make the gravy creamier, mash some of the beans. Add water if the mixture seems too dry. Chunks of ham and pickled meat can be used to supplement the sausage and further flavor the dish. Serve over the rice with hot buttered garlic bread on the side.

If you have leftover rice, it will make a tasty and different breakfast.

Terri Naylor

• FRIED RICE

Prepare and chop all the ingredients in bite-sized pieces before beginning to cook and cook enough rice.

Put about 1½ tablespoons of oil in the frying pan, enough oil to put a *light* coating on all the ingredients. Add bits of bacon, ham or beef fat.

Put this on the stove. Stir occasionally with a spatula. Add slices of garlic. Stir. After a few minutes, tip the garlic onto a plate (to be re-added later). Put slivers of non-fatty meat in the oil, turn until each piece is coated with oil, and cook gently.

When the meat is almost cooked, add onion rounds and stir, so that they are coated with oil. Stir occasionally until the onions are translucent and soft, then tip the onions and meat onto the plate with the garlic.

Add vegetables to the oil one by one, first those which take the longest time to cook. Add bits of shrimp or quick-cooking fish or any precooked meats. Make sure that each piece is coated with a thin layer of oil. You are not really frying the food but actually steaming each piece within its own oil jacket, thereby retaining the natural flavor and sweetness of the vegetable or meat.

When the shrimp and bits of meat are cooked, and before the vegetables become at all mushy, tip out on top of the meat, onions and garlic.

If necessary, add a little more oil. Put in the cooked rice and separate the grains, breaking the chunks with the spatula. Make sure each grain is coated in oil. Simmer for a few minutes, turning occasionally.

When the rice is heated up, return all the previously cooked ingredients and mix the whole thing up. Salt to taste; add parsley and other spices and herbs if you desire.

Break up 1 or more eggs over the whole mass. Keep stirring until the heat of the other food cooks the bits of egg.

This recipe is quick and easy. It requires only one cooking pot and one burner and the actual cooking time is only about 10–15 minutes.

It generally satisfied our cravings for starchy bread products in times when we couldn't get bread and did not have the time or inclination to bake.

Jenny Donaldson

• PIGEON PEAS AND RICE WITH BACON

Many Bahamians specify salt pork for this recipe, but I find bacon to be a more suitable ingredient.

½ cup dry pigeon peas	½ cup tomato paste
2 cups water	2 teaspoons thyme
6 slices bacon cut into small pieces	1 cup white rice
1 medium onion, chopped	Salt and pepper to taste

Wash and soak peas in water for several hours, then cook in a pressure cooker until tender, about 20 minutes. Reduce pressure and be sure to save the liquid. Sauté bacon and onion together in a medium saucepan until onion is soft and most of the fat is gone from the bacon. Add rice, cooked peas and liquid, tomato paste and seasonings; cover and simmer until the liquid is absorbed and rice is cooked, about 20 minutes.

Linda Turner

• TO ONIONS ADD . . .

H. W. Tilman, peripatetic voyager to unlikely places, remarks in his book, "Never go on a boat without onions." Bill Snaith, the blithest soul that ever cruised, suggests that a good cook "sautées onions and then decides what he's going to cook." To onions let me add 3 items to the armament of a well-supplied cook: Lots of rice, lots of instant and real mashed potatoes, and a good supply of various flours and meals.

The rice must be Uncle Ben's, wild or natural brown. Unbleached white flour, whole wheat, couscous, cornmeal and rolled oats can be used in interesting ways. Potatoes should always be cooked in excess of the current need, for the leftovers can generate potato salad, potato cakes or latkes, deep fried potato puffs, potato pancakes, hash browns, curried potatoes, creamed potatoes—the list is endless.

Rice is another variety provider that keeps, takes little space and can provide gastronomic tunes for the virtuoso. The basic approach to rice is to cook it in bouillon in a pressure cooker, take it off after a few minutes of pressure and park it in a bunk, wrapped thoroughly in a blanket, where it will finish cooking while the stove is used to bring the rest of the meal "au point". Leftover rice can be used in casseroles, kedgeree, rice cakes and added to soup.

Variations of Potato Pancakes

Add an equal volume of flour to mashed potatoes, break in about 1 egg per cupful, add some salt, 1 teaspoon of melted butter per cupful and a dash of baking powder.

Cook both sides to brown in a greased pan. Thinned with milk, the mixture makes delicious pancakes; thickened with flour, it makes a sort of hotbread that is delicious with butter. Mixed with grated cheese and finely chopped onions and fried in a well-greased pan, it's a tasty light lunch, with protein, carbohydrates and a vegetable. Vary it further with anything on my "flour" list.

My focus on these additive dishes may seem odd, but I've never known a boat undersupplied wiith the main courses—and I've known too many where peas, beans, potatoes and tomatoes were the whole list of extras and got repetitive on the 24th day.

Norris Hoyt

SANDWICHES

• OUR SVANEN HAMBURGERS

5 pounds ground beef	1 cup shredded onion
1 pound bread crumbs	1 teaspoon oregano
3 or 4 eggs	½ teaspoon pepper and salt

Mix all ingredients together; make sure all is well mixed. Shape into large round firm balls the size of tennis balls. Fry in butter, oregano, salt and pepper, pressing gently with spatula, until medium or well done. Serves 20.

Margaret Havers

• HOT TUNA SANDWICHES

When we drop anchor in some cozy harbor after a long morning's sail, we yearn for something other than the standard lunch fare of cold cuts or cold sandwiches.

This is one of our favorite lunches. Combine a large can of white meat tuna with half a fresh avocado cut into cubes, a quarter cup of American or Cheddar cheese cubes, minced onion and sour cream or mayonnaise to moisten.

Split Syrian or pita bread (try both the white and the wheat for variety) and fill the pockets with the mix.

Put a little butter or margarine in a fry pan. Put in the sandwiches, cover and heat until they are warmed through and the cheese has begun to melt.

Bernice Rieders

• POCKET MEALS

Pita bread keeps for about 1 week or 10 days without refrigeration and stores easily. We eat it often with different fillings.

Hash Sandwiches

Cooked canned corned beef hash and chopped onions in a little oil in a skillet until brown. Stuff into pita bread pockets, then grill pockets in a skillet until brown. Eat with your fingers and save washing up.

One night we had such rough weather we didn't want to use the stove, so we made a cold pocket meal.

Sausage Sandwich

Put thinly sliced sausage (one that keeps without refrigeration), sliced dill pickles and mustard in the pita pocket, serve and enjoy!

The dill pickle helps to satisfy a craving for something crisp when you have no refrigeration.

Bonita Knickmeyer

• BIMINI PIZZA

When we could not face another piece of fish, tasty as it is, we decided to make pizza.

Then we realized our alcohol oven was not in operating condition. We decided to give it a try and do it stove-top. The results were super!

The pizza was cooked slowly at a low temperature until golden brown on the bottom and bubbly on top. We used a good-sized skillet and a kettle, both oiled and floured on the bottom and sides and covered with a tight lid.

Crust

Follow instructions on boxed Hot Roll Mix. (We kneaded dough in pancake mix as we had no flour on board.)

Sauce

Simmer together 2 cans tomato paste, onions, black pepper, a few drops Tabasco (add other ingredients to your own taste).

Topping

Chopped onions, green pepper, small can mushrooms chopped, sliced fresh tomatoes (optional), 8 ounce package mozzarella cheese.

Recipe makes 2 extra-thick medium-sized pizzas. Nothing like pizza-parlor taste at sea!

Nancy Bushneck

SEAFOOD

• CALAMARI

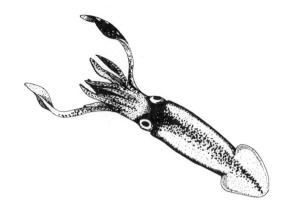

The name squid, in the United States, is associated with dead bait and slimy creatures, so to relax everyone—we will call it by the Italian name, "calamari," and turn it into a most palatable delicacy. Calamari is an inexpensive and highly nutritious meal.

There are 2 ways I know of to prepare calamari: In sauce or fried. Both are very quick and simple.

Fried

Buy 1 pound of cleaned (it makes it so much easier) calamari and wash thoroughly under fresh water. Pat dry with towels.

Using a sharp knife or poultry scissors, cut across the calamari, making bite-sized rings. Salt and pepper, roll in flour and place each ring into very hot oil—olive oil is the best. Cook until golden. Place on paper towel to remove excess oil. Serve with lemon.

In Sauce

Follow the same instructions as above for cutting and washing and place in marinara sauce (2 small jars or 1 large jar).

Cook for 1 hour, longer if desired, and serve over spaghetti or macaroni.

If you're serving guests, it's best not to tell them what they are eating until they start to rave about your cooking.

Kay Aurin

• SEAFOOD MOUSSE

Cool dishes are popular when the temperature soars, but you may be hundreds of miles from the nearest market when the last fresh greens have gone. This dish uses only easily stored items.

Soak 1 package unflavored gelatin in ¼ cup cold water. Add ¼ cup boiling water and stir until dissolved.

Put ¾ cup mayonnaise in a large bowl, add the gelatin solution and fold in 1 cup flaked seafood.

Then add:

½ cup chopped dill pickle or 1 chopped cucumber
2 tablespoons chopped parsley (dehydrated)
2 tablespoons lemon juice (bottled)

8 pitted black olives, sliced
½ cup chopped water chestnuts, celery, almonds or carrots (for a crunchy texture)

Chill at least 1 hour or until firm. Unmold and serve on a bed of bean sprouts.

I have never had a problem keeping mayonnaise without refrigeration. I use the 8 ounce size and keep it tightly sealed.

Bonnie Owra

• BAHAMA FISH BALLS

A Bahamian lady in the Abacos cooked these for me and they were good! It's a great recipe for any large fish or one that tends to be tough.

Cook potatoes in a pressure cooker, take them out and mash them up. Add parsley, onions or other spices to taste. Cook the fish in the pressure cooker, remove, debone and season with salt and pepper.

Make a small open ball with the potatoes, stuff with flaked fish. Close the ball, drop into hot fat and brown.

Serve the fish balls hot with cold Saint Pauli Girl or Beck's Bier, conch salad and hot fresh Bahamian bread. Great lunch!

Jim Tygart

• SEAFOOD À LA FRIED BREAD

We discovered during a number of offshore passages that the crew will absolutely relish practically anything that you serve atop or inside fried bread slices. One of our favorite lunches, a snap to prepare yet gathering consistent rave reviews, is Seafood à la Fried Bread (or use chicken instead).

Lightly fry sliced white bread in butter.

Prepare your sauce with:

1 can cream of mushroom soup	Salt and pepper to taste
1 cup American or Cheddar cheese	Dash garlic
¼ cup milk	Dash onion powder
½ cup white wine	Pat of butter

After it's simmering nicely, add your cut-up seafood or cooked chicken and simmer another 5 minutes. Serve over the fried bread and step back to receive your acclaim. You'll never convince them you didn't learn this at gourmet school.

Jarrett and Stan Kroll

• FISH AMBROSIA

1 pound fish fillets, cut in 1 inch cubes	2 teaspoons sugar
½ cup mayonnaise	½ cup shredded coconut
2 tablespoons lemon juice	1 medium pineapple cut in bite-sized cubes

Simmer fish cubes in 4 cups lightly salted water for 5 minutes. The fish should flake easily. Drain and cool. Combine mayonnaise, lemon juice and sugar. Add to fish and toss lightly. Add coconut and pineapple. Yummy! You can make many variations with this recipe, depending on what you have aboard. Celery or orange slices are good additions.

Sue McBride

• SUSHI

Sushi is a cold dish made with slightly sweet-and-sour rice and eaten with the fingers. It can be prepared ahead and stored until needed. It's great on a hot day. In Japan, sushi is the equivalent of the American hot dog!

2 cups rice	2 teaspoons vinegar
2 cups water	½ teaspoon salt
2 teaspoons sugar	

Soak the rice in the water with the sugar, vinegar and salt for 1 hour. Cover and bring to a boil on high heat until the water begins to spew out. Without lifting the lid, reduce heat to very low and cook for 8 minutes. Remove from heat and let stand for 8 minutes.

When the rice has cooled, wet your hands and shape the rice into 3 inch oblong patties. Spread the patties thinly with Japanese horse-radish mustard (this is hot).

We prefer raw fish such as tuna, yellowtail, octopus, halibut and albacore, or cooked shrimp, scallops, crab or lobster. If we're not too sure of the taste of a raw fish, we fry it lightly.

Cut the fish to fit on top of the patties and serve with small dishes of soy sauce. Dip the sushi in the soy sauce and enjoy!

Tanya Horowitz

• TUNA BURGERS

Since we rarely eat beef, I have found a simple, delicious way to serve tuna as a substitute.

1 can tuna, drained	1 teaspoon dried minced onion
1 egg	Seasoned bread crumbs
¼ cup catsup	

In a bowl, flake tuna and mix with raw egg, catsup and onion. Add bread crumbs until mixture will form patties that hold together. Fry the burgers in a small amount of oil and butter until brown and cooked through. Melt 1 slice mozzarella cheese on top and serve on a bun or bread with your favorite garnish. These burgers are also delicious by themselves for those who are weight-conscious.

Susan Andersen

• BARBECUE TUNA

Combine:

1 can tuna in water or oil
1 tablespoon Worcestershire sauce
1 tablespoon wine vinegar
1 teaspoon chili powder

1 tablespoon prepared mustard
3 tablespoons catsup
1 tablespoon water
½ teaspoon dried onion flakes

We like this on a bun with slaw or as a main dish with baked beans and slaw. Try it; you will not believe this is tuna.

Jill Gaither

• BUMSTEADS

We usually stock cheeses, either aged that require no refrigeration, or dried, and the processed cheeses in jars or spray cans. We also like hard sausages, like summer sausage and the pickled sausages that come in jars. Along with pickles and fresh fruits and vegetables, they make easy, tasty and quick lunches.

This recipe serves 8.

1 can tuna, crab or salmon (drained
    and flaked)
¼ cup chopped sweet or dill pickle
1 tablespoon minced onion

3 hard-boiled eggs, chopped
¼ cup Cheddar cheese, diced
2 tablespoons mayonnaise
8 hotdog buns

Combine all ingredients except buns. Butter the hotdog buns and fill with the mixture. Wrap each in aluminum foil and bake at 350° for 10 minutes.

Lynette Walther

• TOP SHELL FRITTERS

Conch has become scarce in some areas of the Bahamas, but we found an abundance of top shells (incorrectly called whelks by the locals). Not knowing the best way to fix these critters I experimented and found the smaller ones are delicious boiled and dipped in lemon and butter. They have much the same flavor as clams.

The larger ones are very tasty made into fritters.

Let 8 shells stand in fresh seawater for several hours to purge themselves. Steam them for about 10 minutes so that they can be removed easily from the shells.

Discard the round black trap door and mushy end (this can be eaten but is usually sandy). Grind or chop the meat very finely along with 1 medium onion.

Mix the meat and onion with: 1 egg, 1 teaspoon baking powder, 1 tablespoon ketchup, salt and pepper, garlic, thyme, chili powder, ½ cup flour and enough water to make a soft, sticky mixture

Drop small balls into hot cooking oil and deep fry until golden brown. Drain excess oil and eat these delectable fritters dipped in a sauce of catsup, Tabasco and horseradish.

Serve with curried rice and wine, and you'll have a gourmet feast for 2.

Marilee McAlpine

• LINGUINE WITH WHITE CONCH SAUCE

Olive oil (about ¼ cup)
2 cloves garlic (or garlic salt)
Handful parsley (fresh or dry)
¼ teaspoon oregano

Pinch thyme
2–4 cleaned conch, chopped
Salt and pepper to taste

Sauté garlic in olive oil until translucent (not brown). Add parsley flakes, oregano, thyme, about ½ cup water and salt and pepper to taste. Heat to boiling and simmer about 10 minutes. Add conch and cook 5 more minutes, or add conch, cover and remove from burner. Pour over linguini or spaghetti and garnish with Parmesan cheese.

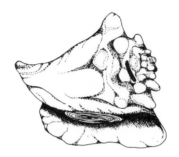

CRACKED CONCH

2 or 3 conch for each person
Flour, cornmeal or pancake mix
Milk and/or egg

Oil to cover bottom of pan, about
¼ inch deep

Pound conch with a tenderizer hammer until soft and quite thin. Soak in milk or milk and egg while you heat oil. Dip conch in flour and then put in hot oil until brown; turn once. Serve with cocktail seafood sauce (very good).

Janet Harbach

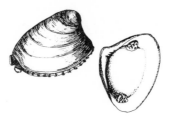

• CLAM AND SHRIMP CRÊPE CASSEROLE

Feeling a bit classy one rainy day aboard *Fria Via* in the Virgin Islands, Jim Larson and I concocted a dish fit for company or celebrations.
Make the crêpe batter 1 hour ahead of time and let sit.

¾ cups all-purpose flour	1 egg
Pinch of salt	1 tablespoon oil
1¼ cups milk	

Mix together with hand egg beater or wire whisk. Set aside.
Put 1 tablespoon of oil in the crêpe pan and heat until hot. Tip out oil. Put a spoonful of batter in the pan and roll around quickly until the base is covered. Crêpes should be thin, so tip out any excess batter. As soon as the batter appears dull and the edges begin to brown, flip over with a spatula and cook the other side. This side cooks more quickly.
Throw out the first crêpe, it absorbs the oil. Do not add any more oil. Keep making crêpes until the batter is gone.

Mix together:

1 can shrimp, drained	1 jar mushrooms, drained
1 can minced clams, drained	1 can spinach, drained
1 can cream of celery soup, undiluted	

In a baking dish alternate the flat crêpes with the filling until all the filling has been used. Bake for 25–30 minutes in oven or pressure cooker.
Any leftover crêpes can be served for dessert. Sprinkle each with about 1 teaspoon sugar and ½ teaspoon of Benedictine or B&B and roll up. Fantastic!

Wendy McKee

• CLAMS IN VERMOUTH

I've just discovered what vermouth and a bay leaf can do for a bucket of clams. My clams will never see water again!

I'm even willing to bet that those who ordinarily can't stand the ugly little things could be tempted.

Make a sauce with: ½ cup dry vermouth (or sweet and dry mixed), ¼ cup melted butter, garlic salt, black pepper, juice of ¼ lemon and 1 bay leaf.

Pour the sauce over 2 quarts washed clams and steam. Remove the clams and serve with the broth in individual bowls for dunking.

The broth is the surprise. It's unexpected, but it sure is better than butter.

Barbara Ashton

• TEN-MINUTE MUSSELS

Mussels can be found in almost any tidal area, on rocks, pilings, even in the sand. All you need to do is pull them off their resting place and throw them in a bucket. Cleaning the mussels is the most time-consuming job in preparing for the feast.

A good metal brush or very stiff plastic brush is needed to scrub each mussel; be sure to pull out the hair-like fibers from the edge of the shell. That's the hardest work for the rest of the evening.

In a large pot put 2 to 3 cups white wine. Chop 4 to 5 scallions very small, not forgetting the excellent green stems, and throw them in the pot of wine with 2 pats of butter.

Turn on the stove, throw in the mussels and cover. In 10 minutes or less you'll have a divine meal.

If you wish to add more elegance to the meal, serve an antipasto before. If not, just a salad and French or Italian bread.

One bucket of mussels is more than enough for 4 people.

Kay Aurin

• CRAB CAKES

This is a recipe for the sailor who has no refrigeration. The main ingredient—crabmeat—can either be caught fresh or taken straight from the can.

1 pound crabmeat	¼ teaspoon Worcestershire sauce
2 eggs, beaten	½ cup cracker crumbs
2 tablespoons minced onion	3 tablespoons mayonnaise
1 tablespoon prepared mustard	Salt and pepper to taste

Mix this mess together and shape into 8 cakes. Fry in hot butter to a golden brown. Serve 'em hot to a hungry crew and you might get 4 servings.

Ron Benner

VEGIES AND PASTA

• VEGETABLE HASH

Vegetable hash can be a side dish or a main course. It will feed 4. Sometimes we top it with fried eggs.

¼ cup butter	½ cup green beans, finely chopped
2 medium onions, finely chopped	1 teaspoon salt
2 garlic cloves, crushed	1 teaspoon black pepper
¼ cup chopped mushrooms	¼ teaspoon Cayenne pepper (if
4 medium potatoes, finely chopped	available)
4 medium carrots, finely chopped	

In a large fry pan melt half the butter. When foam subsides, add onions, garlic and mushrooms and fry for 5 to 7 minutes. Transfer this mixture to a plate and set aside.

Add the remaining butter to pan and melt. When foam subsides, add potatoes, carrots and beans and cook for 12 minutes, stirring occasionally.

Now add the onion-mushroom mixture to the pan and stir in the salt, pepper and Cayenne. Reduce the heat to low and simmer the mixture for 5 minutes or until the vegetables are cooked. Serve at once.

EGGPLANT-ZUCCHINI BAKE

1 eggplant	1 cup mushrooms, chopped
2 small zucchini	¾ cup hard cheese
¾ cup tomato sauce	1 cup water
1 tablespoon soy sauce	2 tablespoons Parmesan cheese
¾ cup green peppers, chopped	

Sauté green peppers and mushrooms in butter. Steam eggplant and zucchini in water and soy sauce until both are soft. Place sliced eggplant and zucchini in casserole dish with tomato sauce, peppers, and mushrooms on top. Sprinkle hard cheese on top. Then add another layer of all ingredients above and sprinkle with Parmesan cheese.

Bake at 300° for about 15 minutes. As an option, more hard cheese can be added and the dish baked for another 5 minutes.

Sonia Walter

• BUCKWHEAT MACARONI

You can substitute whole wheat macaroni for the buckwheat; both are available in health food stores. The amounts can be varied to suit individual needs and taste. (Do not use seawater for cooking any pasta. It will make it much too salty.)

½ pound buckwheat macaroni, cooked	1 or 2 tablespoons grated onion
	1 cup grated Cheddar cheese
2 large firm tomatoes, diced	Mayonnaise to moisten
2 green peppers, diced	Salt and pepper to taste

Combine all ingredients and mix well.

Karen Rankin

CHAPTER 8

MAIN MEALS

BEEF

• QUICK MEAT PIE

I use packaged Flako pie crust mix, which comes wax-wrapped, keeps indefinitely and makes one good thick crust or two thin ones. All you have to do is add water. Any filling can be used—freshly cooked meat or fowl if you have it, the various canned stews (beef, chicken, meatball) or the ubiquitous canned corned beef. With added canned vegetables of your choice and a sprinkle of onion salt, all these fillings are good and quick.

Light the oven. Use an oven-proof dish (deep enough to hold at least 4 1-pound cans of stew) to mix the pie crust according to label directions. Remove pie crust to a slightly floured surface and shape to the size of the dish. Put cans of stew or other filling into the dish. Place the pie crust on top, pressing gently to sides to seal. Make a small hole in the center with a skewer or marlinspike.

Bake at 450° for 15 minutes, then reduce the heat to 350° for a further 30 minutes. By the time the pie crust is cooked, the filling is piping hot. Serve with California red Burgundy or whatever you've got.

Barbara Davis

• BULLY BEEF BURGOO

Because the boat had bare sitting headroom and the galley's alcohol stove was the non-pressurized type, meals under way were of the very simple, quick, efficient kind.

This one takes about 30 minutes to fix and is especially good when night is coming on and the Gulf is getting dusty. Put on your oilskin bottoms or the rubber apron every sea cook should wear and clamp a deep pot onto the stovetop.

While 2 large, cut-up onions and about 3 stalks of celery are sautéing in oil, open a can of parboiled roast beef onto a plate and shred it with a knife and fork.

When the onions are limp, add meat and gravy, stirring to coat the meat with oil. Add 6 cups water, an 8 ounce can green peas, season with salt, pepper, garlic powder and a teaspoon of the ubiquitous, nautical curry powder.

Bring to a boil and simmer for about 10 minutes.

(Now is the time some cooks would stick their heads out the companionway and say to the watch on deck, "I say, lads, there's some awful knocking noise up forward. Do you think something's caught under the bow?" Then, while their attention is distracted, duck below and pour himself a quickie from the medical stores.)

Turn off the fire, add a small can of evaporated milk and stir in instant potato flakes slowly until you reach burgoo consistency, which is, as everyone knows, just a little thicker than stew.

Serve into 3 deep bowls and be sure to top with Waverly crackers. Delicious.

This recipe also makes an outstanding fish chowder base if you leave out the meat and green peas. Top with bacon bits.

In spite of the restrictions imposed by the galley, we three bachelors found our meals quite tasty, although, as the pig in *Animal Farm* said, "Some were more tasty than others."

William Cox

• SINGLEHANDER'S STEW

A few years back, bound for the lower latitudes and sunnier climes, I happened to ship a Teflon saucepan. Before that passage was out I was to hit upon one of the few singularly significant advancements in the history of seagoing culinary art.

The aforementioned small Teflon pan is needed, as well as a moderately large spoon, raw onions (always vital on a cruising boat), instant rice, a collection of optional canned ingredients, a handful of spices and a roll of toilet paper. Seldom have such mundane principals so synergistically contributed to such an important discovery.

The preparation procedure is quickly told, hence its value—any true sailor knows that among the important elements found on any successful cruiser are stout scantlings, simplicity and low maintenance. This singlehander's stew has them all.

Step one: The fire is lit and the pan is containing a dollop of seawater placed in it. A raw onion is added (large, quartered and strong) and the lid placed on. After the onion is boiled briefly, a small can of carrots, beans, peas (including the juice) or what-have-you is added. Then, an additional small tin or portion of whatever cooked meat or fowl is available. Fresh fish will cook up quickly during the preparation.

Things are now moving fast, and it is at this point that the necessary seasoning is added. If a kedgeree is desired, freshly caught fish can be chucked in along with peanuts, raisins and a splash of catsup. If you like curry, canned chicken may be added along with that delectable spice, or saffron and garlic can be substituted to make paella. If the cook is a vegetarian, stick in zucchini, green peppers, olive oil and a light wine to make ratatouille. See how easy it is to move into gourmet-class cooking? The combinations are endless.

It is now only necessary to boil the ingredients long enough to heat them and infuse any spices that may have been added. To this briskly bubbling potion a proper amount of instant rice is then placed. The collection is again brought to the boil, the lid clamped on, the fire extinguished and the instant rice allowed to do its predetermined thing.

The result is light and fluffy, with the stirring spoon now doubling as tableware and the cooking pot becoming the eating dish. No muss, no fuss, no pressure cooker that must be strapped down, no hot grease to inflict a more painful and embarrassing wound on the cook than any Force 9, and very important, no messy cooking tools that must later be scraped, scoured, scrubbed and finally stowed.

The full preparation takes no more than 12 to 15 minutes, the eating from 5 to 50 minutes depending upon the state of the sea and the book you are reading, and the clean-up afterwards a scant 30 seconds or so. The pan is immediately given a quick wipe with convenient and absorbent toilet tissue and the spoon a final cleansing lick by the cook.

With a cat aboard, even these simple chores can be dispensed with (it may be necessary to keep the animal slightly hungry).

Jerry Cartwright

• BEEF WITH BROCCOLI OR ANYTHING

Because the meat is marinated, the toughest meat in any part of the world can be used for this dish.

1 pound beefsteak, sliced	1 slice ginger root or
4 tablespoons soy sauce	¼ cup sliced onion
1 tablespoon cornstarch	5 tablespoons cooking oil
1 tablespoon sherry	½ teaspoon salt
1 tablespoon sugar	½ bunch fresh broccoli or any
¼ teaspoon MSG, optional	vegetable

Mix beef with soy sauce, cornstarch, sherry, sugar, MSG and set aside.

Peel and slice broccoli into flowerets 2 inches long and ¼ inch thick. Pour 2 tablespoons oil into a hot skillet over high heat. Add salt and broccoli, stir and turn until broccoli is dark green, not over 2 minutes. Remove from skillet.

Put remaining oil into skillet, again over high heat. Add ginger or onion, stir in beef mixture and keep stirring until almost done—less than 2 minutes. Add cooked broccoli and mix thoroughly. Serve immediately.

Mushrooms, green beans, green peppers, zucchini or any other vegetable can be used in place of broccoli.

If using green beans do not add MSG to the marinade. Cook the marinated beef first, with the ginger root or onion, remove. Add 2 tablespoons oil to the skillet, stir in beans and ½ cup water. Bring to a boil, then cook over medium heat, stirring occasionally. Add more water if necessary. Cook for 10 minutes, then add salt, MSG and cooked beef.

Robert Kohlman

• SEARCHER STEW

This stew is easy to prepare for any number of people and can't be spoiled by overcooking. It serves 4, so for the 2 of us I serve it the first night with Bisquick dumplings and the second night with noodles.

In a large pot, brown 2 pounds cubed stew meat and 1 small can sliced mushrooms in 1 tablespoon butter. Stir in 2 cans Campbell's tomato soup and 2 cans water. Add 4 or 5 carrots, 4 or 5 celery stalks (both cut in 2 inch pieces), garlic salt, pepper, a bay leaf, ½ teaspoon or so of basil and parsley flakes.

Bring to a boil and simmer 1 hour or so. Add a jar of boiled onions and simmer 15 minutes more before serving, or add the dumplings according to directions.

Jayne McLean

• CARBONNADE DE BOEUF FLAMMANDE

Sauté 4 good-sized onions in plenty of butter until translucent. Fish out onions and reserve them in a baking dish. Sauté and brown in the same pan 2 pounds beef cubes (¾ to 1 inch square) that have first been seasoned with salt, pepper and whatever and dredged with flour. Keep cleaning the pan into the onions as it gets crusty, by adding a little water and making gravy.

Flavor the mix of gravy and onions with whatever is needed to thicken gravy and improve taste. I use bay leaf, sweet basil, salt, pepper, oregano and a touch of Worcestershire sauce. Add to the dish some sliced raw onions, cubed potatoes equal in volume to the meat (but cubed smaller) and carrots if you wish.

Pour enough beer over the mix barely to drown it and bake an hour or so at 350°. Serves 6.

Norris Hoyt

• UNEXPECTED DUMPLINGS

Sue, first mate and hostess-cook on *Tao*, was having to discard 10 pounds of eye-of-round (from a freezer on the fritz)! Anchored at Staniel Cay, we had sumptuous steak that night, then I popped the rest into the pressure cooker for 15 minutes at 15 pounds pressure to preserve it until mañana.

Tao's crew came over for lunch the next day, and I made a big pot of eye-of-round dumplings. It must have been good, for they each had 3 helpings.

Into a 6 quart pot place:

2 pounds eye-of-round, cut into bite-sized chunks and well-cooked. Frying improves the flavor. Mine was pressure cooked to halt possible bacterial growth.	3 beef bouillon cubes
	3 garlic cloves, crushed
	1 tomato, mashed
	1 teaspoon salt
	1 teaspoon chili powder
	1 teaspoon vinegar
3 stalks celery, chopped	1 teaspoon soy sauce
3 large carrots, diced or sliced thin	3 tablespoons flour, dissolved in
3 large onions, chopped and sautéed	1 cup cold water

Add water (or stock) to come 2 inches above all the ingredients. Stir and heat until the gravy thickens—it should be on the thin side. Bring the stew to a boil and meanwhile prepare the dumplings:

2 cups flour (half white/half whole wheat or oat is tasty)	3 teaspoons baking powder
½ teaspoon salt	1 heaping tablespoon Parmesan cheese (adds a bit of zing)

Mix the dry ingredients thoroughly and add enough milk to make a stiff batter, about ⅔ cup. Spoon the batter into the boiling broth until the entire top is batter. Cover tightly. Reduce heat and simmer for 10 minutes, not peeking until the time is up. Dumplings are often wet and waddy, but these are light and fluffy. You can, of course, use another cut of beef.

One of the reasons we don't have refrigeration on *Mariposa* is to avoid the hassles and cost of a breakdown. This was one breakdown that didn't bother us a bit!

Diane Taylor

• BOURBON STEAK

Sauté 2 thinly sliced onions in margarine until they are pale yellow. Remove from pan and keep warm. Rub 2 rib steaks (or equivalent), about ½ inch thick, with a mixture of salt, pepper and garlic salt.

Quickly brown both sides of the steak and remove to a warm serving platter. Stir 1½ ounces bourbon into the pan drippings over low heat.

Pile the onions on top of the steak and pour the hot gravy over. Serve at once. Delectable!

Lillian Morris

• BISTECCA MILANESE

Use 2 medium-sized beef cutlets for each person. Dip the cutlets in a mixture of 1 egg beaten with 2 tablespoons milk. Then coat with a mixture of:

½ cup bread crumbs   Salt and pepper to taste
1 bunch parsley, chopped

Fry in butter in a hot skillet for about 2 minutes each side. Serve. Buon Appetito!

Robin Harris

• SEVEN DISH BEEF CURRY

This is a good cruising meal as canned beef can be substituted for fresh, sprouts for lettuce, dried onions for fresh (put in gravy) and bacon bits for fresh bacon. Cheese keeps 3–4 weeks unrefrigerated if wrapped in a vinegar-soaked cloth.

I usually serve a good Burgundy with it and dessert later in the evening.

½ cup cooked rice per person (keep warm)
2 cans Franco American beef gravy
3 pounds top round (or similar) trimmed to 1 inch cubes

½ pound washed and sliced mushrooms
3 tablespoons curry powder

Condiments:

1 pound can pineapple chunks, drained
6 ounce package shredded coconut
1 pound Cheddar cheese, shredded
12 ounce package slivered almonds

½ small head of lettuce, shredded
Small bunch green onions, chopped
1 pound bacon, diced, crisply fried and drained

Prepare beef and mushrooms. Start the rice and while it is cooking fry the bacon. Prepare the rest of the condiments, putting each in a separate bowl in the center of the table.

Lightly brown the beef in a skillet, draining off any liquid. Add gravy and mushrooms. Stir in curry powder, less or more to your taste. Cover and simmer until cooked.

Serve rice on plates and top with curry. Everyone helps themselves to the condiments, and the flavor of everything together is indescribably good. Serves 8.

Gay Thompson

• CLAY BAKER COMBINATION DINNER

Any or all of these in amounts to serve your crew:

Short ribs of beef	Chicken legs
Pork neck bones or chops	Smoked sausage

One or more:

Potatoes	Onions
Carrots	

Scrub potatoes and carrots, but do not peel unless absolutely necessary. Peel onions and leave whole or cut in quarters, according to size.

Place the vegetables at the bottom of the clay baker with the meat at the top where it will brown. Sprinkle with salt and pepper and place a bay leaf on top. Bake until the meat is done and the vegetables are tender.

This dinner is also excellent cooked on a bed of sauerkraut.

If you do not have a clay baker, you can prepare this meal in any ovenproof container. You will not, however, get the brown, roasted flavor the clay baker produces so beautifully.

Anna Patrick

• GLAZED RIBS

This recipe will serve 4 people.

Trim the fat from 2 pounds of beef spareribs and put in a shallow baking pan. Combine 1 can condensed beef broth, 1 cup dried apricots, 2 tablespoons vinegar, dash cinnamon, dash ground cloves and pour over the ribs.

Bake in a moderate oven about 2 hours or until tender.

Lillian Morris

CORNED BEEF

• RIDING LIGHT RECIPE

Mealtime, and I'm the ship's cook. Sometimes I like to forget the clock and linger on deck, after a passage of perhaps a day or a week when we've shared the excitement of a strange landfall and found our way into a quiet anchorage. This is one of my best times cruising, when together we coil down and put the sailcoats on against tomorrow's sun, look around, smell the land and listent to the birds. Strolling around the deck, itchy feet are stilled. But come on, we're tired, we're hungry, and on such occasions I produce a quick, hot, simple meal that we've not complained about for years:

Peel and cut in small chunks 2 potatoes and boil for 7 minutes. Slice 2 onions and cook in a skillet with a little oil until the rawness has gone. Strain the potatoes and add to the onions. When they start to brown, add a can of corned beef cut into chunks. Tomatoes or peppers, if still aboard, are added or a can of peas for color and bulk. Leave the lot to brown.

By now, Eric has set the riding light and poured a sundowner: I turn the burner low until we're ready.

Susan Hiscock

• THE ORIGINAL PISUPO

As a U.S. Marine, I departed for American Samoa less than a month after Pearl Harbor during World War II.

The local Burns Philip store in Pago Pago had been providing the Samoans with the ingredients of pisupo for years and it was called "pea-soup-o" because it consisted solely of the contents of one can of peas and one can of corned beef, heated in a single black cooking pot over an open cooking fire. Neither the Marines nor the Samoans had anything else to add to pisupo and any additions would destroy the unique blend of the separate, distinctive flavors of canned peas and corned beef.

Because of its unique flavor and its simplicity (2 cans, 1 pot and heat), pisupo has been a favorite emergency meat-and-vegetables dish for nearly 40 years for our family in Rockport, Texas.

The good old original is hard to beat.

Bob Mullin

• CORNED BEEF AND VEGETABLE ROLL

We were the smallest entrant in the Cape Town to Rio Race, 1,780 miles from Cape Town with approximately 1,800 left to run to Rio de Janeiro. Conditions were close to perfect—little or no sea, a big southern ocean swell that we could scarcely feel, and 15 knots of warm trade winds filling the big blue and white tri-radial spinnaker that sent us racing ahead at a good 6 knots.

"Special" meals are very important in a sea cook's repertoire. So what to have this mid-South Atlantic evening?

Mix 2 cups flour, ½ teaspoon salt and 2 teaspoons baking powder and rub in 2 rounded tablespoons shortening until the mixture is crumbly. Add just enough water to make a stiff dough, then roll out to a rectangular shape approximately ¼ inch thick.

Chop 2 onions and add to a mashed-up can of corned beef. Add chopped carrot and some diced potato, sprinkle in some dehydrated peas and moisten the lot with tomato sauce and a good dash of soy sauce. A pinch of thyme, sage, salt and pepper comes next.

Mix well and spread over the dough. Roll up and pinch the ends together. Place on a tray with seam side down, and brush the top of the roll with milk. Bake in a moderate oven about 1 hour. Serve with thick onion gravy.

Judy Harrison

• TRADITIONAL CORNED BEEF AND CABBAGE *(With No Corned Beef)*

Cut up 1 onion, slice 4 to 5 carrots and quarter 4 potatoes. Fill the pressure cooker halfway with water and add 2 beef bouillon cubes. Turn the heat on and let the water boil. Cut up 2 thick pieces of salami in small chunks and add with the vegetables to the pot. Put the lid on the pressure cooker and the weight. Turn the heat to low and simmer for 45 minutes.

Add a quartered cabbage on top and simmer 30 minutes more. Be sure to let the steam out of the pressure cooker by releasing the weight before you open the lid to add the cabbage. Even then, it's always safe not to put your face too close to the pan when you open the lid so you won't get a steam burn.

This makes a good hearty meal when served with scones or biscuits. It can be prepared using ham rather than salami and is just as delicious without meat at all. It should depend on how much of what you have on board. Salami adds a lot of flavor just using a small amount. This is especially good for the last days of the carrots. An awful, soggy carrot will perk right up and taste great in this 1-pot dinner.

Doyle Ann Anawalt

• WILD MAN'S MEAT ON SLEEPING BAG RICE

When you're down to the end of the fresh vegetables and left with the ends of celery, a tomato, a bit of lettuce, a carrot or two, an onion or whatever, and it doesn't look like there's enough for a respectable salad, try this. Wild Man's Meat is a recipe we got from an expatriate merchant marine who claimed to have been to Borneo and gotten the recipe from the Wild Man himself.

Essentially, it's a warmed salad made with corned beef and served over rice. Our version needs only 1 burner but requires 2 pots.

First, the Sleeping Bag Rice. Yes, it's rice cooked in a sleeping bag. You'll need fair weather for this or at least a tight cover for the pot. Measure slightly less water than twice the amount of rice you want to prepare (e.g., for 1 cup of rice, slightly less than 2 cups of water).

Bring the rice and water to a boil, cover tightly, wrap with newspaper or something waterproof, then stuff the pot inside a sleeping bag. It'll stay hot enough to cook itself while you make the Wild Man's Meat.

In the 18 minutes it takes for the rice to cook itself, put a large pot on your 1-burner stove with a couple of tablespoons of oil in the bottom. Break up a can of corned beef into the hot oil, and while it's warming, fix the vegetables. (Use a low flame.)

Cut your variety of vegetables very fine, as you would for a Chinese dish. When they're all ready, dump them in the pot with the corned beef, stirring quickly until the mixture is warm. It must not cook! The vegetables must remain crisp.

Season to taste with white pepper, salt and your favorite spices. Serve with soy sauce over the Sleeping Bag Rice. You'll find the rice flaky and perfect—never stuck to the bottom of the pot. If some water remains, use less next time.

Harley Sachs

• BAD WEATHER STEW

1 can corned beef
2 large onions
3–6 slices bacon
½ fresh cabbage

1 can potatoes
1 can carrots
Salt, pepper, red pepper, bay leaf

Sauté onions and bacon in margarine or butter in a large, deep pot. Add corned beef (break up with fork), juices from canned vegetables, cut-up cabbage, bay leaf and spices to taste.

Cook at low to medium heat for 20–30 minutes. Add canned vegetables and cook until hot (1–2 minutes). Serves 2–4.

Marilyn Steinhuebl

HAMBURGER

• CHILI-RITOS

While trying to do something different with some left-over chili, I came up with Chili-Ritos.

These consist of my chili (today's is O.K. but yesterday's is better), fresh Maui onions (grown only on the island of Maui and the sweetest in the world), sharp Cheddar cheese, La Victoria mild red taco sauce and flour tortillas.

To make the chili use:

1 pound ground beef
1 medium Maui onion, chopped
16 ounce can Hunt's red chili beans
16 ounce can Hunt's tomato sauce

Salt and pepper
La Victoria mild red taco sauce to
    taste

Brown the ground beef and drain off the fat. Combine with the remaining ingredients and simmer about 30 minutes.

When the chili is ready, steam several flour tortillas. I do this by placing a round cake pan in a frying pan with ¼ inch of boiling water and then put the tortillas in the cake pan, cover for about 3 minutes or until they are soft and hot.

Now comes the good part. Place about 2 tablespoons chili in the center of the tortilla and sprinkle generously with chopped Maui onion and sharp cheddar cheese. Top off with La Victoria mild red taco sauce to taste.

Now roll up the tortilla and fold over one end and you have a Chili-Rito. Wash down with ice cold beer and you are in heaven!

Robert Finan

• ENCHILADAS FEO PATO

10 ounce can Ashley's tortillas
1 pound ground beef or 2 small cans boned chicken
1 envelope dry mix or one can enchilada sauce
2 cups grated cheese (when cruising offshore I use Velveeta)

2 large onions, coarsely chopped
2 cups dry green pepper flakes or 1 whole green pepper, coarsely chopped
16 ounce can stewed tomatoes

In fry pan brown beef, add onion, green pepper and stewed tomatoes. Cook vegetables until still slightly crisp. Salt and pepper to taste. Add some bottled hot sauce if desired.

Pour reconstituted or canned enchilada sauce in shallow bowl. Dip each tortilla into sauce before layering in a deep 2 quart baking pan in the following manner:

Cover bottom of pan with layer of meat mixture, then a layer of dipped tortillas, another layer of meat, a layer of cheese, then tortillas and so on. Make the last layer meat, topped with the rest of the cheese.

Bake 30 minutes at 350°. Serve with a tossed green salad or canned three-bean salad.

Arliss Newcomb

• HOT AND PUNGENT CHILI CON CARNE

We are all particularly fond of hot, spicy foods. This chili, with the interesting addition of coffee, makes a favorite meal that can be made from scratch or can be brought aboard practically ready to eat. It is especially welcome during the cooler days early and late in the season on Lake Ontario.

1 pound lean ground beef
Oil
½ cup coarsely chopped onion
    (more if you like them)
2–3 cloves garlic, minced
1 tablespoon paprika
2 tablespoons chili powder
Pinch Cayenne
1 teaspoon salt
1 teaspoon ground cloves

½ bay leaf
2 teaspoons Italian seasoning
½ teaspoon cumin (if you have it)
6 ounce can tomato paste or 19
    ounce can tomatoes
2 cups leftover coffee or stock (If
    using coffee add one Oxo cube
    or 1 teaspoon liquid Oxo)
19 ounce can kidney beans

Brown beef well in the oil. Add onions, garlic, paprika, chili powder, Cayenne, salt and cloves. Toss and fry until onions are soft. Add remaining ingredients and simmer gently at least 1 hour—the longer the better. Add more stock or coffee if necessary.

Add beans just prior to serving and continue cooking just long enough for them to heat up.

Serve with tortillas and garnishes of one or more of the following:

Shredded Cheddar cheese
Shredded lettuce
Chopped green and/or red pepper
Chopped Spanish onion
Sour cream or plain yogurt, or a combination of the two

This is a good recipe to make ahead of time and freeze. Simply double the quantities of everything but the beans and remove half the mixture prior to adding beans. When you reheat the meal, just add the beans when the mixture is hot and serve as above. If I plan to use aboard on a weekend, I prepare my garnishes at home as well, saving a lot of washing and chopping at the last minute.

Anna Patrick

• SOUTHERN SUPPER

1 pound ground beef
1 medium onion, cut up
7 ounce can mushroom stems and
  pieces
1 small can spinach, drained and
  chopped

1 egg, scrambled and cut up
2 tablespoons soy sauce
Garlic powder to taste
2 tablespoons margarine

Sauté onions with mushrooms in margarine until semi-transparent. Add meat and brown while sprinkling with garlic powder and soy sauce. When meat is brown, add spinach and egg. Simmer, covered, long enough for flavors to blend (10–15 minutes). Serve with or over rice.

Binnie Bowman

• HAMBURGER STROGANOFF

1 pound hamburger
½ cup chopped onion
2 garlic cloves (chopped)

1 package brown gravy mix
1 cup sour cream (fresh or dry)
½ cup mushrooms

Brown hamburger, onion and garlic in heavy skillet. Add gravy mix and half the water called for on the package. Simmer 10–15 minutes. Stir in mushrooms and sour cream. Serve over egg noodles.

Janice Cunningham

• STOVE-TOP SPECIALS

During our 3 month cruise of the North Channel and Georgian Bay, we discovered that cooking aboard a 23 foot sailboat is an exercise in patience.

Our galley consisted of a 1-burner camp stove, an icebox and a cold water pump-your-own sink. Our cookware was limited to a Dutch oven, a 4 quart saucepan, a 1½ quart saucepan, a 6 inch frying pan and a whistling teakettle.

Despite these "primitive" conditions, we were not condemned to canned foods. We usually stopped at small towns along the way and stocked up on fresh meats, vegetables and fruit every four to five days.

Two of our favorite recipes used interchangeable ingredients:

Spanish Rice

1 pound ground beef
1 or 2 green peppers, diced
1 onion, chopped

1 can tomato soup
Instant rice
Seasonings

Brown ground beef in skillet; add green peppers and onion and sauté. Drain grease. In a saucepan make soup according to directions. Add seasonings. After soup comes to a boil, remove from heat and add 1 soup can of instant rice. Let sit for 5 minutes. Add soup-rice mixture to beef; serve. Makes excellent reheated leftovers.

Stuffed Peppers

3 green peppers
½ pound ground beef

1 cup instant rice
1 can tomato sauce or soup

Core peppers and place in saucepan. Fill pot half full with water and heat to boiling to soften peppers. Brown ground beef and prepare rice. Spoon beef and rice alternately into peppers and heat for a few more minutes. Warm tomato sauce and pour over peppers on serving dish.

Carol Kristl

• PAWPAW MONTESPAN

Everyone around Bermuda knows how to make this dish, but this is my adaptation for ovenless cooking.

Wearing rubber gloves (remembering that green pawpaw is an excellent meat tenderizer) peel, seed and quarter 3 small green pawpaws. Bring to a boil a mixture of ½ seawater and ½ freshwater in a big pot then drop in the pawpaw. Cook for about 20 to 30 minutes until quite well done.

Butter your largest skillet and mash the pawpaws in it. In another pan cook 1 or 2 chopped Bermuda onions in a little butter until yellow and transparent. Add 1 pound hamburger, salt and pepper to taste and cook until done.

Spread this mixture on top of the pawpaw, top with ½ can Campbell's tomato soup, lots of grated cheese and cracker crumbs. Cover and cook very gently for about 30 minutes until the cheese is bubbly.

Penny Voegeli

• BEEF AND LIMA STEW

I am a reluctant cook and am often found half an hour before dinner peering sadly into *Kim's* lockers and muttering about missing ingredients. But with three children to feed, I have developed a system of sorts and collected some foolproof recipes.

2 cups or 1 pound small dried
    lima beans
2 tablespoons fat or oil
1 pound ground beef
1 cup sliced onions or 3 tablespoons
    instant chopped onion

Salt to taste
19 ounce can tomatoes (reserve
    liquid)
2 teaspoons sugar
2 teaspoons Worcestershire sauce

Wash lima beans, soak for 2 hours, then cook in fresh water for 10 minutes. Drain. Fry sliced onions in a skillet with the fat. Add rest of ingredients including beans. If needed, add tomato liquid. Cover and cook until beans are soft, 15 to 20 minutes. Serves 5.

Jenny Evans

• HAMBURGER HOTPOT

Bring the hamburger patties on board frozen, let them thaw during the day and you won't need to put them in the icebox or cooler.

1½ pounds ground beef, in 4
    patties, frozen
4 potatoes, peeled and thickly sliced

4 carrots, peeled and thickly sliced
1 large onion, sliced

Brown the hamburgers on one side in a skillet, turn and place one slice of onion on top of each burger. Cover with layers of sliced potatoes, carrots and the rest of the onion. Season liberally with salt and pepper, cover and simmer on low heat for 30–45 minutes until potatoes are tender.

Don't peek too often.

Nancy Pittman

• FIRST NIGHT OUT PASTA

Pasta and meat sauce is a good first night meal, with green salad from the garden and wild greens harvested on foraging trips ashore.

Meat Sauce

½ cup chopped onions
1 small clove garlic, chopped
¼ cup olive oil
1 pound ground beef
2½ pound can Italian tomatoes

6 ounce can tomato paste
1 teaspoon salt
½ teaspoon oregano
Fresh ground pepper to taste

Cook onions and garlic in oil until transparent; add meat and cook until redness disappears. Add rest of ingredients and cook until desired thickness.

Elbow macaroni is easier to handle afloat than spaghetti for the pasta. Pour some Gallo Hearty Burgundy—and enjoy!

Lorraine Hall

• PRACTICAL PASTA

I'm 6 feet, 5 inches tall, weigh 215 pounds and sail a Guppy 13 (the one with the little cabin), to the everlasting delight of the rest of the population.

I also do considerable cruising and cooking on friends' boats (Folkboat and Abbott 30) on Lakes St. Clair and Huron and have even become quite adept at producing meals over Sterno on the foredecks of 14 foot outboards.

While pasta—principally spaghetti and elbow macaroni—is undeniably among mankind's all-time blessings, it is hard to handle on small boats. It needs lots of water and a big pot. It has to be strained after boiling, which isn't easy on a wildly pitching little vessel.

But there is a way, as I learned from an Italian-Swiss chef who consistently served superb pasta in his restaurant.

To make:

Cook a lot of spaghetti, using a gallon of water per pound of pasta. Salt liberally and add 3 or 4 tablespoons salad oil to the water *before* adding the pasta. Keep boiling rapidly and turn with tongs while it's boiling. The moment it is "al dente" (very slightly chewy) dump the whole potful into a strainer, then immediately into a large pot of ice and ice water.

Chill for a few minutes, then strain, divide into serving portions and package between wax paper. Pasta will keep for a week if refrigerated.

To use:

Melt some unsalted (or lightly salted) butter in a pan and gently sauté the portion(s) of spaghetti until heated through.

Then, instead of turning the pasta out onto a plate and pouring the sauce over, pour the sauce into the pan with the pasta and simmer until the whole lot is piping hot.

The cold-pasta-butter-warmup method is the best way I know to serve a spaghetti meal on board. Great imbibings often accompany pasta eating, and crowd control is difficult. But with this method, the pasta will always be perfect.

Joe Reisner

• QUICK SKILLET LASAGNA

1 pound ground beef
2 tablespoons butter
2½ ounce envelope spaghetti
   sauce mix
2 cups creamed cottage cheese
3 cups medium uncooked noodles
1 tablespoon basil

1 tablespoon parsley flakes
1 teaspoon salt
2½ pound can (or 3½ cups)
   tomatoes
1 cup water
2 cups shredded Monterey Jack
   cheese

In skillet, lightly brown meat in butter. Sprinkle half the spaghetti sauce mix over meat. Spread cottage cheese over meat. Next arrange uncooked noodles in a layer. Sprinkle with remaining spaghetti sauce mix, basil, parsley flakes and salt.

Add tomatoes with liquid, and water, being sure all is moistened. Cover tightly and simmer 30 to 35 minutes or until noodles are done. Sprinkle cheese over top. Replace cover and let stand 10 to 15 minutes before serving. Serves 8.

With the lasagna I like to serve boat-grown alfalfa sprouts mixed with finely shredded green or red cabbage and tossed with store-bought oil and vinegar dressing.

Don't forget a glass of red Burgundy to make the meal complete!

Irene Westbye

• COLD MEAT LOAF

½ pound ground beef
½ pound ground ham
½ pound ground pork
1 teaspoon salt

½ teaspoon garlic powder
1 teaspoon onion
½ teaspoon Season-All
1 egg

Mix the meats well, until they look like one uniform hamburger mix. Add the rest of the ingredients and mix well. Divide in half and shape into loaves. Wrap them well in aluminum foil. Boil in the pressure cooker in 2 cups of water for 35 minutes. Refrigerate until cold, then slice. It's delicious in sandwiches, with potato salad, or with crackers.

Maryellen Farinas

CHICKEN

• ORIENTAL CHICKEN

¼ cup oil
2 chicken breasts
1 tablespoon sherry
1 tablespoon soy sauce
1 tablespoon cornstarch
8 ounce can bamboo shoots

3 tablespoons hoisin sauce
½ teaspoon crushed dry red pepper
   (optional)
1 tablespoon chopped onion
1 teaspoon grated fresh ginger

Bone and cube chicken. Mix sherry and soy sauce. Marinate chicken for ½ hour or longer in mixture. Sprinkle chicken with cornstarch and fry in hot oil for 3 minutes; stir while frying. Add remaining ingredients and fry for 5 minutes over a high flame; stir while frying. Serve with boiled rice. I have used canned boned chicken and added ¼ cup water with the final cooking. Fresh or canned pork, beef or fish can be used instead of chicken. This same recipe is great using plum sauce instead of hoisin sauce.

Dianna Schwierzke

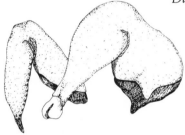

• CURRIED CHICKEN

1 small can chicken, flaked, with
   juice
1 can cream of mushroom soup

1 small can mushrooms with juice
Curry powder to taste

Cook ingredients in saucepan, stirring frequently. Serve over hot fresh rice and top with slivered almonds or fresh grated coconut. Fried plantains are especially good with this dish.

Marg Desfosses

• POTLUCK PAELLA

The word *paella* comes from the name of the pan in which the dish is cooked and served in Spain. If I'm lucky enough to have power, I use a large electric skillet; if not, I use my paella pan.

Sofrita is the base, or minimum ingredients, for the paella and is stowed before departure.

Sofrita

Olive oil	Large can pear-shaped tomatoes
Rice	Can whole cooked chicken
Garlic	Dried mushrooms
Onions	Parsley flakes
Saffron (or curry if saffron is too expensive)	Small can garbanzo beans

Method: Soak a handful of dried mushrooms in water. Drain the liquid from the mushrooms, chicken, tomatoes, garbanzos; also from minced clams and canned vegetables if these are to be added. Add enough water to this to make 3 cups liquid.

Cut all vegetables in rather large chunks. Quarter tomatoes. Leave bones in chicken where possible (like legs) and chunk the rest of the meat.

In paella pan, using olive oil, sauté 1 zucchini, 1 green or red bell pepper (saving some seeds to add to rice), 1 medium onion and any other fresh vegetable, especially celery. Remove from pan and set aside.

To paella pan add: 1½ cups rice, 3 cups liquid (heated to boiling point), 1 clove garlic (crushed), mushrooms, 2 tablespoons parsley flakes, 2 tablespoons bell pepper seeds, garbanzos, salt, pepper, saffron or curry to taste and a little Tabasco if you like.

Cover, return to a boil and simmer about 15 minutes (total cooking time is a minimum of 30 minutes).

Now, go mix yourself a martini and visit the other boats to collect their contributions.

Add:

Catch-of-the-day: Any fresh fish, cleaned, filleted and cut in medium-sized pieces. Shellfish scrubbed and added whole the last 10 minutes or clams until they pop open.

Leftovers: Any meats, especially ham or sausage, beef or fish. Add late enough in cooking time for the leftovers to stay identifiable, except for ham or sausage, which should be added with the fresh vegetables. Olives are a good addition.

Now go back to the burner, add fresh vegetables and cook for 5 minutes. Add fish, meats and cooked vegetables. Add chicken broth or water to keep paella moist but not runny. Taste and adjust seasonings.

Serve with French bread, if available, and fruit and cheese for dessert —and lots of good wine.

Fritz Kinney

• EXTRAORDINARY CHICKEN

This will serve 6 and can be frozen and reheated.

4 ounces mozzarella cheese
12 ounce jar plain spaghetti sauce
1 green pepper, diced
1 large onion, diced
½ pound mushrooms, sliced
1–1½ pounds Portuguese chourico,

hot or mild Italian sausage, or any spicy sausage
6 chicken legs with thighs
1 sliced zucchini or equivalent of green beans, peas or other green vegetable

Separate thighs from drumsticks. Salt, pepper and bake 30 minutes in oven at 450°. Remove from oven and drain off fat.

Slice sausage into small wheels and brown in skillet. Add onions and brown. Pour in spaghetti sauce, lower heat and allow to simmer. Add peppers and mushrooms, simmer covered for 30 minutes until the sausage is cooked through.

Pour sauce over chicken to cover. Grate cheese over the top and sprinkle with Parmesan for an extra zing if you wish. Bake for 15–20 minutes at 300°.

For one pot, stove-top cooking: Cook chicken until done in a large skillet. Remove chicken to keep warm while sauce is cooking, then replace and add cheeses. Cover to heat through and melt cheese.

Kate Davis

• CHICKEN CASSEROLE

4–6 chicken breasts, cooked and boned (canned will work)

2 cups sour cream (can be powdered)

2 cups cream of mushroom soup

1 package Stove Top stuffing

Put the chicken in the casserole, mix sour cream and soup and pour over. Add some sherry and mushrooms if you wish. Prepare the stuffing as directed on the package, cool, spread over the casserole and bake uncovered for 30 minutes at 350°.

Stephanie Kaufhold

• CHICKEN FLORENTINE

This dish, made from all canned ingredients, rivals many I've made on land with all fresh ingredients.

Take your chicken out of the can. If it's your first time opening a canned chicken, go slowly. Canned whole chickens are very fragile and very ugly but make very good meals. I found it best to drain the liquid out of the can by holding the lid on, saving just a small amount of the juice in the bottom of the can, and then carefully pulling out the chicken. A canned chicken may fall apart without using a knife, and I usually bone all but the wings and the drumsticks.

Lightly coat the chicken in flour and brown in a little oil. Remove chicken from the pan and add to the pan 1 large can of spinach, well drained. Add a few drops of the chicken broth to the spinach and heat through.

In a separate bowl mix 2 cans Aunt Penny's Hollandaise Sauce, 1 egg if you have it, and ¼ cup milk. I use dry milk, but you could also use evaporated milk or even fresh. Aunt Penny's is good straight from the can, but if you have the time and the extra ingredients, these additions make a smoother sauce that goes farther.

A splash of wine and/or lemon juice is also good mixed with the sauce.

Add a little sauce to the spinach with a dash of nutmeg and mix it all together. Place chicken pieces on top of the spinach in the frying pan and cover with the remaining sauce. Sprinkle top with seasoned salt, lemon pepper and a little paprika. Put lid on and simmer until the sauce is bubbly, and it's ready to serve with rice or noodles.

Doyle Ann Anawalt

• SCOTCH CHICKEN

Chop 1 medium onion and sauté in 3 tablespoons oil. Add 2 chicken breasts or 4 thighs and brown slightly. Add 1 can Italian zucchini and tomatoes, ¼ to ½ cup Scotch whiskey and season with oregano, salt, pepper and Worcestershire Sauce.

Simmer covered for 30 minutes and serve on rice or mashed potatoes. This dish has a very calming effect on crews!

Marian Saffo-Cogswell

• POLLO CON CERVEZA

This is chicken cooked in beer. The small coastal chickens weigh approximately 2½ pounds, just right for 2 hungry people. This is a simple recipe that uses some of the best local produce in South America.

In a mixture of butter and oil, cook until soft and transparent, but not browned:

2 tomatoes, peeled and seeded
1 onion, chopped
1 green pepper, chopped

½ teaspoon cumin seed
Salt and pepper to taste

Add cut up chicken and a bottle of beer. Cook for 1 hour either in a heavy frying pan with a good cover or in the oven at 375°.

Ted Squier

• RUMMY BAKED CHICKEN

4 pounds chicken, cut up
3 tablespoons soy sauce
½ cup honey
1 tablespoon ground ginger
1 egg yolk, beaten

3 cloves garlic, crushed
½ cup chicken stock or chicken
   bouillon
½ cup rum

Arrange chicken in a baking pan. Combine all other ingredients and pour the sauce over the chicken. Bake 1 hour in a preheated 375° oven, basting several times.

Wanda Parker

• THREE WAYS WITH HATCHET BAY CHICKEN

In the Bahamas, chicken is one of a few locally grown products. No matter how small the shop or commissary, chicken always seems to be available, either fresh or frozen. It's as good as the chicken back home, which I can't say for the pork and beef we've tried.

Chicken Oriental

3–4 pound fryer, cut into serving
    pieces
½ cup Catalina salad dressing

1 envelope onion soup mix
⅔ cup apricot preserves

Mix all ingredients and pour over chicken pieces in a baking pan. Marinate for 20 minutes. Bake for 1¼ hours at 350°. Serve with rice.

Chicken Ragoût

3–4 pound frying chicken, cut into
    serving pieces
2 large potatoes, cut up
2 large carrots, cut up
1 onion

1 chicken bouillon cube
3 tablespoons flour
2 tablespoons cooking oil
1½ cups water

Dredge the chicken with flour and brown in oil in the pressure cooker. Add water, bouillon cube, and bring cooker up to 10 pounds of pressure. Cook 15 minutes. Cool cooker normally for 5 minutes, then reduce pressure by pouring seawater over it. Open cooker and put in onion, carrots and potatoes. Close the pot and cook 8 minutes at 10 pounds of pressure. Cool cooker again as described above.

Chicken With White Wine

3–4 pound fryer, cut in serving
    pieces
2 tablespoons flour
½ cup water
½ cup white wine

2 tablespoons cooking oil
    (preferably peanut)
1 chicken bouillon cube
Oregano and rosemary
1 small can mushrooms

Brown the chicken over low heat, skin side down, in the oil, for about 10 minutes. Turn and brown for about 5 minutes. Sprinkle flour over the chicken and stir so all of it is coated. Add water, wine, bouillon cube and mushrooms.

Lower the flame and stir things around. If you are cooking on a kerosene stove, put an asbestos pad under the pot so that it will simmer and not boil. Add oregano and rosemary. Simmer 20 minutes, stirring occasionally.

Phyllis Solakian

• HONEY CHICKEN

Honey chicken is an embarrassingly simple recipe for the elegance of it. It can be done in an oven or on a burner in a heavy skillet.

In either case, for 4 breasts melt ¼ pound butter in the pan, stir in 6 tablespoons honey, 3 tablespoons prepared mustard and 2 teaspoons curry powder. When I'm organized enough, I mix the mustard, honey and curry at home and bring it aboard in a plastic container.

Place the chicken in the sauce, turning to coat evenly. Cook uncovered in a moderate oven; on top of the stove, cover part of the time. Baste and turn pieces several times. Make rice to pour the rich sauce over.

Phyllis Mabrey

• WEST INDIAN CHICKEN

3–4 pounds chicken parts	4 tablespoons raisins
Lemon	1 teaspoon brown sugar
Flour	2 tomatoes
2 large onions	Rice

Cut up chicken into small chunks. Squeeze lemon over it, sprinkle with salt and pepper, and dust with flour. Brown chicken in generous amount of butter in a large skillet. Cook until tender. Add chopped onions, raisins, sugar and tomatoes. Season with oregano, thyme, dash of Tabasco, soy sauce, ginger and add a bit of dry vermouth near the end of cooking time. Simmer 20 minutes.

If available, slice whole pineapples lengthwise and remove the fruit so the shells are intact. Fill the bottom with rice and serve the chicken mixture scooped on top. Serves 6.

Susan Siegel

• MIRACLE CHICKEN

This is just the thing when you've made port, bone-tired but sick of canned or instant foods.

1 pound boned chicken breasts	Olive oil
2–3 medium sized onions	Butter (a bonus if you have it)
1 cup mushrooms	Thyme (a sprinkle)
1 clove garlic or garlic salt	

Cut the chicken into reasonably sized pieces and brown in the butter and oil. Dice the onions, removing the first tough layer under the skin. Sauté the onions, mushrooms, garlic and thyme with the chicken until onions are transparent.

Serve with plain or flavored rice to 2 people.

The whole thing takes two pans and 10 minutes. If you have a little white wine to spare, splash it in when you are browning the chicken.

You can use canned chicken, but if you're going ashore to stretch your legs anyway, try it first with fresh.

Bill Deighton

• CHICKEN OVERBOARD

After stumbling up the companionway with both hands full of the best parts of our last chicken, Ted lovingly lowered them onto the grill. Then we both watched with horrified fascination as the inadequately tightened set screw let the grill slip slowly and majestically downward, neatly dumping the breasts, drumsticks and the wire cover of the grill itself down through two crystal fathoms to a sandy grave in the British Virgins.

Then the squall hit. With the rain drumming on the cabin top and the fleet plunging and swinging on their rodes like a herd of tethered horses spooked by a coyote, I used the chicken wings, backs and necks to make what we now call "Chicken Overboard," a useful dish for when you have run out of practically everything.

1 can kidney beans with sauce
7 ounce can Mexican hot sauce
2 chicken bouillon cubes

Whatever bits of chicken (or
    anything else) are left

Simmer 15 minutes, accompany with ice cold vodka and water.

The key, of course, is the Mexican hot sauce, which we always carry with us for emergencies or simply to dress up tired food. The brand we like best is "Herdez Home Style Mexican Sauce," which is available all over Latin America. In the U.S. you can find it in specialty stores in big cities and in groceries and supermarkets in areas with large Mexican populations.

Priscilla Squier

GOAT

• CABRITO DE LA ISLA

The options here are how to obtain the *cabrito*, young goat, are Mode #1—the supermarket, or Mode #2—hunting in the islands of Mexico. Taking a firearm into Mexican waters legally is difficult, but it can be accomplished after reams of paperwork. If you elect Mode #2, the next hurdle is a hunting permit, but in all cases the law of self-preservation is foremost and if you happen to be under attack by a 20-pound cabrito in one of those remote areas, you must protect yourself.

To waste the carcass of such a fine animal would be a sin. My first terrifying experience came at West Partida, in the Sea of Cortez, in the winter near the singing caves. (The singing caves troll at West Partida in the winter when the north wind blows—expressing the misery of Indians long departed.)

While dressing this vicious animal, protect the meat from the fur. A touch of the aromatic hide can spoil the delightful flavor of the flesh. With the basics in hand, use some imagination with the following, depending on whether you will cook on the beach or the boat:

3 pounds meat, in strips, cut wide and thin	¼ cup sugar
2 teaspoons dried mustard	2 small onions, smashed
1½ tablespoons curry powder	2 cloves garlic, smashed
1½ tablespoons salt	4 tablespoons soy sauce

Mix ingredients and let meat soak for 1 hour or more. String meat on wood sticks and barbeque on the beach, or use the ole' frying pan on the boat.

I. H. Lee

• CURRIED GOAT

2 pounds goat	½ pound carrots
2–3 onions	1 tablespoon curry powder
1 bunch herbs	1 teaspoon sugar
1 clove garlic	2 tablespoons tomato catsup
1 teaspoon salt (or to taste)	1 tablespoon butter
Water to cover	

Cut meat into bite-sized cubes, fry lightly in butter. Add curry powder, seasonings and water to cover. Simmer until meat is tender (about 1½ hours). Add sliced carrots and continue cooking until meat and carrots are tender. Serve with boiled rice.

Lollie Dreizen

LAMB

• LAMB, ANY WAY, ANY DAY

We are lamb eaters. Admittedly, some of the lamb should be classified as mutton, but if cooked properly it is delicious. The secret to cooking lamb is to use a high temperature. This gets rid of most of the fat and leaves a brown crispy surface.

Roast Lamb should be seasoned with salt and white pepper and cooked at 425–450° for at least 45 minutes, then reduced to no lower than 375° for the remaining cooking time. (I reckon on 20 minutes per pound for small pieces and 15 minutes for large ones.) If cooked at a low temperature the juices leach out and the meat is dry and tasteless. Baste several times during cooking, draining off excess fat. For the last hour of cooking I put peeled potatoes around the meat, baste several times and by the time the meat is cooked, the potatoes are crisp and brown and cooked through.

Swede Bash is our favorite vegetable with roast lamb; in England, big yellow turnips are called "swedes" and are best for this dish. Equal quantities of swedes and carrots are chopped small and cooked in salted water until tender, not mushy. Drain, then mash and drain again, thoroughly. (Reserve liquid.) Mix in lots of white pepper and a pat of butter. (Other types of turnips or hard squash could be used if swedes are not available.)

Good Gravy is an essential with roast meat. I have never been able

to master the roux method for gravies and sauces, ending up with a nasty, lumpy mess each time. Out of desperation I made up my own method.

After removing the meat and spuds from the baking dish, put them back in the oven to keep hot. Drain off all except about 2 tablespoons of fat from the pan. Pour in the vegetable liquid, adding extra water if necessary and simmer over low heat, scraping in all the little brown bits that remain in the pan. Mix together 2–3 tablespoons all-purpose flour in a cup or more of *cold* water. When thoroughly mixed—no lumps—gradually pour into baking pan and stir constantly over low heat. As the flour cooks the gravy thickens. Color and flavor with Kitchen Bouquet, Maggi seasoning, bouillon powder or whatever, and salt and white pepper. Just before serving, drain into the gravy any juices that have leached from the meat.

Mint Sauce is a must with roast lamb and for me it must be more mint than sauce and *never* cooked! In a small jug or tumbler put lots of washed and coarsely chopped fresh mint, sprinkle with a teaspoon of sugar and pour over a few teaspoons of boiling water to dissolve the sugar. Add malt vinegar to cover. Dried mint can be used; crumble a little but do not turn the leaves into a powder. (If the "lamb" is really mutton, serve with red currant jelly.)

Lamb Stew is one of the side benefits of roast lamb, as cold roast lamb is not particularly appetizing and if re-cooked is revolting. So, I always buy a bigger piece for roasting than we can eat, leaving enough for lamb stew. Once you have finished dinner and before the remaining meat has congealed, chop it up into bite-sized pieces, put into a foil pan, cover with gravy and add a few sprigs of mint. Cover with plastic wrap, then cover tightly with aluminum foil and freeze. The lamb retains its freshly roasted flavor and is delicious served with rice or noodles and peas. (Remember to make enough gravy to do this.)

Stuffed Rolled Lamb is made from an inexpensive cut—the flank or breast of lamb. Bone it, then spread thinly with stuffing. I use fresh

white bread crumbs, onions, sage or thyme, salt and pepper and an egg. Roll up like a jelly-roll and tie with string. Cook for at least 1½ hours at 425°, basting and draining fat.

Lancashire Hotpot also uses inexpensive cuts—neck chops or packages of meal labelled "stew meat." Bake the pieces at high heat until brown and most of the fat has cooked out. Put the drained meat in a casserole or deep ovenproof dish. Make enough gravy to barely cover the meat. Chop up onions and carrots and layer over meat. Slice peeled potatoes ¼ inch thick and layer carefully in overlapping slices, salting lightly . . . there should be at least 4 or 5 layers. The potatoes act like a piecrust or lid and all the flavors are sealed in. Bake in the oven at 300–350° for at least 1½ hours uncovered. The top layer of potatoes will brown.

This can also be done in a skillet on top of the stove on low heat, but must be covered. The top layer of potatoes will not brown, but a few sprinkles of Worcestershire sauce will improve the appearance.

If you haven't thought of cooking lamb before . . . try it, you might like it! It's available in lots of cruising areas where other meats are unobtainable.

Barbara Davis

• LEG OF LAMB À LA DIESEL

While making the passage to Deshaies on Guadeloupe, we used our motoring time to cook a leg of lamb on the diesel. This way we saved on butane gas and kept the galley nicely cool.

The recipe is quite simple:

Take a 5 to 6 pound leg of lamb (ours was boned), rub it thoroughly with your favorite spices and salt and pepper to taste. Wrap it tightly in several layers of aluminum foil to prevent any grease from dripping on the engine. Place the package securely on the manifold of the diesel.

Check the leg after approximately 3–4 hours. Turn the package after this check and let bake for another 3 hours until done.

Other big pieces of meat (e.g.; roasts, tenderloins or ham) can be substituted for the leg of lamb, though cooking time will vary.

Ingeborg Gregory

• MOUSSAKA

3 or 4 large eggplants	1 cup milk
3 large onions, sliced	2 eggs
1 pound minced lamb (or beef)	Meat stock or fresh tomato sauce

Slice the eggplants and fry them; also fry the onions and meat. Put a layer of eggplant in an oiled oven dish, then a layer of the meat, followed by a layer of onions; repeat until the dish is full. Add 1 cup seasoned meat stock or fresh tomato sauce, then pour over the top the milk, seasoned with salt and pepper, into which the 2 eggs have been beaten. Cook in a moderate oven for 30 minutes until the batter forms a golden crust.

This dish brings back all the Balkans for me and is found also in the Middle East and Turkey. There are many variations; I often substitute slices of cooked potato when no meat is available. Grated cheese sprinkled on top doesn't do any harm either.

Gwenda Cornell

MYSTERY MEAT

• SPECIALITÉ DU BATEAU

We had been joined in the Gulf of Aden by David Eals, an officer of the Bedouin Legion in order to sail as far as Musseina'a, the limit of his responsibility. He was a charming and sophisticated guest, not unaccustomed to gourmet meals, as he had at one time been A.D.C. to the Viceroy in India.

He sent two Land Rovers, manned by a patrol of his picturesquely uniformed Bedouins, along the coast, suitably provisioned so that we might dine ashore each night. The vagaries of wind and current prevented us from making the rendezvous in time for supper, and on two occasions Beryl was forced to provide us with an unpremeditated meal.

As she cooked below, the smell on deck was delicious. David and I could hardly wait for the plates to be passed up to the cockpit: Liver and onions and Beryl's wonderfully dry fried rice. The sun set behind a rocky headland astern, and the sea was alive with the movement of fish. *Tzu Hang* ghosted along close-hauled in only a breath of wind, towards a dim light that blinked on the coast a few miles ahead.

"That will be my men," said David, "and that was a wonderful meal."

"Have some more?" suggested Beryl.

"Yes, please," he said enthusiastically, and I passed my plate to Beryl just as eagerly. I noticed a pleased and rather amused look on her face but put it down only to her appreciation of our enthusiasm for her cooking.

Next day we failed to make another rendezvous on time, and Beryl asked us what we'd like for supper. "I don't suppose that we could have the same as we had last night?" asked David. "It was delicious."

"Of course," Beryl replied. "I've got masses." Again I thought that I saw a slight look of amusement.

Next day we arrived at Musseina'a, and instead of Beryl's cooking we had a meal ashore with the Bedouin Legion under the walls of their fort; a whole sheep, running in grease, cooked with mounds of rice, and eaten with the fingers round a communal dish. We sailed the following morning and could just make out David, standing by the two Land Rovers, parked below the walls of the Beau Geste fort and waving his red and white checked headcloth in farewell.

It was some days later, when Beryl and I were talking about our sail with David and how much we enjoyed it, that she said, "I've got to tell you. That fried liver and onions that you both enjoyed so much. It was cat food."

"It was what?"

"It was "Whiskas." You know. That case of cat food we got in Aden.

The label said 'Best beef liver for cats,' and cats are such choosey people that I knew it would be good."

"How ghastly," I cried. "For heavens sake don't give it to me again."

"But you both enjoyed it so much," she protested, "and anyway it was an emergency. I hadn't been expecting to cook you a meal.

"Isn't he stupid?" she said, turning to the cat.

Recipe:

Slice two onions, fry until golden brown. Add a little flour and brown. Empty in 2 cans 'Whiskas' liver for cats. Serve hot, with rice.

Never allow the can to be seen, but you can explain that the meal is 'out of a can' in an offhand way. Do not encourage further inquiries.

Miles Smeeton

BACON

• BACON-CELERY-LIMA MEDLEY

You can prepare this dish at home . . . put it in a covered casserole dish in the bottom of the reefer and heat up a day or two out.

6 or so slices bacon, or
    3 or 4 slices ham
	Savory leaves, coarse pepper,
	    paprika

Several celery stalks	1 can condensed cream of
1 medium/large onion	celery soup
½ medium-sized green pepper	A dash of milk
1 can lima beans or 1 package frozen limas	Cheddar cheese

Fry bacon or ham until crisp, in a wide deep fry pan. Lift out, drain, cut into small pieces and set aside. To the drippings add 3 cups celery cut in ½ inch slices, chopped onion and seeded pepper cut in ½ inch squares.

Cook until onion is limp, then remove from heat. Stir drained limas into cooked onion mixture with ¾ teaspoon savory leaves and ⅛ teaspoon pepper, and add the crumbled bacon or diced ham.

Combine celery soup and ⅓ cup milk (or water) and stir into vegetables. Sprinkle with 1 cup shredded Cheddar cheese and a dash of paprika. Cook covered over medium heat for about 25 minutes or until hot throughout.

Guaranteed to lift the spirits of 5 to 6 crew members . . . providing you stoke them up with plenty of wine, cheese, pickled herring and crackers while the dish is bubbling on the alcohol stove.

Ed Rhodes

• BLACK BEAN CHILI

1 cup dried black beans	1 large green pepper, diced (or
4 cups water	dehydrated pepper)
8 slices bacon cut into	Salt and pepper to taste
1 inch squares	Vinegar (optional)
1 medium onion, chopped	

Wash, then soak the beans several hours in the 4 cups water. Sauté bacon and onion in pressure cooker until onion is soft. Add beans and original water, salt and pepper and cook under pressure for 25 to 30 minutes.

After reducing the pressure and removing the lid, add the chopped pepper and simmer (without pressure) for 10 minutes more. Adding a bird pepper to the pot gives the chili an extra "bite," but resist the temptation to add 2 or 3 because these tiny, innocent-looking critters pack quite a wallop. You may vary the taste by adding a few tablespoons of vinegar to your bowl. I am sure this recipe could be prepared in a conventional soup pot, but the cooking time would naturally be longer.

Linda Turner

• MACARONI 'N BACON

This is one of my favorites for an impromptu dinner for unexpected guests. The quantities can be increased to feed any number.

Cook up a potful of macaroni shells. While they're cooking, fry ½ can (½ pound) bacon until crisp. Drain the shells and combine with the crumbled bacon, 1 can mushroom gravy, 1 can sliced mushrooms, a little garlic powder and a dash of Worcestershire sauce.

When you're cooking any sort of pasta, the directions always call for an awful lot of water. You can use less water, and if you have only a small pot, you can fill it quite full if you add a little margarine to the water or rub margarine around the top of the pot—this will keep the water from boiling over.

Katy Burke

HAM

• PORTLAND CANAL THUNDERMUG

I used to fish around the Ketchikan area (Dixon Entrance to Bradfield Canal) and usually stayed out about 10 days.

I've named this version of the recipe after the Portland Canal. I whipped it up while camping at a prospect up there.

Use a reliable brand of baked beans and empty a 1 pound can into a pot. Add 2 teaspoons of Worcestershire sauce and spice it up with hot sauce. Chop up some ham and onion and mix with mayonnaise.

Stir into the hot beans. Serve with bread and butter for a good filling meal.

Paul Bowman

• APPLE HAM GALLEY SUPPER

This is a good way to use up leftover baked ham.

Dice cooked ham—enough to fill 3 cups—and place in a well-greased deep skillet. Spread 2 tablespoons mustard over ham.

Core and slice 2 apples. Arrange over top of ham and sprinkle with 2 tablespoons lemon juice.

Combine ¼ cup firmly packed brown sugar, 1 teaspoon grated orange rind and 2 tablespoons all-purpose flour. Mix and spread evenly over apples. Bake in ship's oven at 350° for 35 minutes or cook, covered, in the skillet over medium heat for 20 to 25 minutes or until ham/apples are hot and sugar-flour-orange rind mixture has melted.

Serves 4 with sliced peaches, French bread and any kind of jam, but strawberry or raspberry are best.

Ed Rhodes

• HAM CROQUETTES

½ pound ground ham
2 tablespoons flour
⅛ teaspoon pepper
⅛ teaspoon garlic powder

¼ teaspoon onion powder
½ teaspoon salt
¼ pound butter or margarine
1 to 2 tablespoons milk

Melt the butter and mix in the flour. Add 1 or 2 tablespoons milk to soften the paste slightly so it's manageable. Add the ham and spices to form a stiff dough. Shape into small cylinders about 2 inches long and refrigerate for 2 hours. Dip in egg and bread crumbs and fry until brown in 350° oil.

Norma Gaffron

• WATERLESS HAM DINNER

5 slices ham
4 green onions, sliced
2 stalks celery
2 tomatoes, sliced

1 can green beans (reserve liquid)
1 can tomato soup
Various seasonings—oregano, basil,
    garlic powder, pepper, salt, etc.

Layer sliced ham with tomatoes, celery and onions in aluminum foil or shallow baking pan. Put drained green beans over layers. Mix green bean liquid with tomato soup and seasonings and pour over all. Bake, covered, 1 hour at 350°. If you have mushrooms or grated cheese, add these to the top.

Mary Jane Robinett

• YO-HO-HO-HAM

Into a baking pan, put a ham and cover with ½ jar orange marmalade and about ½ cup rum. Bake approximately 1 hour at 325° before adding a can of green beans (drained) around its base. While the beans warm, you can fix instant potatoes and open a can of fruit.

Norma Gaffron

• HAM AU GRATIN

1 pound canned ham
1 package au gratin potato mix

Try to find the mix which requires no milk, as it eliminates ingredients. If milk is required, try powdered milk. Cut approximately ½ to ¾ of the ham into bit size pieces. Prepare the potato mix according to the directions. Stir in the ham pieces.

I cook the meal in a Teflon skillet, covered, stirring frequently to keep from sticking. If you have an oven, follow the directions on the package. Good with a vegetable or salad. You can use the whole ham if you're really hungry.

Fred Bingham

• HAM WITH APPLES AND DUMPLINGS

Being physically disabled, I'm always looking for simple, but good, recipes that don't take a lot of time and effort. I discovered this one in New England.

All you need is one small canned ham—there are several brands that need no refrigeration and are great to have on board—a package of dried apples and a package of biscuit mix.

Place the ham and its juices in a large pot with a cover. Add the dried apples and 2 cups water. Let simmer while you make the dumplings from the mix. Add dumplings to the pot and simmer until done.

The dumplings absorb the ham and apple flavors. It's a quick and easy meal with only one pot to clean and it tastes oh-so-good!

Millie Beals

PORK

• THROW-TOGETHER BOILED DINNER

1 pound pork or any meat cut into small pieces. Add any vegetables you have on hand—I especially like to use cabbage, carrots and onions as a base. Then I add anything else I should use up. Add 1½ cups water and a bouillon cube and pressure cook for 10 minutes. Serves 4.

Fiona McCall

• PIRATE'S PORK AND PEAS

Put about 1 cup rice (converted or regular) in a baking pan and add 1 can peas, juice and all. Then arrange pork chops over the rice and bake —slowly. (If you're sure you have enough moisture in the pan, the dinghy ride can last an hour and a half and all will be well.) This is good with a crisp green salad.

Norma Gaffron

• MENUDO

1½ cups diced pork
1 cup diced potatoes
⅓ cup cooked garbanzos (chick-
   peas)
1 medium tomato, sliced
1 medium onion, sliced

1 clove garlic, crushed
2 bay leaves
5 peppercorns
Cooking oil
Salt to taste

Sauté garlic in oil until brown, add onion and tomatoes. Add pork and continue sautéing for 5 minutes. Add water to cover, salt, pepper-corns and bay leaves and continue simmering for 15 minutes. Add po-tatoes and garbanzos. Simmer for another 20 minutes. Serve hot. Makes 4 servings.

Shirley Young-Shannon

• PEANUT PORK KABOBS

We use long skewers with loop handles that can be attached around the grill to avoid losing dinner overboard to the fishes.

2 pounds boneless pork, cut into
    1½ inch chunks
¼ cup peanut butter
4 onions, grated
1½ tablespoons lemon juice
1 tablespoon brown sugar
3 tablespoons soy sauce

1 garlic clove minced
½ teaspoon pepper
½ teaspoon Cayenne pepper
1 teaspoon ground coriander
1 teaspoon ground cumin seed
1½ teaspoons salt

Mix together peanut spice sauce, then stir in pork until well coated. Cover and cool for several hours. Thread on skewers and broil over coals for 25 minutes. Serves 6.

Andrena Huntsman

SAUSAGE

• TOAD IN THE HOLE

Precook 1 pound or more of sausage, drain. Prepare a Yorkshire Pudding batter. Put 1 tablespoon fat from sausages into an 8-inch pie pan, pour in the batter, then drop the sausages into the batter. Cook as for Yorkshire Pudding (at 425° for 30–40 minutes).

Other cooked meat can be used, e.g., canned corned beef, cubed. This dish is especially good served with onion gravy.

Barbara Davis

• STOCKTON BEACH SAUSAGE/POTATO DINNER

Looking ashore through a port as he peeled the potatoes, the cook concluded that if there ever was a "golden crescent beach, sheltered by rocks on each end, lapped by crystal-clear (but cold) water," this was the place. And Stockton Bay is *not* ringed with cabanas or thundering hordes of beach joggers. All he could spot with the glasses was one couple, from a Pearson 30 anchored up the beach, skinny dipping . . . burr!

So, it was back to the potato peeling and a good slug of a cold, mountain Chablis.

2 pounds franks or smoked sausage links	3 carrots
	1 jar (small) dill pickles
2 pounds medium-sized potatoes (or 2 pound can whole potatoes)	Mustard
	Caraway seed
1 large onion	Salt and pepper
Several stalks celery	

Fry thinly sliced sausages over medium heat, lightly coat with mustard and cook until brown on all sides. Lift out with spatula. Cut scrubbed, unpeeled potatoes into small chunks or ¼ inch slices. (If using canned potatoes, drain, then slice and allow less time for cooking.)

Melt 3 tablespoons margarine in fry pan. Add potato slices—a few at a time—coating each slice or chunk with margarine. Turn potato slices frequently, dabbing on margarine as needed. Add cooked sausage slices, plus sliced onion, diced celery, carrots and chopped dill pickles. Turn often with fork or spatula until vegetables are heated through.

Combine ¾ cup dill pickle juice, 1 tablespoon sugar, ½ teaspoon each of caraway seed and mustard, and pour over potato/sausage mixture.

Cover fry pan and let everything simmer on low heat while the potatoes get fork-tender and the cook pours another jelly glass of cold, mountain Chablis.

Hail the crew on the beach. By the time they row back out (allow about 20 to 30 minutes, depending on the size of the potato chunks and the distance you're anchored from shore), dinner will be ready. Shake on salt and plenty of ground pepper and you're ready to serve as they clamber aboard.

Serves 6 with extras for the swimmers. (If you should have some left over, store in a jar in the reefer and heat up for breakfast.)

Ed Rhodes

• PEPPER-UPS

1½ pounds pork sausage meat
½ sweet pepper, finely chopped
1 tablespoon Worcestershire sauce
1 tablespoon mayonnaise

2 teaspoons mixed herbs
1 egg, beaten
Salt and pepper
Rolled oats

Combine everything except the egg and oats. Divide into 6 flat cakes, dip in egg and coat with oats, pressing oats on them well. Chill for 30 minutes and fry until golden on both sides.

Pauline Hancock

• SAUSAGE MEAT AND NOODLE CASSEROLE

This dish happened accidentally when my 1 pound roll of sausage meat went mushy before I could get it sliced.

1 pound sausage meat
1 onion, diced
1 teaspoon garlic salt
½ teaspoon oregano

Black pepper
Squeeze of lemon
1 package Betty Crocker
      Noodles Romanoff

Fry sausage meat and onion until brown and crumbly. Drain off fat. Prepare noodles according to directions. Add remaining ingredients.
Mix in sausage mixture and heat until hot.

Pam Pelletier

FISH

• NEWFOUNDLAND FISH AND BREWIS

Hardtack, 1 cake per person plus
      1 for the pot
Fish, whatever you have

¼ pound salt pork
Onion

Break the hardtack into pieces and soak all day if the fish and brewis is for dinner. Should all the water be absorbed, add more when you start cooking to keep the hardtack from burning. Bring the hardtack to a boil. Remove from heat, drain and break into bite-sized pieces.

While the hardtack is heating, cut the salt pork into small pieces and render over low heat until the pork is browned. In Newfoundland the product of this rendering is called "scrunchions." Cook the onions in the rendered fat until golden, add the hardtack and fry lightly. Add the fish, stirring the mixture.

That, though, is my version. Traditionally, the fisherfolk did not use onions but simply rendered and fried the salt pork separately, then dribbled the fat and scrunchions over the fish and brewis on the plate.

If you don't have hardtack and are having boiled potatoes with your fish, you might like the scrunchions and fat dribbled over the fish and potatoes. I like it because it adds a little something to the bland potatoes. No matter how you serve fish and scrunchions, they are delicious.

Chuck Patrick

• FISH NEWBURG

Fish and vegetables are our main diet, so imagination plays a large part in my cooking. This dish can be made with any kind of fish, but tastes like Lobster Newburg!

In a saucepan, melt ¼ cup butter and blend in enough flour to slightly thicken. Then add:

1 tablespoon tarragon	1 pint heavy cream (or 1 can
1¼ cups Chablis	Nestlé's cream and 1 large can
¾ cup grated cheese	evaporated milk)

Poach the fish in water in a frying pan. Sprinkle with a generous amount of thyme, salt and pepper. Poach until flaky, then break up into 2 inch square pieces. Put into a baking dish with the sauce. Mix, then sprinkle with paprika. Bake at 350°–400° until brown and bubbly.

Sara Ackley

• TIMBALE

Silver Girl has no oven, but I do have a Presto pressure cooker which is invaluable, as is their instruction and recipe book.

Mix together:

2 cups cooked boneless or canned fish, flaked in bite-sized pieces

2 eggs

½ cup evaporated milk, half and half or whole milk

1½ cups bread cubes or pieces

Add one or more of these:

1 tablespoon lemon or lime juice, sherry, melted butter

1 teaspoon Worcestershire sauce

2 tablespoons chopped parsley, celery, onion, pepper or olives

Do not over-season if the fish has a delicate flavor.

Place in a bowl or pan that will fit on the rack inside the pressure cooker. Put 4 cups water in the pressure cooker, place the bowl on the rack and cook with the top on but the steam regulator off for 5 minutes. Then set the regulator and cook for 10 minutes. If you have an oven, this dish can be baked for 30 minutes at 350°–400°.

Jeanne Gail

• FISH AND POTATO SCALLOP

½ cup butter

1 medium onion, sliced and separated

½ cup flour

1 teaspoon salt

Dash pepper

3 cups milk

4 thinly sliced raw potatoes

2 pounds fish fillets

Cheese slices

Melt butter. Sauté chopped onion until transparent. Blend in flour, salt and pepper. Gradually add the milk, boil and set aside. Grease a casserole and wash fillets. Lay half the fish in the casserole and top with cheese slices. Pour approximately half the sauce over the fish. Add the remainder of the fish and top with the slices of raw potato. Add remaining sauce. Bake in a 350° oven for 30 to 40 minutes.

Rhode Island Seafood Council

• FUN WITH FISH

On a good passage on *Discovery* we ate fresh fish every day, and on one in particular, we devoured the finny flounder for 15 feasts in a row. The challenge was always "how to cook it this time?"

I was awarded the piscatorial Medal of Honor (with Three Scales), denoting meritorious action in the galley, for serving this recipe.

½ cup butter or margarine (or vegetable oil)

⅓ chopped green pepper (¼ cup if dried)

⅔ cup finely chopped onion (or dried, according to package directions)

½ cup light brown sugar (or maple syrup)

¼ cup vinegar

1 pound can pineapple chunks

2 tablespoons cornstarch

1 teaspoon salt

1 tablespoon water

1–2 pounds freshly caught fish

2 tomatoes, cut in wedges, or 1 can whole tomatoes

1½ cups rice cooked in 3 cups water with 2 tablespoons butter or margarine

Melt butter in saucepan and add green pepper and onion. Sauté until tender. Remove from heat. Add sugar, vinegar and pineapple with juice.

Mix cornstarch, salt and water to a smooth paste and add to sauce, cooking well. Stir constantly until mixture thickens, then set aside.

Poach fish in water, drain and add to sauce, but don't cook. Cook rice in water, salt and butter. Add tomatoes to fish and sauce and spoon over rice. Should make 4–6 servings.

Carol Hogan

• BAKED FILLETS

This is a delicious way to prepare mild white fillets such as cod or bass.

Beat lightly together 1 egg and ½ cup milk. Combine ½ cup Parmesan cheese and ½ cup flour. Add paprika, salt and pepper to taste.

Dip fish fillets into the milk and egg mixture, then into the flour and cheese mixture. Place on a foil-lined baking dish and pour melted butter or margarine over the top. (I use a pastry brush to make sure each piece is coated.)

Bake in 375° oven for 10 to 15 minutes.

Great eating!

Linda Cummings

• FISH DINNER IN A POT

2 pounds fish fillets	1 can whole tomatoes with liquid
½ cup flour	½ cup water
1 teaspoon salt	2 tablespoons catsup
½ teaspoon pepper	2 teaspoons salt
1 large onion, sliced	½ teaspoon pepper
4 medium potatoes, sliced thin	Oil for cooking

Cut fillets into serving-sized pieces. Combine flour, 1 teaspoon salt and ½ teaspoon pepper. Roll fish in flour mixture. Sauté fish in oil until brown on both sides; 1 or 2 minutes per side should be enough. Spread onions and potatoes over fish. Combine tomatoes, remaining salt and pepper, catsup and water. Pour over fish. Cover and simmer until potatoes are done. Usually this takes 30 minutes.

Sue McBride

• BETTER THAN FRYING

Freshly caught fish, poached, boiled or broiled, is a heavenly repast, a natural source of calcium, phosphorus, iron and copper, providing protein of first-rate quality. Fish is also rich in vitamins A and D, thiamine, riboflavin and nicotinic acid as well as niacin, an element of the vitamin B complex.

Poached Fish

1 large fish, filleted	2 slices lemon or lime
1 cup of white wine or water	3 peppercorns or parsley sprigs
1 small onion, sliced	

Place all ingredients in a heavy frying pan. Heat or simmer about 5 minutes and cook until fish flakes easily. Garnish with slices of lemon, lime or oranges.

Zippy Broiled Fish

1 pound fresh fish fillets	⅛ teaspoon chili powder
1 tablespoon light margarine or oil	⅛ teaspoon garlic powder
1 tablespoon soy sauce	Tabasco sauce to taste—just a dash
1 tablespoon Worcestershire sauce	

Place fillets in single layer in an oiled shallow baking dish. Combine other ingredients. Pour over fillets. Broil about 4 inches from heat for 10 or 15 minutes or until fish flakes easily with a fork. Don't overcook. 4 servings.

Garnish with green grapes. Serve with a salad of bean sprouts and marinated green beans or a tossed green salad.

Beatrice Levin

• FISH CAKES

On *Karma* we sometimes have a catch of fish that are too small to cook except by boiling, but they can still make a tasty meal.

This recipe will feed 4 people.

1 cup raw brown rice	1 large or 2 small eggs
2½ cups boiling water	¾ to 1 cup cornmeal and oatmeal
2–3 small fish, cleaned	(half and half)
1 medium onion, chopped	Vegetable salt to taste
1–2 stalks celery (optional)	1 tablespoon soy sauce
1 carrot, diced (optional)	Cheese

Add brown rice to boiling water, cook on high for 10 minutes then turn to low for 30–45 minutes or until rice has absorbed all the water.

Boil fish until it flakes off the bones, drain and cool. Pick out bones and skin and put crumbled fish in with the rice.

Sauté vegetables in oil and add to mixture. Stir in the eggs and slowly add cornmeal and oatmeal to make a nice dry mixture that holds together.

Add vegetable salt and soy sauce to taste. Form into patties and fry in oil until golden brown on each side. Top with a slice of cheese for the last minute of cooking and serve hot.

Leftovers can be stored for later. If you prefer, use mashed potatoes in place of the brown rice.

Rhonda Harris

• FISH LOAVES, GREEN TURTLE STYLE

I've been visiting Green Turtle Cay for years and each time enjoyed the hospitality of Dr. Curtis Mendleson and his wife, Marie. They are retirees, and Dr. Mendleson runs the clinic on Green Turtle.

These recipes were given to me by Marie, and any type of fish can be used. She uses grouper, snapper or any of the excellent fish available in the Abacos.

2 cups cooked fish	½ cup finely chopped celery
2 tablespoons butter or margarine	½ cup grated Cheddar cheese
¼ cup flour	1 tablespoon chopped parsley
½ teaspoon salt	½ cup bread crumbs
1 cup milk	1 teaspoon lime juice
⅓ cup finely chopped sweet pepper	

Melt butter or margarine and add flour. Stir until smooth and well blended. Gradually add milk; cook until thickened and smooth. Add remaining ingredients. Mix well and place in a well-greased loaf pan. Bake for 30 minutes at 350°. Serve with the fish sauce of your choice. Creole sauce is a good accompaniment. Yield: 4 servings.

Variation: To vary the fish loaf, line greased loaf pan with sliced raw potatoes. Spoon fish mix in pan, dot with catsup and butter or margarine; sprinkle with bread crumbs and bake.

Another loaf recipe is:

2 cups cooked fish, flaked	1½ cups bread crumbs
½ teaspoon baking powder	⅔ cup chopped celery
⅓ cup chopped onion	1 tablespoon lemon juice
1 cup milk	1 tablespoon pimento, minced
1 tablespoon chopped green pepper	Salt and pepper to taste

Mix ingredients together and form loaf in an oiled pan. Bake at 350° until brown and firm. Serve with desired cream sauce. Yield: 4 to 6 servings.

Jim Tygart

• POISSON HAPATONI

This dish was prepared for us after a successful fishing expedition with islanders from the village of Hapatoni on the island of Tahauta in the Marquesas. We used kahi (tuna) but any firm-fleshed fish would do.

2 pounds fish	Oil, vinegar and sugar
Small onion	Soy sauce
Garlic	

Cut fish into small pieces, wash, drain and pat dry. Add onion, garlic, salt, 3 tablespoons sugar and enough oil and vinegar to coat all the fish with the marinade. Marinate for 30 minutes (the fish will soak up a good deal of the liquid). Add soy sauce to taste and pour off extra liquid. Fry quickly in hot oil. Cooking too long will make it tough.

Nancy Lewis

• SALT COD SUPRÊME

Salt cod from Canada is available, wrapped, inside little wooden boxes that make it ideal for stowing aboard a boat. The salt cod has to be "freshened" by soaking in freshwater for 24 hours, so it is not a meal you throw together in rough weather.

Cover 1 pound salt cod with freshwater and soak for 24 hours (if you can change the water once or twice, do so). Drain, cut into 1 inch chunks, cover with fresh cold water, bring to a boil and simmer for 30 minutes. (Do not add salt.)

Melt 2 tablespoons butter or margarine in a saucepan, add 1 cup milk (fresh or reconstituted) and heat almost to boiling. Mix 2 tablespoons all-purpose flour with 1 cup milk until smooth. Remove saucepan from flame and stir in the flour/milk mixture. Return to low flame and stir continuously to avoid lumps while the sauce thickens. More milk can be added if it is too thick. Add salt and white pepper to taste and throw in lots of chopped fresh parsley or dried parsley flakes.

Heat a 1 pound can of chick-peas (or any type of pea bean) in their juice. Drain and put into a dish with the drained cod. Pour the sauce over them. Serve with plain boiled potatoes and a strong young white wine.

Parsley sauce is also good with any fresh, coarse, white fish or with hot boiled ham.

Barbara Davis

• DISGUISED BLUEFISH

While cruising the northeast coast of the U.S. we found that by trailing a feathered lure we could catch a bluefish almost every day. Well, bluefish is fine for a while, but there are limits!

Bluefish is somewhat oily, and that taste can pall. We dried some, which is useful as we have no refrigeration on *Jona*.

Our days began by weighing anchor, setting sail, adjusting the wind vane and throwing a handline overboard. Generally, a couple of hours later our supper was on the end of the line. Bluefish—again? Finally, I came up with a way to doctor bluefish so that even John likes it.

Fillet the fish as soon as possible, rinse well with fresh water, salt and pepper liberally, then let stand for a few hours.

Poach fillets in 1 inch water with diced onion, salt, pepper and a bay leaf. Simmer, covered, for 5 to 10 minutes until fish flakes.

Make a cream sauce: Melt 2 tablespoons butter, add 2 tablespoons flour and blend until bubbly. Add ½ cup milk (fresh or reconstituted) and bring to a boil, stirring constantly. Season with salt and pepper. Pour over the fillets for a delicious bluefish dinner.

Variations: Add 1 teaspoon dried mustard or ½ teaspoon curry powder or 1 teaspoon catsup—each seems to change the flavor just enough to disguise the fact that it's bluefish again!

Nancy Light

• THOSE CHESAPEAKE BLUES

Nothing, but nothing, beats the taste of freshly caught fish, especially if it's bluefish from Chesapeake Bay.

Breading and Seasonings:

Crushed crackers of any sort, preferably mixed, provide the breading. Salt, pepper, bouquet garni or the premixed French seasonings provide more than enough variations in flavor. The slight sweetness of the crackers accepts the seasonings and beautifully enhances the delicate flavor of the fresh bluefish fillet.

Bluefish Luane

Toast ½ cup almonds in 2 tablespoons butter and set aside. Dip fillets in evaporated milk and dredge in seasoned (salt and pepper only) crushed crackers. Fry in butter 3 to 4 minutes per side over moderate heat. Serve with toasted almonds over top.

Bluefish Roast Garlic

Roast 5 or 6 large garlic cloves (slivered) in hot olive oil and set aside. Yes, it will smell pungent! Dip fillets in evaporated milk and dredge in seasoned (bouquet garni seasoning, salt and pepper) crushed crackers. Fry in olive oil over moderate heat until done (3 to 4 minutes per side). Serve with roasted garlic over fish.

Bluefish in Sour Cream/Wine Sauce

Prepare 1 package of sour cream dry mix and set aside. Assemble and have ready: ½ cup finely chopped scraps of fish salvaged from the carcass, ¼ cup white wine, 2 tablespoons minced onion, salt and pepper.

Dip fillet in evaporated milk and dredge in seasoned crushed crumbs. For seasoning, use bouquet garni, or I prefer to use a French premix of thyme, basil, savory, fennel seed and lavender flowers. Fry fillets in butter till done and transfer to serving platter or plates.

Prepare sauce: Lightly sauté fish scraps in 1 teaspoon butter with wine, onion, and salt and pepper to taste. After a few minutes, remove from heat and carefully stir in sour cream, being careful not to curdle the cream. Heat to serving temperature and serve over fillets. It is wonderful!

Just Plain Bluefish

Follow the above steps but omit seasonings except for salt and pepper. A teaspoon of minced onion and a splash of white wine added during the cooking process will greatly enhance the flavor and the aroma is fantastic!

Roger Olson

• WHOLE ROAST STUFFED BUFFALO

In all my years of cooking I have enjoyed some exceptional dishes, but none were better than the succulent flesh of roasted buffalo. Your first need is to get a buffalo.

We use the same methods the Indians used to get these critters. We spear them, at night, while they feed in the shallows along the river and creek banks. We've got electric lights to help, which are better than the pine-knot torches the Indians used.

After you get your buffalo, you must prepare the animal for cooking. Open the body cavity and remove all organs, discard them and wash the cavity thoroughly. Buffalo are grass feeders and may ingest a lot of grit. Cavity clean, prepare the outside of the carcass, but do not skin. A layer of fat beneath the skin provides a self-basting effect that assures succulence.

Salt and season the inside of the body cavity, and then generously salt and pepper the exterior. Cut up enough celery, in pieces 2 or 3 inches long, to cover the bottom of the roasting pan. Add two bay leaves. It goes without saying you need a large pan to roast a whole buffalo.

Make sufficient bread stuffing to fill the body cavity of the buffalo. If you can get crabmeat or shrimp or both to add to the stuffing, it makes it much better. Stuff the buffalo with the stuffing and sew, pin or skewer closed.

Place the buffalo in the roasting pan and scatter a mixture of celery, quartered medium onions and quartered small tomatoes around it. Pour enough chicken bouillon into pan to cover the bottom to a depth of about ½ inch.

Liberally lace the exposed parts of the buffalo with Worcestershire sauce. Salt and pepper again, lightly, to replace that washed off by the sauce.

VERY IMPORTANT! Sprinkle the outside of the carcass with Mc-Cormick's Seafood Seasoning. Be very careful not to overdo it, as this stuff is potent. But when a Gulf Coast Creole cook admits any Yankee seasoning is good, it's got to be good!

Garnish the buffalo with sliced lemons or limes. Sprinkle generously with paprika. Place in the oven and cook until done at 325° to 350°, no hotter. Use lower heat for smaller critters.

If your boat does not have an oven, place the pan on asbestos heat diffusers, across two burners, on top of the galley range and cook, covered with aluminum foil, over low to moderate heat. Use a heavy pan such as a deep cast iron platter for stove top cooking. The average buffalo should cook in about 45 minutes to an hour on top of the stove or in the oven. Test the flesh with a fork to check for doneness.

When the fish is cooked on top of the stove, it will not brown under the foil. Remove the foil and brown with—can you guess?—a blow torch!

Yes, I said fish. Buffalo is a delicious fish. The meat is snow white and comes off in large chunks. Except for "feather bones" that taper off into fine feather-like tines, it is relatively boneless. These feather bones are only a slight nuisance. Call your guests' attention to them.

Can't catch any buffalo? The recipe is just as good with red snapper, redfish (channel bass) or any fish large enough to bake. It looks good and tastes better.

How do you prepare the outside of the carcass? You scale it after dressing it. Buffalo have large, easily removed scales.

Warren Norville

• CARIBBEAN GROUPER

Blend together (an egg beater will do):

3 very ripe bananas
1½ cups mayonnaise
¼ cup evaporated milk
Sugar to taste

Pour sauce over a 2 to 3 pound filleted fish and bake until golden brown on top.

Linda Bosley

• BAHAMIAN FRIED FISH

Bahamian ladies are terrific cooks. This is their, and our, favorite way to cook fish.

Use whole cleaned, scaled, but not filleted grouper, snapper or runner. If large, cut into serving-sized pieces; otherwise just slash diagonally through the skin. Sprinkle slashes with lime juice and hot sauce. Flour the pieces and fry in smoking hot oil about 10 minutes each side, less if pieces are small.

Anne Beard

• SKATE RAY

Many people overlook the skate ray as a source of excellent meat. Oddly enough, it doesn't have a fishy taste to it at all. For those of you wondering what it tastes like . . . it could be described as a cross between lobster and turtle meat. It is known as the "Pork of the Sea."

Ray is easily speared, either from a boat or in the water. Many people shy away from it because of the myth that the barb is at the end of the tail. Fortunately, it is not. It is located in the tail near the body.

If you are fortunate enough to spear a ray, eat only the meat from the wings—discard the body portion.

Barbecued Ray

On a grilling skillet or a hibachi, grill ray meat, marinating continuously with barbecue sauce, for about 35–45 minutes. Tastes just like barbecued pork.

Golden Fried Ray

2 well-beaten eggs
1 cup white flour
½ teaspoon Lawry's Seasoned Salt
½ teaspoon pepper
Crisco or oil

Fillet ray. Dip into eggs. Add salt and pepper to flour. Roll ray in flour, covering thoroughly. Add 1 to 1½ cups Crisco to frying pan. Heat shortening on a low to medium flame until about 225°. Fry about 4–5 minutes on either side.

Carmen Iturra

• POT ROASTED BONITO

From Mexico to Panama everyone else caught mahi-mahi, sierra, wahoo and albacore. All *we* were catching, however, were bonito. When that's all you have, you can't afford to be choosey and throw them back. And after a time at sea, anything fresh is welcome. But there's a difference between edible and tasty. Prepared this way, even bonito tastes good.

Clean fish and cut into ¾ inch to 1 inch steaks. Heat 1 tablespoon cooking oil (or other shortening) in a frying pan with a lid. Brown fish steaks on both sides (about 2 minutes a side). Top each with a slice of onion. Add 2 tablespoons liquid—water, wine or bouillon. Cover and cook over low heat until tender, about 20 minutes.

Joanne Sandstrom

• BONITO WITH DAD'S-LAST-BEER MARINADE

Combine 1½ cups beer with ½ cup cooking oil. Add:

Clove garlic (or ⅛ cup teaspoon
  garlic powder)
2 tablespoons lime or lemon juice
1 tablespoon brown sugar (or
  molasses or honey)

1 teaspoon salt
½ teaspoon ground cloves (or 3
  whole cloves)

Pour marinade into shallow pan. Marinate bonito steaks at least 1 hour, turning several times; drain. Heat 1 tablespoon cooking oil in frying pan; fry bonito steaks until done, about 3–5 minutes on each side.

But if you actually use the last can of beer, as we did, be sure you have something else to pacify the captain.

Joanne Sandstrom

• POACHED SEA BASS

While fishing in Turtle Bay, Baja, Mexico, a 16 inch kelp bass took an orange spoon, then a 42 inch white sea bass took them both!

A simple but elegant way to serve mild white fish like sea bass is as follows:

Make an aromatic chicken broth using fish herbs or a pinch of what have you. Cut the fillets into 3 inch squares. Then poach the fish in the broth until just flaky. Do not overcook or it will crumble. Remove from broth and mound in a bowl or serving dish.

Add 1 cup white wine and some parsley flakes to the broth, then thicken with flour or cornstarch to the consistency of heavy cream. Salt and pepper to taste. (I use white pepper.) Pour over fish and serve.

Ernie Copp

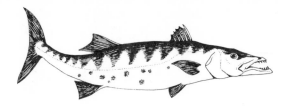

• ESCABECHE

I remember when my grandmother made escabeche. She used to go into great detail explaining its preparation, especially when complimented on her culinary ability.

This dish, however, is one of the simplest to make, and it is also designed to keep fish in areas where there is little or no refrigeration. When finished, the best way to have it is cold, since I feel it tastes better in the company of beer.

The best fish for escabeche is barracuda. In California we used yellowtail or other similar fish. Here in Puerto Rico barracuda are plentiful, so we make it almost every week and we never get tired of it.

3–4 pound barracuda	½ teaspoon oregano (you can use
Olive oil	fines herbes)
Dark vinegar (Heinz Apple Cider	2 or 3 cloves garlic, not too small
preferred)	2 or 3 bay leaves
1 large onion	1 teaspoon peppercorns
	Salt to taste

Cut the barracuda into 1 inch cubes, salt and pepper and fry until golden. You can use regular cooking oil. After the fish is fried, take it out and drain on a paper towel to soak out the extra oil.

Cut the onion into slices approximately ¼ inch thick. Place layers of fish and layers of onion rings in a deep dish.

Drain the cooking oil from the pan and wipe clean. Crack the garlic cloves and place in frying pan with oregano, peppercorns, bay leaves and salt to taste. Mix vinegar and olive oil in a ratio of 2 cups vinegar to 1½ cups olive oil and pour into frying pan. Bring to a boil and then immediately reduce to a simmer for 1 minute only.

Let it cool a bit, then pour the whole concoction over fish and stir gently so fish will be soaked.

You can let it sit until it cools, or you can let it stand for a week. As long as fish is kept well soaked, it will not spoil. However, in our vessel it never gets a chance to last that long!

Manny Varela

• STOVE TOP OVEN-BROILED FLOUNDER

This is simplicity itself, and the less you do to a fish as delicious as flounder, the better.

Flounder, 1 large or enough small ones (with some for seconds)
Limes, several big ones, lemons as a last resort
Bacon strips
Salt, pepper, paprika and Worcestershire sauce
Suitable pan
Blowtorch

Scale, dress, head, wash and drain the flounder. Treat the pan with a non-stick spray (Mazola or Pam), put in flounder, add salt and pepper to taste and sprinkle with Worcestershire. Cover flounder with thin slices of limes alternating with strips of bacon. Squeeze lime juice over and sprinkle with paprika.

If you have an oven, cook for 30 to 45 minutes, then brown under broiler.

To cook on top of the stove I have a long cast iron pan about 1½ inches deep that fits over 2 burners. Put an asbestos heat diffuser pad over each burner, cover the flounder with foil and simmer for 30 to 45 minutes or until done. Peep to check, but do not turn or disturb the fish.

Enjoy your happy hour.

When the flounder are done and ready to serve, light your blowtorch and play over the flounder until it is browned and the bacon crispy.

Serve with pommes de terra à la tin can, green peas and a good dry sauterne.

Your imagination will dream up other uses for the blowtorch. Baked Alaska, maybe?

Warren Norville

• STUFFED SQUID

I got this recipe for fixing squid from a shrimper down at Dauphin Island many years ago. Having been in the Mediterranean and the Far East, I'm not one of those who thinks squid should be used only for bait. Our local fishermen don't believe that either, because I suspect they keep them off the market so they'll have plenty for themselves.

Anyhow, we had been dragging all afternoon and managed to catch quite a few nice sized squid, 6 or 8 inches long. Here is the recipe this old shrimper gave me:

First, take the squid and pull the head and tentacles out of the mantel. Remove the quill and the ink sack and discard. If you are squeamish, you can also discard the eyes. Now set the mantel—this is the big sack-like body of the squid—aside and take the head and tentacles and chop them up into not too small chunks.

Then make a stuffing just as you would for turkey or chicken, but if you are lazy like I am, take a box of prepared Stove Top dressing as it does just as well. I like to add a little extra onion, celery and chopped bell pepper to the Stove Top dressing. While sautéing these additional vegetables, I also sauté the chopped portion of the squid.

Now when the dressing, vegetables and squid are ready, add about an equal part of crabmeat to the volume of the dressing and mix well. When this is all mixed, take the mantels of the squid and stuff them with the crabmeat dressing stuffing. Make an egg and milk dip, dip the stuffed squid in it and roll them in corn meal, cracker meal or flour and fry them in deep fat.

The fat should be hot, and on a boat where there is no way to tell the temperature of the grease, simply float a kitchen match in the grease and when the match ignites of its own accord, the grease is hot enough to fry seafood.

Do not overcook the stuffed squid, but fry only long enough for them to turn a light golden brown. Experience will tell you exactly how long this should be and may vary slightly according to individual taste.

When done, drain the squid on a paper towel and serve. While cooking, it would be a good idea to steal as many as you can from the main stock because once you get going with this, there won't be much time left for you to eat.

Warren Norville

• SHARK!

Shark! The word immediately brings forth visions of "Jaws." I used to feel somewhat the same way until this past summer when I had the opportunity to turn the tables and sample "Jaws" instead of the other way around.

To my delight I found that shark is a snowy-white meat with a subtle flavor that I can only describe as somewhere between lobster and sole. Not only are they excellent eating, they are also plentiful in most areas and are easily caught. The best size for eating are the smaller ones, 4 feet or less, which also provide great sport fishing when caught on a rod and reel.

Preparation: The secret to good shark is in the care and preparation of the meat immediately after the shark is caught. The most important thing is to bleed and clean the shark *immediately* as follows:

1. Cut off the tail and hang head up until bleeding stops; 1 to 2 minutes.
2. Slit the underside and remove entrails. Be sure to remove the dark red blood vessels on either side of the backbone.

The shark can now be filleted just like any other fish and cooked immediately or frozen for future use. As an alternative, the meat can be kept for up to a week by cutting the head off and packing the carcass in ice.

You may cook shark using any of your favorite recipes. It is equally delicious baked, broiled, fried or made into chowder. My absolute favorite, however, is:

Shark à la Bruno

2 pounds shark	1 teaspoon mustard
1 cup mayonnaise	1 package crispy saltine crackers
3 tablespoons honey	

Blend the mayonnaise, honey and mustard together in one bowl and crush the crackers in another. Dice the shark meat into 1 inch cubes. Dip the cubes in the mayonnaise mixture, then roll in the cracker crumbs. Place the prepared cubes in a shallow baking pan lined with foil. Do not grease the pan. Bake in a 350° oven for 10 to 12 minutes or until golden brown. Do not overcook. That's it. The result is a gourmet delight just this side of heaven.

Bernard deKeyser

• FILLET OF SHARK

Before cooking . . .
Trim the thick steaks between the 2 dorsal fins on both sides of the backbone. Remove the skin and slice the fillets into slabs. Ice the fillets immediately.

Soak the meat in a diluted lemon juice solution overnight in the refrigerator to remove all blood and neutralize ammonia compounds.

Broiled Mako Steaks

Cut fillets into ¾ inch thick steaks. Sprinkle with salt and paprika. Brush generously with melted butter. Place steaks under broiler 6 inches away from source of heat for 5 minutes.

Baste with butter, turn steaks, baste again and continue broiling for 5 to 8 minutes. Keep the meat moist, adding more butter as needed.

Baked Blacktip Fillets

Blacktip fillets (or other medium-tasting shark)	1 green pepper, sliced thin
	½ cup white wine
3 tomatoes, sliced	3 tablespoons butter
1 onion, sliced	Paprika, salt and pepper

Place enough tomato slices in an oven-proof dish to cover the bottom. Place fillets on tomato slices and season with salt, pepper and paprika.

Spread butter over fillets and distribute onion, green pepper and remaining tomato slices over top. Pour wine over all. Bake at 325° for 30 minutes.

Hammerhead Hors d'Oeuvre

Hammerhead fillets (or other shark meat)

½ cup melted butter
Onion salt, pepper and paprika

Slice meat into ¾ inch cubes. Soak cubes in melted butter for 15 minutes, then remove and season generously on all sides with onion salt, pepper and paprika.

Place cubes on foil-lined rack under broiler for 10 to 12 minutes, turning pieces frequently and basting with butter as needed to keep meat moist. Serve on platter with toothpicks and plenty of tartar sauce within reach.

Bob Hueter

• TUNA TEMPTER

¼ teaspoon celery seed
4 teaspoons instant chopped onion (or ¼ cup fresh chopped onion)
2 tablespoons margarine
1 can cream of celery soup

1 soup can milk (powdered or fresh)
1 small can tuna, drained and flaked
2 tablespoons diced pimento
1 cup egg noodles
¼ cup Old London toasted bread crumbs

Cook onion and celery seed in margarine until crisp-tender but not brown. Blend in soup and milk, add tuna and pimento. Cook noodles as directed. Combine noodles and tuna mixture in 2 quart casserole, top with bread crumbs and dot with margarine. Bake at 350° for 25 to 30 minutes or until lightly brown.

Irene Westbye

• TUNA PANCRÊPES

This is super quick to prepare if you make a double batch of pancakes for breakfast one day and save half, tightly wrapped, for the next day. (Pancakes keep without refrigeration for a couple of days.)

Mix 1 can cream soup (any kind), 2 tablespoons flour, 1 to 2 cups milk and dehydrated onion to taste in a saucepan. Bring to a boil, stirring frequently.

Take ½ cup of the mixture, add ¼ teaspoon salt, ⅛ teaspoon pepper, 1 small can drained tuna (more if you like) and leftover cooked or canned vegetables (drained).

Spoon about 2 tablespoons of the mixture onto each pancake, roll up and place seam-side down in a baking dish. Pour over remaining soup mixture and sprinkle with ½ to 1 cup grated cheese (Cheddar is good).

Heat in oven until bubbly. If you have a broiler you can brown the cheese under it for an elegant finishing touch.

Judy Gainor

• TUNA PILAF

1 box Minute Rice (2 cups)	1 small can light chunk tuna
4 ounce can mushrooms (drained)	(drained)
4 ounce can water chestnuts	1 can golden mushroom soup
(drained)	Tablespoon of Indian curry

Mix soup with enough water to make 2 cups. Bring to rolling boil and add all other ingredients. Remove from heat and let pot sit, covered, for 5 minutes. Fluff with fork and serve. Goes great with side order of crusty bread and cold white wine.

Variations include: fresh or canned shrimp in place of tuna, bouillon in place of mushroom soup and regular rice instead of Minute. The only difference is longer cooking time for the rice. Other ingredients that add to the combination include quick-cooked vegetables and small sausages or shellfish, which results in an excellent paella if you substitute saffron for the curry.

Bon appétit!

Bob Burgess

• SALMON LOAF

I used to do all my baking in a pressure cooker, but now I have a propane oven on board. This dish is ideal for long voyages.

1 can salmon	¾ cup milk (powdered or
½ onion, chopped	evaporated)
Dried parsley	Salt and pepper
2 eggs	½ cup wheat germ

Mix all ingredients except milk and eggs; whip these together with a fork and add last. Bake in an oiled casserole at 350° for 40 minutes. If you have no oven or pressure cooker, a covered saucepan over low heat will work. Serves 3.

Jan Upton

• SEAFOOD TETRAZZINI

This recipe will serve 2 starving sailors or 4 normal appetites and uses only 1 pan.

Cook ½ pound spaghetti or macaroni, drain, rinse and set aside. In the same pan, melt 3 tablespoons butter, blend in 3 tablespoons flour, season with salt and pepper and gradually add 1¼ cups liquid milk (fresh, canned or powdered). It will thicken.

Add:

1 crumbled chicken bouillon cube	⅓ cup sautéed chopped onions
¼ cup sherry or white wine	2 teaspoons lemon juice
⅓ cup Parmesan cheese	⅛ to ¼ teaspoon thyme or
½ cup mushrooms (fresh or canned)	marjoram
2 cups seafood	Ripe olives

Heat but do not boil. Carefully stir in spaghetti, heat and serve topped with slivered almonds (optional). Shark is especially good for this dish.

Jan Stroeber

• MEDITERRANEAN FISH STEW

This is an excellent dish for supper after sailing, especially when we have guests along and have worked up hearty appetites.

1 large can tomatoes in purée, crushed
2 onions, chopped
2 cloves garlic, chopped fine
1 teaspoon basil
1 teaspoon salt
½ teaspoon pepper
2 bay leaves
¾ cup white wine (or vermouth)
1 bottle clam juice (optional)

1 large chicken bouillon cube dissolved in 1 cup water
2–3 pounds fish, cut into 2 inch pieces (I use about 1 pound cod and ½ pound each flounder, haddock, shrimp (shelled and deveined). All cod can be used, and a few clams and mussels can be added.)

Optional, but each adds to the flavor:

Dash or two Tabasco
½ teaspoon oregano
Few strips dried orange peel

1 teaspoon crushed fennel seeds
½ teaspoon thyme
Pinch of saffron

Film a large frying pan with oil and sauté onions until soft but not brown; add garlic and cook a minute or two more.

Add tomatoes, clam juice, bouillon (if not using clam juice use 2 bouillon cubes dissolved in 2 cups water and omit salt), wine or vermouth, seasonings and optional items.

Cook for at least 15 minutes or up to 2 hours, adding more liquid as needed. Add fish and cook for about 15 minutes until fish is opaque and flakes easily.

Serve with lots of crusty bread and a tossed salad.

Margo Waite

SHELLFISH

• SPANISH CLAMS

Clean about 2½ pounds clams and place in a saucepan with just over 1 cup cold water. Heat quickly until shells are open and remove from heat. Drain the water they've boiled in through a thin cloth to remove the sand.

Heat 2 tablespoons oil, cook 1 finely chopped onion and 1 grated garlic clove until golden, add 1 tablespoon of grated bread to fry for a moment, then the drained water, ½ glass wine, ½ bay leaf, the juice of ¼ lemon and ¼ teaspoon black pepper. Bring this to the boil, pour over the clams and boil again about 10 minutes. Add salt to taste and parsley flakes.

Don't waste this on poor weather—it needs a romantic anchorage, a full moon, softly lapping water and chilled white wine.

Gwen Skinner

• LINGUINE WITH WHITE CLAM SAUCE

Once the proud owner of a 46-foot yacht on Lake Michigan, I now find myself living on the Arizona desert with just memories of spending my summers sailing and enjoying cooking and eating aboard.

2 cans white clam sauce	1 teaspoon oregano
1 can chopped clams	Dash of salt and pepper
3 tablespoons butter	½ to ¾ pound cooked and buttered
3 cloves garlic, minced	linguine
1 cup minced fresh parsley or 3 tablespoons dried parsley flakes	4 tablespoons grated Parmesan or Romano cheese

Melt butter with garlic, add clams and clam sauce, parsley and seasoning. Simmer together until liquid is reduced by a third. Mix into cooked, drained and buttered linguine and toss with cheese. Great with a big tossed salad and French bread. Serves 4.

Janet Slatin

• RICE WITH CLAMS

Sailing up the Oregon coast en route to the San Juan Islands aboard *Chanticleer,* our Valiant 40, we were lucky to have Sue McAvoy as chief cook. She makes especially good Italian dishes, and this one can be made with fresh or canned clams.

Sauté in ¼ cup olive oil:

Large handful parsley, chopped fine   1 clove garlic
1 onion, chopped fine

Cook for 10 minutes. Then add:

2 cups cooked rice   1 teaspoon paprika
1 tablespoon Worcestershire sauce   1 cup Parmesan cheese
½ teaspoon salt and pepper

Put into a baking dish and pour over the top fresh clams sautéed in butter or 1 10-ounce can clams with juice. Bake at 350° for 30 minutes.

Cathy Reed

• CLAM STEW

Clams are my weakness, but they are also one of the easiest and tastiest dishes to prepare.

Chop 3 to 4 slices bacon, 2 onions, 1 green pepper, 2 stalks celery and sauté until the onions are golden.

Cut 2 or 3 small potatoes into bite-sized strips and add to pot with 1 large can tomatoes (or 3 to 4 fresh with 1½ cups water). Simmer 15 minutes with salt, pepper, 2 pinches oregano and a pinch of caraway seeds.

Scrub 1 to 2 dozen clams (or whatever your catch) and add to the pot, shells and all. This way you conserve the precious juices and don't have to bother opening the clams.

Cover and simmer for 10 minutes or until the clams are fully open. Remove the clams, chop the meat and return to the pot to cook for another 10 minutes.

A few minutes before serving add a cup of white wine and presto—it's out of this world!

Kay Aurin

• PICHILINGUE PISMO PIE

My wife and I discovered the prolific chocolate (pismo) clam in beds near La Paz soon after we cruised in aboard our Tahiti ketch *Traildust*. Pichilingue, one of the favorite anchorages of cruisers in the Sea of Cortez, is a short 9 miles from La Paz and loaded with all types of delicious sea food; pin shell clams, butter clams, octopus, lobster and many types of fish. The pismo is probably the most abundant and easy to take in this area.

In most cases you'll have to locate them by siphon holes in the sand, two holes situated about 1 inch apart. Once the holes are spotted, just a swipe with your hand down into the sand under the holes, about 3 inches, will produce a clam. I learned this purely out of academic interest while watching Mexican nationals fishing.

Now that you have acquired all the almejas (Spanish for clams), by whatever method you deem necessary for a hearty meal, proceed as follows to make your P.P.P.:

2 pints clams, shucked and chopped
¾ cup dry prepared poultry stuffing
1 clove garlic
3 tablespoons cooking oil or
    bacon fat

½ cup dry white wine
½ cup ground Parmesan cheese
1 large chopped onion

Save the liquor when you shuck the clams. Sauté chopped onions and crushed garlic in the oil in a heavy frying pan. Mix in the remaining ingredients except the clam liquor. Add liquor as needed to give the mixture a consistency of soft dough. Cook either on top of the stove, covered, over medium heat, or in a 350° oven for 30 minutes.

I. H. Lee

• DULL DAY CLAM PUDDIN'

Some days it just doesn't seem worthwhile to get out of your berth. A dull grey fog has stubbornly settled in. The larder is empty of anything tasty. You've finished your book. And it's Sunday and everything in the closest town is closed.

Spend the morning clamming. We don't have a proper rake, so Colin dives for any sort of clam he can get his hands on while I use the dinghy as a "float boat." (Don't forget to take your fog bell if it's really socked-in!)

Steam the clams (any kind will do) and chop them. While they're steaming, trim crusts from 5 slices of white bread, butter one side and cut into cubes. Put the bread cubes into a bowl with 1 cup milk, some chopped onion, a dash of Worcestershire, salt and pepper. Add 3 beaten eggs and the clams. Turn into a buttered pan and arrange a can of well-drained tomatoes prettily on top (if you have them). This meal-in-a-dish will be crusty and delicious when baked about 45 minutes, uncovered, in a 350° oven.

If you're not in clam territory a can of minced clams will do just fine.

Pat Day

• CONCH, ITALIAN STYLE

This recipe uses easily stored ingredients and conch, which is readily available in the Bahamas.

4 conch, cleaned and boiled for 20 minutes in saltwater	½ cup red wine
1 large onion, sliced	1 teaspoon each parsley and oregano
2 packages dry spaghetti sauce mix	Salt and pepper

Slice conch into 1 inch strips. Sauté onion in olive oil until tender, add conch and sauté for 5 minutes. Prepare sauce according to package directions, then add to conch and onions.

Add remaining ingredients, simmer 20 minutes, then serve over spaghetti.

Beverly Salkin

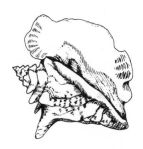

• HOT AND SPICY SHRIMP JAMBALAYA

Canadian weather has a tendency towards the bottom half of the thermometer so, although the Folkboat's tiny galley has produced some magnificent gourmet meals in its time, such as Beef Wellington and Fish and Chips, curry dishes and warming concoctions made with rum are the ship's specialties.

You do need a small pressure cooker for this dish, but I imagine most serious cruising people have one anyway.

Frank spent many years in India and Burma and acquired a love for curry and spicy foods which, although doing little for his choleric temper and blood pressure, are most popular among guests who come aboard in the evening.

Jambalaya can be made well in advance and warmed up when needed. This recipe serves 8.

1 tablespoon fat or margarine	Shake garlic to taste
1 cup long grain rice	½ cup chopped onion
19 ounce can tomatoes	½ pound diced ham
1 small can mushrooms (drained)	½ cup water
1 pound frozen or fresh shrimp	½ sliced green pepper or celery
Pinch, or two, or three, red pepper	Pinch ginger
Salt and pepper to taste	

Heat pressure cooker, add fat, fry onion and garlic until golden, stir in ham and rice. Cook till rice is golden. Add seasonings, water, tomatoes and mushrooms. Mix well. Add shrimp and sprinkle green pepper over all. Close cover securely and cook 5 minutes at 15 pounds pressure. Cool in lake or ocean, remove cover, stir and serve.

Kit Pratt

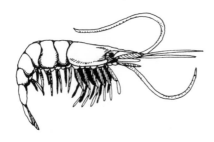

• CAP'N JACK'S SHRIMP GUMBO

Along the rivers and bays of North and South Carolina, Georgia and Florida, shrimp abound. They are easy to catch with a drop or cast net. However, you'll need local instructions if you are a novice with the nets.

3½ cups canned tomatoes
2 cups tomato juice
4 cups water
10 bay leaves
Salt and pepper to taste
3–4 tablespoons Worcestershire
    sauce
2 pounds fresh okra, sliced

4 strips bacon
4 tablespoons flour
2 large onions, cut small
2 cloves garlic, minced
3 cups cooked shelled shrimp
1 tablespoon gumbo filé (optional)*
4 cups hot boiled rice

Combine tomatoes, juice, water and seasonings in a large kettle. Fry bacon crisp, add flour, onion and garlic and cook till flour is brown. Add to large kettle, then add shrimp. Simmer for 1½ hours. Add gumbo filé and serve on mounds of hot rice in deep soup dishes. Serves 8 to 10.

I am not an okra fan, but it belongs in gumbo. Try canned if you can't find fresh locally. Ten bay leaves may sound a bit much, but they settle in nicely.

This dish can be prepared in advance and warmed up for deckhands coming off watch!

* Gumbo filé is a flavoring made from the sassafras tree. It adds a distinctive New Orleans taste to the stew. You might have to try a gourmet shop, because it is not often found in your corner market.

Jack Koneazny

• SHRIMP SCAMPI

No one should cruise in Key West or the Dry Tortugas without tasting the local shrimp. If you approach an anchored shrimper during the day, you may be able to trade some cold beer for a few pounds of shrimp. If you buy it at a local store be sure that it has not been frozen.

2 pounds shrimp	3 diced garlic cloves
¼ pound unsalted butter	1 teaspoon garlic powder
3 lemons	Enough olive oil (do not use a
½ teaspoon salt	substitute) to cover the bottom
½ teaspoon pepper	of a heavy frying pan with
1 teaspoon oregano	¼ inch of oil

Shell and clean the shrimp. Heat oil and butter in a frying pan over medium heat until hot. Add shrimp and the juice of 1 lemon. Stir gently for 1 minute. Continue stirring and add the spices and the juice of ½ lemon. Simmer until shrimp begin to curl (5 minutes or less). Add the juice from another ½ lemon, stir gently, remove from heat and spoon shrimp onto bed of white rice garnished with lemon wedges. Pour liquids from pan over the shrimp and serve.

Babbie Connett

• ORIENTAL SHRIMP AND RICE

This dish can be served hot or cold as a salad.

1 pound can Chinese vegetables, drained	2 cups diced, cooked and deveined shrimp
1 cup diced celery	½ cup seasoned vinegar and oil dressing
1 cup diced onion, or scallions with tops	3 cups cooked rice
1 cup chopped or slivered almonds	

Combine all ingredients. Toss lightly with dressing just before serving. This will serve 8. Schooner, the cat, loves to help us eat shrimp whenever he gets the opportunity!

Gail Childs

• BBQ SHRIMP

½ cup chili sauce
2 tablespoons vinegar
2 tablespoons dark corn syrup
¼ cup salad oil

½ clove garlic
½ teaspoon salt
¼ teaspoon pepper

Blend at high speed. Thread 2 pounds shrimp and lemon wedges on skewers. Brush with the sauce and broil over medium coals 6 to 8 minutes on each side, brushing occasionally with the sauce. Serves 4 to 6 as a main course (or 10 to 12 as an appetizer).

Joan Young

• SAUTÉED SCALLOPS AND SHRIMP

Living aboard *Miracle* on the Delaware shore of the Chesapeake Bay, where fresh seafood is abundantly available, I concocted this dish in the middle of winter when I needed a taste of the ocean.

½ pound scallops
¼ pound shrimp
1 clove garlic, minced
Dash of thyme
Dash of salt

Dash of paprika
1 small onion, minced
Butter
Olive oil

Combine butter and olive oil over medium heat in a large skillet. Add everything except paprika and sauté for 8 to 10 minutes turning a few times.

Remove to a serving dish and sprinkle with paprika. Serve the sauce separately in individual bowls. Serves 2.

Although this really smells of garlic while cooking, the seafood picks up less flavor then you'd expect. I serve this with fried zucchini and lightly flavored rice.

Bill Deighton

• STANIEL CAY CASSEROLE

Sometimes in the Exumas, the hunting can be slow. One such day the Captain (mighty hunter) did manage a small lobster and a small grouper—neither a meal for 2 by itself.

1 small lobster	1 package Hollandaise sauce
1 small grouper (or margate,	Pinch of sweet basil
schoolmaster, etc.)	Pinch of tarragon
15 ounce can spinach (squeezed	
dry)	

Steam lobster and poach fish. Cut into bite-sized pieces. Line bottom and sides of a casserole with spinach. Add fish and lobster. Make Hollandaise sauce, adding basil and tarragon while cooking. Top fish with the sauce and bake for 25 minutes at 350°. Serves 2.

Dewey Durnford

• SPINY LOBSTER DELIGHT

Every successful diver has muttered, at some time or other, "I'm tired of lobster." This dish is different and can be cooked on a 1-burner stove.

1 large spiny lobster (enough for 4	2 tablespoons curry powder, more if
hungry people)	you like
2 cans cream of mushroom soup	Salt and pepper to taste
1 cup or more canned milk, water,	2–3 cups cooked rice
or mixture of the two	

Cook rice in pressure cooker with 2 parts water to 1 part rice. When the valve jiggles remove cooker from stove and put aside. Do not open until ready to serve.

Cook 1 lobster in second pressure cooker with 1 cup seawater. Steam for 10 minutes after valve jiggles. Cool immediately. Put lobsters into a bucket of seawater to cool. Remove shells and cut meat into bite-sized pieces.

Put mushroom soup in a large pan and gradually add milk or water (if too thick, add more). Stir and simmer for a few minutes. Add salt, pepper and curry powder to taste. Add lobster and stir until heated through.

Serve over the rice. It's unlikely there'll be any left. Our guests often ask for third helpings!

Ilene Blankman

• KOWLOON EXOTICA

Desired cooked seafood (see below)
1 head Chinese cabbage, shredded
1 large can mushrooms
4 medium carrots, sliced Chinese style (slice lengthwise, then chop into small lengthwise sections)
1 can bamboo shoots

½ chopped onion
2 tablespoons teriyaki sauce
2 tablespoons soy sauce
1 tablespoon Lawry's Seasoned Salt
1 tablespoon black pepper
⅓ cup cornstarch
3 tablespoons water

Desired seafood may include one of the following: 2 lobsters, 2 cups chopped conch, or 2 cups chopped turtle meat.

On a low heat, mix cornstarch, water, teriyaki sauce, soy sauce, salt and pepper in a Chinese wok. Simmer for 5 minutes, then add onions, carrots, mushrooms (drained) and bamboo sprouts. Add seafood.

Cook for about 10 minutes. Add Chinese cabbage.

Chicken, lobster and turtle meat should be precooked for at least 10–15 minutes before adding to other ingredients. Conch, if used, should be raw. Simmer for 20 minutes. Serve over rice. Feeds 4.

Carmen Iturra

• LOBSTER COCONUT CURRY

½ cup minced onion
2 cups coconut milk
6 tablespoons butter or margarine
2½ cups cooked lobster
6 tablespoons flour
2½ teaspoons curry powder

1½ teaspoons granulated sugar
½ teaspoon ginger
1 cup chicken broth (fresh, canned
   or bouillon cubes)
1 teaspoon lemon or lime juice
Boiled rice for 4 people

Sauté onion in butter until tender, stir in flour, curry, sugar and ginger. Add broth and milk, and cook over asbestos pad, stirring constantly until thick.

Add lobster, cut into bite-sized pieces, and lemon or lime juice. Heat well and serve over rice. Side dishes of mango chutney, chopped salted peanuts, freshly grated coconut and pineapple chunks add extra flavors.

This dish is guaranteed to satisfy 4 very hungry sailors!

Nancy Hitchins

• LOBSTER OMELET

If lobsters are available, try this way of serving them.

2 lobsters, boiled and diced
4 eggs, beaten lightly
4 tablespoons milk

2 tablespoons butter
⅓ cup port wine cheese
Salt and pepper

Add milk to eggs, melt butter in an 8 inch skillet and pour in eggs. As mixture sets, loosen edges with a spatula, letting the uncooked top part of eggs run underneath.

When omelet is mostly cooked but still creamy on top, spread cheese over half of it, put lobster on top of cheese and fold other half over top of it. Cover skillet, cook for 3 minutes and serve.

Beverly Salkin

VEGETARIAN

• MILD, MEATLESS CHILI

16 ounce can whole peeled
    tomatoes
15½ ounce can kidney beans
Small onion, chopped

1 teaspoon chili powder
¾ cup uncooked, Uncle Ben's
    converted rice
1 stalk celery, sliced thinly

Brown onion in oil; add celery, kidney beans and tomatoes (break up). Add the rice and chili powder. Cover and simmer, stirring occasionally. Chili is done when the rice is cooked and the celery is tender.

This chili will be thick. If you desire a thinner chili, add about ½ cup water or an 8 ounce can tomato sauce.

Salt and pepper is optional. If you prefer a zestier chili, add 2 tablespoons chili sauce and more onion. Even more chili powder will do the trick.

Serve with crackers and a large fresh salad.

Kathy Port

• HOT STUFF

It is important to observe that the spicier the food, the longer it is likely to last. However, the addition of spices such as chili should be to taste and worked up to slowly. Fresh Rio Grande chilies are preferred. If these are unavailable or you are on a long voyage, get El Paso brand hot chilies and mash them up with a fork. I generally use ½ cup El Paso chili (hot) per gallon of food prepared. With this addition it will last up to five days without chilling during a Chesapeake summer and longer in cooler waters.

When eating these chili dishes it is important to remember that all those intrepid seamen who discovered this continent did so in search of spices (like chili) that would preserve food. It is therefore a salute to these intrepid mariners to eat heavily spiced and unrefrigerated foods in North American waters.

Chili Ratatat

Obtain eggplant, zucchini and/or summer squash, tomatoes, celery and mushrooms. Parboil the eggplant to remove the skin and cut all vegetables into ½ inch sections. Cook in pot or pressure cooker with one can of mashed hot chili peppers per gallon of Ratatat. Serve on a bed of rice with soy sauce to taste. This dish is good for saving and reserving. It gets better each time it's heated. Be sure to serve with muchas cervezas (beer) on hand for gringos.

Joe Bossom

• VEGETARIAN TACOS

1 can Mexe-beans	1 cup chopped cheeses—Cheddar
1 small can green chilies	and Monterey Jack with
1 onion	peppers
1 can or package fresh	Thinly sliced lettuce, tomatoes
corn tortillas (12)	Your favorite taco sauce

In an oiled pan quickly fry on both sides all the corn tortillas. Put them on paper towels to thoroughly drain. While you are cooking the tortillas, pan fry the sliced onions and diced green chilies. Add the Mexe-beans and cook until hot.

Spread out the cooked tortillas and in the center of each put 1 or 2 spoonfuls of the cooked beans, onion and chilies. Sprinkle each with the cheese mixture; roll up and toothpick each tortilla. Put them back into the pan you used to cook the tortillas. Heat just until the cheese melts.

Serve with lettuce, tomato and taco sauces. Also try rice for the main filler instead of beans.

Sally Schroeder

• WILD RICE AND MUSHROOM CASSEROLE

The Santa Barbara Channel and Islands offer us year-round challenging sailing, protected anchorages and warm waters. Most are as primitive today as they were centuries ago and have an abundance of marine and plant life.

I've developed a number of dishes over the years. Most of them can be adapted to use available ingredients, to personal tastes and for number to be fed.

This is a favorite for mushroom and cheese lovers:

Pour 4 cups boiling water into a large rectangular baking dish. Add 1 cup wild rice and 1 cup brown rice. Bake 20 minutes in a 325° oven. Chop 1 large onion and put in a large bowl; add 1 can whole ripe olives, 1 medium chopped pepper, 1 or 2 cups chopped walnuts (optional), 4 or 5 cups grated Cheddar cheese and 3 or 4 cups sliced mushrooms. Stir.

Remove rice from oven, add approximately 5 tablespoons oil and stir well. Add cheese/mushroom mixture and stir well. Place foil on top and bake at 350° for 20 minutes. Serves 7.

Randi Sanger

• HOT LENTIL SANDWICH

During our winter sailing when we bundle up to keep warm in the chilling air, foods prepared at home and reheated on our propane stove add just the right amount of warmth to the day. Our all-time favorite is a hot sandwich high in protein and flavor.

1 cup lentils	1½ teaspoons salt
2 large onions (cut into thin slices)	¼ teaspoon pepper
¼ cup oil	½ cup brown rice
4 cups water	

Heat oil and fry onions until lightly browned. Rinse lentils and place in 3 quart pot or casserole. Add water, bring to a boil and cook covered over low heat for 20 minutes. Add rice, salt, pepper and the onions with oil. Continue cooking, covered, over low heat until the lentils and rice are tender but not mushy, about 25 minutes. Serve spooned into warmed pita bread with fresh sprouts and tomatoes.

Robert Rose

• HAMBURGER-LESS STEW

This is a real stomach warmer, especially after a cold day's sail battling the elements.

16 ounce can whole peeled
  tomatoes
8 ounce can tomato sauce
2 large stalks celery, thinly sliced
1 medium onion, sliced
2 carrots, thinly sliced

Fresh or canned mushrooms
  (optional)
Macaroni
Italian seasoning
Salt and pepper (optional)

Brown the onions in a small amount of oil. Then add the tomato sauce, whole tomatoes (breaking up with a fork), celery, carrots, mushrooms and seasoning. Cover and simmer, stirring occasionally.

Prepare macaroni according to directions and quantity desired. When vegetables are tender, add cooked macaroni and simmer until everything is hot.

Romano or Parmesan cheese sprinkled on top is a delicious addition.

Kathy Port

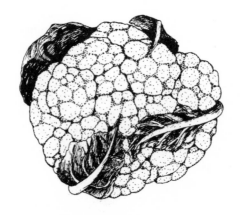

• NO BUM STEER

Granburger is packaged in thick, waxy, milk-carton type containers that are durable at sea. It is dehydrated and will keep indefinitely, is more potent in food value than "real" ground beef, contains no cholesterol, is rich in protein, low in fat and calories and has vitamins and minerals.

It is a *real* substitute for every ground beef use—except the creation of a hamburger! (I have tested everything from eggs to Crisco as a possible adhesive and as yet have found no way to provide a juicy hamburger at sea.) Rehydrated Granburger looks, tastes and acts enough like ground beef to be invaluable in dishes like chili, tacos, spaghetti or Chinese noodle casseroles.

Granburger is saltier than ground beef, so reduce or omit the salt called for in a given recipe. The lack of fat in the product does mean a flavor that is actually distinct from hamburger, but it is a subtle and pleasant distinction.

Spaghetti with Meatless Sauce

1 cup Granburger granules
¾ cup hot water
2 tablespoons polyunsaturated oil
1 tablespoon instant minced onions
  (or fresh)
4 mushrooms, sliced (optional)
½ cup chopped green pepper
  (optional)

1 stalk celery, chopped (optional)
⅛ teaspoon garlic powder
¼ teaspoon black pepper
16 ounce can tomato purée
2 tablespoons parsley
¼ cup sliced black olives
Parmesan cheese
Spaghetti

Rehydrate Granburger by adding hot water to granules in skillet and soaking 3–5 minutes, stirring occasionally. Make a well in center and add oil, stir to spread oil over skillet. Add onions, garlic powder and black pepper, cooking on medium heat until onions are softened, about 5 minutes. Add any optional vegetables, tomato purée, parsley and sliced olives. Stir and simmer over low heat. Add spaghetti and 1 teaspoon oil to rapidly boiling salted water on other burner and cook for 8 minutes.

Spoon sauce over cooked spaghetti and serve, if possible, with French bread (heated with Italian-seasoned margarine?) and a green salad. Instant Roma!

Carolyn Taylor

• STUFFED SQUASH

Squash, especially the winter variety, is a very good storage vegetable, rich in vitamins A, K and B and iron. It is available in some form in probably every country in the world. It is also very versatile in that it can be used as a vegetable, pickle, pie filling, or even as a decoration, while in many places the dried skin is used as a utensil.

One of the ways we like to eat it is stuffed. It can be stuffed with a hamburger or leftover cooked meat and rice combination, but it can also be done as a vegetarian dish. The addition of cheese in combination with rice makes the supply of protein adequate. One idea for this uses:

Packaged rice dinner such as Rice-a-Roni or Rice Pilaf
Fresh onion or dehydrated onion flakes
Canned tomatoes and/or tomato sauce
Edible squash of any type

Wash the squash and cut in halves or circles to make convenient and attractive servings. Remove seeds and strings. If the squash is of a very tough winter variety, you may wish to parboil it at this time to begin tenderizing it.

Prepare the rice dish as directed, adding some of the extra onion if desired, and some tomatoes or a small amount of the tomato sauce to the mixture. It is not necessary to completely cook the rice mixture at this time.

Stuff the squash with the rice mixture and pour tomato sauce over it. Sprinkle generously with the grated cheese and cook in a pressure cooker or bake, covered, until the squash is tender and the rice is heated through.

Anna Patrick

• BROCCOLI CASSEROLE

1½ cups cooked broccoli
½ cup mayonnaise
1 small grated onion or equivalent
    of dried
1 tablespoon lemon juice

1 egg
1 cup shredded Cheddar cheese
1 can Campbell's cream of
    mushroom soup

To cook in oven: Lightly grease a casserole dish, arrange broccoli in it. Combine rest of ingredients and pour over. Top with a bit more cheese. Bake at 400° for 20 minutes.

Stove top cooking: Lightly grease a heavy skillet (with a tight-fitting lid) and prepare as above, then cover and heat over a low flame until cheese is melted throughout.

If you don't have a flame-tamer, crush a disposable aluminum tray or pie plate and use under the skillet.

Elaine Thomas

• STOVE-TOP CHEESE PIE

I'm really pleased with my Optimus Mini-oven. With just a 2-burner kerosene stove I can bake breads, cakes and even pies that taste fantastic!

Mix 1 cup wheat flour, dash of salt and 6 tablespoons margarine until it resembles cornmeal. Pat into stove-top oven pan and bake at medium heat for 10 minutes. Fill crust with 1 sliced onion (sautéed or not, or any vegetable you desire) and 1 cup sliced processed cheese. Pour 2 eggs, beaten with a little milk, over the cheese and cover with sliced tomatoes and seasoned bread crumbs. Bake until golden and eggs are set. This is just as good as a traditional quiche, without the cook having to spend time rolling out a crust.

Debbie Blank

• VEGETARIAN INDIAN CURRY

In a large pan sauté ½ cup onions in butter and add these spices, cooking until the onions are nearly clear:

½ teaspoon mustard seeds (black)
½ teaspoon tumeric powder

¼ teaspoon each cumin powder, Cayenne, coriander powder and garam masala*

From here you can be creative. Use whatever fresh or canned vegetables you have available. Indian favorites are potatoes, eggplant, broccoli, cauliflower, snow peas, cabbage or sweet green or red peppers. Be sure to allow enough cooking time for each vegetable to be done and tender. Along with your choice of vegetables, add 2 cloves of finely chopped garlic. After perhaps 30 minutes of cooking, when all vegetables are tender, add the juice from half a lemon or lime. Serve over steamed rice. Makes a delicious hot and spicy dinner for 2 to 6, depending on the quantity of vegetables added.

* Garam masala is a mixture of cinnamon, cloves and cardamom seeds ground together in equal amounts.

Sally Schroeder

• CHEESELESS MACARONI AND CHEESE

Almost everyone likes macaroni and cheese, but if you are cruising, cheese is sometimes unavailable. We discovered four ways to have a cheesey sauce.

With soup: Heat undiluted cream of Cheddar cheese soup and pour over the macaroni.

With dehydrates: Dehydrated Cheddar cheese can be made into a sauce with a little water, powdered milk, butter and cornstarch.

With dressing: Drain macaroni, return to pot, pour blue cheese dressing over and reheat. Blue cheese dressing will keep if stored in a cool place.

With real cheese: Hard cheese can be stored for several months if wrapped in a vinegar-soaked cloth.

Elaine Kerr

• MEATLESS MOCK CASSEROLES

During our 30-day passage home from Hawaii to California with miles of ocean ahead bringing days and days of humdrum meals from myriad cans, I longed for an oven aboard for the first time in my sailing experience.

Cravings for favorite baked casseroles became an obsession that finally forced me to my knees. Somewhere under the settee amongst all those tins had to be a remedy.

Mock Macaroni and Cheese Bake

1 box macaroni and cheese dinner
4 ounce jar sliced mushrooms

1 cup crushed potato chips

Substitute whatever you like in place of the mushrooms—olives, pimento. No chips? Use buttered cracker or bread crumbs.

Prepare macaroni dinner as instructed on box. Add mushrooms and ½ cup potato chips. Heat thoroughly. Top with remaining ½ cup chips and serve.

Mock Tamale Pie

1½ to 2 cups Fritos corn chips
15 ounce can tamales (Dennison's
  Tamalitos are great!)

4 ounce can sliced black olives
1 cup whole kernel corn
½ cup grated sharp cheese

The basic ingredients are the Fritos and the tamales. The chips absorb the liquid and give the "baked" consistency. Adding the combination of olives, corn and cheese enhances the end result, but these ingredients won't be missed if you don't have them on board.

Spread the chips (mine were stale—I never throw anything away unless it's slimy or shriveled) across the bottom of a coated skillet (Teflon or lightly greased). Pour tamales, juice and all, over the chips and with a fork blend the mixture until tamales are mashed into small pieces. Add remaining ingredients and heat thoroughly.

Donna Freeland

• ALMOST INSTANT LASAGNA

I applaud the invention of the pressure cooker.

This recipe makes great lasagna quickly. Using all the cheeses makes it fabulous, but you can use whatever combination you like.

Sauté in olive oil: 1 onion, sliced

2 cloves garlic, minced

Add:

10 ounce can stewed tomatoes   2 teaspoons each salt and oregano
10½ ounce can tomato purée   ½ teaspoon each garlic powder and
12 ounce can tomato paste   marjoram
2 cups broth   1 teaspoon each basil and thyme
3 tablespoons honey

Simmer 1 hour so it's quite thick. I make it the night or morning before to let it really season.

In a pan to fit inside pressure cooker layer:

Uncooked lasagna noodles   Mushrooms and/or black olives
Mixture of 1 pound ricotta and/or   Spinach, well-drained
    cottage cheese, 2 eggs, and 1   Tomato sauce
    teaspoon each oregano and   Parmesan cheese
    thyme

Top with olives and mozzarella. Cover tightly with foil and place in pressure cooker with 1 cup water. Cook at 10 pounds pressure for 20 minutes. Let cooker cool to reduce pressure. Makes 6 to 8 servings.

Carlynn Ashley

• SPAGHETTI FOR A CROWD

This quick spaghetti recipe has never failed to be a great success with those hordes of starving friends who suddenly arrive on board, wedge themselves in unbelievable numbers around the cabin, and clearly won't get a square meal until the next day unless you provide one (it's raining, their outboard isn't working, the whiskey bottle's still got 3 hours hard drinking in it, and Fred's only just started recounting the story of the typhoon of '64).

It's a mouthwatering and filling supper dish and will feed 4 or 5.

Package of spaghetti	Salt and lots of black pepper
4 eggs	Variety of herbs (almost anything
2 tablespoons butter, margarine or	you care to put in, e.g., thyme,
vegetable oil	oregano, basil)
1 tablespoon hard grated cheese	
(e.g., Parmesan)	

The quantities of the ingredients can be varied as much as you like, depending on what you have available. Cook the spaghetti until it is al dente (tender but firm), drain off the water and add the butter. Turn the spaghetti to distribute the melted fat. Beat the eggs well and pour over, turning again to get an even distribution. Put over a low heat, stirring regularly.

Add herbs, salt, lots of black pepper, and cheese. After about 5 minutes the spaghetti will become sticky, which means the egg is cooked and the dish is ready.

In summer it's nice served with a crisp green salad, or, if you really want to go mad, some fresh double cream beaten in with the eggs is sensational.

Clare Francis

• VEGETARIAN SPAGHETTI

Quantities depend on number of people served.

Celery, onions, carrots, eggplant,
   green beans, fresh okra,
   peppers, christophene or any
   other vegetable you might
   think compatible
2–4 tablespoons vegetable oil
1 large can tomato purée
1 small can tomato paste
2 tablespoons honey

2 tablespoons wine vinegar, sherry
   or wine
¼ teaspoon oregano
1 teaspoon basil
1 teaspoon tarragon
2 bay leaves crushed
2–4 garlic cloves pressed
Salt and pepper to taste

Chop vegetables and sauté in oil until onions are clear, about 15 to 25 minutes. Add remaining ingredients.

Simmer until vegetables are done to your liking, adding enough water to control the consistency.

Good served on spaghetti or rice. Also great the next day, placed unheated in a cheese omelette or combined with black pitted olives and chilled as salad at lunch.

Sue Thorpe

• EGGPLANT PARMESAGNA

1 large eggplant
1 onion
1 clove garlic
12 ounce can tomato paste

2 packages spaghetti sauce mix
1 pound cottage cheese
½ cup Parmesan cheese
¼ pound wide noodles

Cook noodles and make up spaghetti sauce adding onion and garlic. Flour and fry pared and sliced eggplant in oil until light brown. Layer all ingredients in large skillet or Dutch oven starting with sauce, then eggplant, noodles, cheeses and sauce again until all is used. Bake on top of stove using an asbestos pad over a medium fire until heated through.

Beverly Salkin

• THE VERSATILE EGGPLANT

Cruising in the Mediterranean, we savored many delicious ways of cooking eggplant. In 4 years of world cruising I have found this vegetable everywhere, always looking tempting in the market with its shiny purple skin. It keeps excellently without refrigeration for at least two weeks even if the skin wrinkles slightly, so I always buy some when provisioning for a long passage.

Ratatouille

3 sliced onions   3 sliced green peppers
3 eggplants   6 peeled tomatoes

Sauté the onions slowly in plenty of oil. When soft, add the peppers and diced eggplants (unpeeled). After 10 minutes add the tomatoes, salt and pepper and stew slowly for 30 minutes. It is important to *stew* the vegetables in the oil, *not fry* them. For authentic Provençale flavor, olive oil should be used. I also add a few coriander seeds, basil or parsley.

This can be eaten on its own or alongside grilled meat or sausages. It is even better cold the next day.

Eggplant Beignets

One of the simplest ways to prepare eggplant is to slice it, salt it, drain, squeeze out the water, dip the slices in batter and fry in hot oil.

Zucchini is excellent like this too, and in fact can be substituted for eggplant in most recipes.

Stuffed Eggplant

The ambitious cook might try stuffing eggplant, mixing the scooped out flesh with cooked rice, chopped tomato, fried onion, garlic, seasoning and herbs such as marjoram or basil. Stand the stuffed eggplant in a pan with a little oil. When this is hot, add hot water halfway up, cover and simmer very slowly until cooked (45 minutes).

Gwenda Cornell

• CASSOULET

Shifting from the spacious galley of our old wood yawl *Kittiwake* to the sitting head room of our new Stone Horse, *Curlew III*, required a major readjustment, and for the first month or so the little cabin seemed very cramped and crowded. Before very long, though, I began to think of it as cozy rather than cramped and came to agree with Mr. Herreshoff (I forget which one) who said that standing headroom below is necessary only if you intend to give a dance, adding that very few people sleep standing up.

I've also come to enjoy cooking while sitting in the comfortable chair between *Curlew's* two berths and having food supplies, chopping board, sink, icebox, utensils and stove all within easy reach.

Cassoulet is a cold-weather meal, best to cook and eat before there's skim ice on Chesapeake Bay but after the Canada geese and diving ducks begin to sweep in at masthead height (in our case 32 feet, 4 inches).

It's at its best at anchor with the kerosene lamps and cabin heater all burning merrily after a hard thrash to windward.

1 can Campbell's Home Style beans	1½ teaspoons Grey Poupon mustard
1 can lima beans, drained	¼ teaspoon chili powder
½ cup sharp Cheddar cheese, grated	Cayenne pepper to taste
1 cup plain low fat yogurt	Parmesan cheese (optional)

Place beans in a saucepan over low heat (not too difficult with an alcohol stove) and add cheese. In a small bowl mix yogurt, mustard and spices. When the beans are heated through and the cheese is melted, stir in yogurt sauce and reheat.

Top with a sprinkling of Parmesan cheese and serve with chilled red jug wine, which may also be sipped while the cassoulet is heating.

Priscilla Squier

• HAPPINESS IS A GOOD BEAN STEW

On my voyage from England to America in 1980, I sidestepped canned food and instead found my protein and indeed my variety in the humble bean. Lima beans, navy beans, black beans, brown beans, red beans, soya beans, kidney beans, Great Northerns and, for good measure, split peas, black-eyed peas and lentils all found space in *Iskra's* bilges.

I stored them in plastic bottles with screw tops, given to me by a kindly and provident hospital nurse who had saved them from the trash bin. They fitted nicely under the bunks in the main cabin. They lasted the voyage across.

They were the basis of my diet, and they were an unqualified success. I have never eaten better or arrived fitter from an ocean passage although conditions otherwise were not good. Together or separately, depending on my whim, they formed the nucleus of countless bean stews which seemed to develop a life and personality of their own, proliferating themselves from meal to meal as new delights were added and what one might describe as the tone and texture of the stew passed through its inevitable metamorphosis.

The key to bean cuisine is preparation. Beans must be thoroughly rinsed (saltwater will do), boiled for no more than 3 minutes in an open saucepan and then soaked in half fresh and half saltwater for at least 10 hours. This is to clear away the oligosaccharides, the sugars—they can be poisonous in red beans if they are not properly cooked—that cause flatulence, even diarrhea. Soaking breaks down these sugars into digestible form. The liquid must be discarded.

Now the beans can be teemed into a pressure cooker and vegetables added. Root vegetables should be put in whole—onions, potatoes, carrots and anything else on hand. A can of tomatoes is a good addition—they are the only fruit that survives canning without significant loss of food value. Marmite or Bovril make good flavoring or curry powder or garlic or spices—I usually kept the spices for second day stew.

Second day bean stew was something of an adventure, and by day three anything could be expected. I added eggs, dried fruit, sultanas, nuts, raisins, or sometimes a tin of anchovies, tuna or mackerel. The whole thing added a new dimension to my travels.

Frank Mulville

CHAPTER 9

MUFFINS AND BREADS

MUFFINS

• BRAN BOFFINS

In Pago Pago we were invited to a party at a friend's house, and we got to know Mike and Susan from *Chrysalis*. Susan and I helped cook for the party, enjoying the luxuries of a "real" kitchen.

We met up with *Chrysalis* again and cruised together in Tonga, and the recipes started flying back and forth. Sometime during this month of gourmandizing Susan made boffins, and I realized that it was, besides being delicious, a perfect recipe for an ovenless boat that can also be made successfully without eggs.

1 cup sour milk (add 1 tablespoon lemon juice or vinegar to milk and let sit for 5 minutes)	1 egg ¼ cup oil

Mix together well and set aside. In a large bowl mix:

1 cup bran	½ teaspoon salt
1 cup whole wheat flour	1 teaspoon baking soda
½ cup brown sugar	

Add liquid ingredients to dry and blend well. Pour batter into greased and floured 8 inch square pan or muffin tins. Bake for 25–35 minutes in 350° oven. Yield: 12 muffins or 9 large squares

To cook on top of a stove I use a lidded pan with the baking tin sitting on a cake rack.

Brew up a pot of tea, butter boffins and pass the jam, please!

Roxy Darling

• CINNAMON RAISIN BEER MUFFINS

When I am asked how I keep a little one busy on board my answer is, "We bake nearly everyday."

12 ounce can beer (at room temperature)
2 tablespoons sugar or honey
2 teaspoons cinnamon

½ cup raisins
3½ cups self-rising flour
½ cup whole wheat flour

Put all ingredients in a bowl and mix thoroughly. Place batter in greased Teflon muffin pan. Bake in preheated 375° oven for 20 minutes. Serve warm with plenty of butter or margarine. Makes 1 dozen.

Linda Soltysik

• ENGLISH MUFFINS

These are easy to prepare, can be eaten with jam for breakfast, with a favorite sandwich filling for lunch or with butter any time.

Dissolve 1 package yeast in ¼ cup warm water.

Combine:

½ cup milk, scalded
1 tablespoon sugar
1 teaspoon salt

¼ cup butter or margarine, melted
½ cup water, cool

Mix in the yeast mixture, then gradually add 3 cups flour or more until the dough is smooth and elastic. Let rise for about 1 hour. Form into muffins about 1 inch thick and 3 inches in diameter.

Let rise again for about 1 hour, then bake 9 minutes each side in an ungreased fry pan, covered, on low heat. They also can be baked in the oven at 350° for 10 to 15 minutes and will turn out more like rolls than muffins. But they are just as delicious!

Lucie Bridgstock

• BERMUDA TEA SCONES

This is an old Bermuda recipe, and they can be cooked in an oven or in a covered skillet on top of the stove.

¼ cup margarine	Handful sultanas (white raisins)
1 cup self-rising flour	A little sour milk

Mix all ingredients to a smooth paste. Drop by spoonfuls onto a greased baking sheet. Bake in a hot oven for about 10 minutes. Serve warm with lots of butter.

As I have no oven aboard *Ocean Spirit* I use my 10 inch heavy aluminum covered skillet lined with several rounds of greased aluminum foil which have been cut to fit the skillet.

Preheat the pan, then cook over a low flame for about 8 minutes.

This method is great for making Christmas cookies or any other sort of cookie.

I sour the milk by adding a little lemon juice or vinegar.

Penny Voegeli

• GRANDMA'S SCONES

When we left Cabo San Lucas we had no idea that it would take us 31 days to reach San Diego.

We were 700 miles offshore—700 hundred miles from the nearest grocery store—when I realized I was out of salt. I could not believe it! I had everything but the kitchen sink on board but no salt! I was mixing up a batch of our favorite wheat scones so I just substituted chicken bouillon for salt. The scones received rave reviews. The next time I made them I used beef bouillon, and they were also good.

This is an old Irish recipe that my grandmother taught me. The scones are very tasty with the texture of a yeast bread, and because of their simplicity they are perfect for shipboard cookery.

3 cups flour (all white or any proportion white and wheat. I use 2 cups wheat and 1 cup white.)	½ teaspoon salt (or chicken or beef bouillon)
2 teaspoons baking soda	1 cup milk soured with 1 teaspoon vinegar or lemon juice. (I use powdered milk.)

Add milk to dry ingredients and mix thoroughly. Dough will be sticky. Divide into 4 parts. Using generous amounts of flour, pat each portion into ½ inch thick round patties. Cut into wedges and cook on ungreased griddle or heavy pan 10 to 20 minutes on each side over medium flame. (I use paper plates to pat out the dough for easy clean-up.)

Dianna Schwierzke

• DROPSCONES

I don't think there is anything special about this, but we made these regularly on *Moonraker* for our afternoon tea, making enough at one go to last for a day or two. We used an iron griddle which we kept lightly oiled with olive oil. A frying pan would probably do just as well.

Mix together:

1 egg

1 tablespoon margarine or butter

1 tablespoon sugar

Add to this mixture:

2 cups self-rising flour

Mix together. Very slowly add milk to this mixture while stirring, until you have the right consistency (it should run off the spoon like thick syrup).

Warm the griddle on the stove and let the mixture run from the spoon onto it to form round pancakes about 3 inches in diameter. Flip them over when the underside is cooked. They will not stick if the griddle is kept lightly smeared with oil and is not too hot.

These quantities will make about 20 dropscones. With three of us on board *Moonraker* we had to make 18, 21 or 24 to ensure equal shares!

Jock McLeod

• SOURDOUGH BREAD

In the 30,000 miles we have sailed in *Tzu Hang*, from the west coast of Canada, down to the tip of South America, through the Patagonian Canals, up the east coast and through the Caribbean and Bahamas, we have baked a lot of loaves of bread!

Even in port we often make it if the local bread isn't good.

We do carry yeast, but it is not essential for bread making if you make sourdough. The only drawback is that sourdough bread must rise for 24 hours.

Make the sourdough starter by mixing ½ cup white flour with 1 cup water and leave uncovered for 5 days.

Ingredients:

Up to 2½ cups warm seawater (108°F)	2 tablespoons cooking oil or melted butter (optional)
1 tablespoon sugar	5½ cups flour
½ level tablespoon salt	

Put 1½ cups flour into large mixing bowl with seawater, sugar, salt and oil. Add sourdough starter and stir the mixture until smooth. Keep adding flour until you have a dough that is easy to handle.

Knead the mixture in the bowl, to avoid spreading flour all over the boat, for about 10 minutes. Once the dough has a spongy feeling, it is ready. Reserve ½ cup dough, then split the dough into 2 loaves, brush all over with butter and put into bread pans to rise. Cover with a cloth and leave in a draft-free warm area to rise for 24 hours.

Bake at 375° in a preheated oven for about 35 to 45 minutes.

Place reserved dough in a container with a cup of water and several tablespoons of flour. The mixture can be covered but not sealed as the bacteria need oxygen. This will be the starter for your next batch.

White flour works best for sourdough bread, but you can use some wheat or other flours with it and add wheat germ, oatmeal, cracked wheat, currants, etc., to add to the flavor and nutritional value.

When extra ingredients are added, decrease the amount of flour accordingly. Powdered, fresh or canned milk can be used in place of water, but if seawater is not used double the amount of salt.

If liquid milk is used it should be boiled and allowed to cool to 108° to avoid a bacterial action that causes the center of the loaves to become soggy after a few days.

Rye flour must have white flour added as rye contains no gluten and will not rise on its own.

Bob Nance

• WHOLE WHEAT BEER BREAD

2½ cups self-rising flour
½ cup whole wheat flour
3 tablespoons sugar

12 ounce can lukewarm beer
3–4 tablespoons bran flakes

Mix all together. Let rise for a while if you have time and bake until light brown on top.

The whole wheat flour and bran flakes make a deliciously different texture.

Randi Sanger

• BISQUICK BEER BREAD

20 ounce box Bisquick
1 can beer

2 tablespoons sugar

Mix all ingredients and pour into a greased bread pan. I use a non-stick vegetable oil spray in the doughnut of the Optimus Mini-oven and bake for about 40 to 50 minutes. (The time varies with the type of stove.) This bread is cake-like in texture but very good. If you are using a regular oven bake at 325° for 1 hour.

Wait 10 minutes before slicing.

Jill Gaither

• BEER BREAD

Mix together:

3 cups self-rising flour
3 tablespoons sugar

12 ounce can warm beer

Bake in a greased loaf pan at 350° for one hour. Spread butter on top of the loaf when it comes out of the oven. Let it cool a little before you slice it (it's easier to slice) if you can stand the tantalizing aroma!

Brenda Hazell

NON-YEAST BREADS

• NO-FAIL WHITE BREAD

Aboard *Fung Ngen* I have reduced the time and fuss required for bread making by eliminating yeast and concentrating on a variety of quick breads. These are useful on coastal cruises as well as ocean passages.

4 cups self-rising flour
1 teaspoon salt

2 cups buttermilk (will keep for baking at least 1 week unrefrigerated and will still work if separated)

Mix all together and place in a well-greased loaf pan. The batter should be sticky. Bake at 350° for 1 hour or until the top is golden.

Variations:

Herb Bread—Add ½ teaspoon each dried parsley and sage or other herbs.

Poppy Seed Bread—Add 2 tablespoons poppy seed to batter and sprinkle 1 tablespoon seed on top.

Cheese Bread—Add 1 cup shredded cheese to batter.

Raisin Bread—Add 1 cup raisins and 1 teaspoon cinnamon to batter.

Dill Seed Bread—Add 2 teaspoons dill seed and 1 tablespoon grated onion to batter. Sprinkle top with dill seed.

Quick Wheat Bread (*no eggs*)

4 cups whole wheat or brown flour
1 cup flour
1 teaspoon salt
1½ teaspoons baking soda

1 teaspoon cream of tartar
1¼ cups milk
2 tablespoons molasses

Mix together dry ingredients. Gradually stir in the milk, then the molasses. Bake in a well-greased pan at 400° for about 40 minutes until golden brown.

Mid-Ocean Wheat Bread (with eggs)

2½ cups whole wheat or brown flour
1½ cups bread flour
1 teaspoon salt
1 teaspoon baking soda

2 teaspoons *each* brown sugar,
    honey, molasses
1½ cups milk
2 eggs, separated

Mix together dry ingredients. Stir in the milk, egg yolks, honey and molasses. Fold moderately stiff beaten egg whites into batter. (You don't need to separate the eggs, but doing so will make a lighter, fluffier bread.) Add a little more flour if batter seems too runny. Bake in a well-greased pan at 375° for 45 minutes until bread is golden brown.

Variations:

Modified Swedish Limpa—Omit honey, increase molasses to 4 teaspoons. Add 1 teaspoon fennel or anise seed and the grated rind of 1 orange.

Modified Pumpernickel—Omit honey, increase molasses to 4 teaspoons. Add 2 teaspoons caraway seed to batter. Sprinkle caraway seed on top.

Crunchy Wheat Loaf—Decrease bread flour to 1 cup, add ½ cup rolled wheat to batter. Sprinkle wheat germ on top.

Modified Ukranian Black Bread—Decrease honey to 1 teaspoon, increase molasses to 3 teaspoons. Add 1 teaspoon each coriander and cinnamon to batter.

Pumpkin Bread

2 eggs
¾ cup brown sugar
½ cup salad oil
1 heaping cup grated raw pumpkin
1¾ cups flour

½ teaspoon each salt, baking
    powder, baking soda
1 teaspoon cinnamon
¼ teaspoon ground cloves
Nuts and/or raisins (optional)

Beat eggs gradually, adding sugar and oil. Stir in pumpkin. Mix together rest of dry ingredients and gradually add to batter. Mix well. Add nuts and raisins. Bake for 1 hour at 350° in a well-greased pan.

Beverly Larson

• LEE SHORE BREAD

This recipe was arrived at after many trials and experimentation. During a 3-day blow with Cuba for a lee shore I had a first mate who was allergic to yeast, and along with my other troubles I had to listen to a running lecture on the need for a good yeast-free bread. The experience made an indelible impression.

3½ cups sifted flour
½ cup toasted wheat germ (toast to a golden brown color)
3 heaping tablespoons baking powder
4 heaping tablespoons honey

1 tablespoon butter
1 egg
1 cup milk (or 2 tablespoons dried milk in 1 cup warm water)
½ cup seawater (or 1 teaspoon salt in ½ cup warm water)

Mix well all dry ingredients. Softly heat milk, salt-water, butter, and honey, allow to cool and stir in the beaten egg. Add the liquid slowly to the mix, stirring all the time.

When dough forms, place on a well floured surface and gently knead the dough. After about 5 minutes elongate the dough and cut in half. Form 2 loaves about 3 inches by 6 inches and erase any dry breaks that might occur in the dough with a wet finger.

Place the 2 loaves about 5 inches apart on a greased cookie sheet and bake in a 300° oven for approximately 40 to 45 minutes.

Please note that unlike yeast dough, this dough should be quite moist during the kneading process.

Dennis Langlois

• ALDERNEY BREAD

We lived in a 300 year old cottage whose massive exposed wooden beams were timbers from the many wrecked ships on Alderney's coast-line.

In the winter the island receives the full force of the Atlantic storms, and from its shores extend several reefs. It still has its quota of wrecks, but now the hulls are usually steel, and they, but not their contents, are left to rust away.

Alderney is only 3½ miles long and 1½ miles wide and supports a close-knit community. We sailed there many times, and after our ordeal in the Pacific it was the perfect place to recuperate.

Here we learned to walk again while planning our voyage to Patagonia. We were readily accepted by the people, and their hospitality was often overwhelming.

I have adapted one of the island delicacies for use on board. It is a moist loaf that will keep for well over a week if it is wrapped in aluminum foil or kept inside an airtight container.

Mix together in a bowl:

¾ cup all-purpose flour
1 tablespoon baking powder

4 tablespoons Ovaltine or
    equivalent
¼ cup sugar

Place in a saucepan and heat gently until the margarine has melted:

1 tablespoon margarine
1 tablespoon black treacle
    (molasses)

⅔ cup milk

Add the liquid to the dry ingredients, mix together quickly and put into a greased loaf tin. Bake in a moderate oven for 60 minutes. I usually make 2 loaves to use the oven economically.

Maralyn Bailey

• SCONE BREAD

The only way to have fresh bread on board is to make it. At certain times there is a great deal of satisfaction from traditional bread making, but most of the time it's a chore to be avoided.

On passages I bake various substitutes. A great favorite of ours is known on *Auralyn II* as Scone Bread, which is good with either jam or cheese. It is simple to make and the ingredients are easily stowed.

1¼ cups all-purpose flour	1 tablespoon margarine
2 teaspoons baking powder	Milk

Put flour and baking powder into a bowl, rub in the margarine and add sufficient milk to make a stiff dry dough.

Divide in 2 and place each half on a greased plate and mold into a flat round disc about 2 inches thick. Cook in a moderately hot oven for 15 minutes, preferably with both plates on the top shelf. Cut into quarters to serve.

For variety, add 3 or 4 chopped bananas to the mix before adding the milk. Cooking time is the same.

Maralyn Bailey

• HARDTACK

Hardtack is a thin, flat, unleavened bread that has gone to sea for ages. It is as nostalgic as a three-stick schooner, easy to make, tastes scrumptious and lasts forever if kept in a dry, airtight container.

You can experiment and substitute different types of wheat and liquids to get the recipe you like best. Try rye flour in place of wheat, buttermilk instead of milk, and so on.

The hardest part about making hardtack is rolling the dough as thin as possible. The lazy way out is to roll the mixture on the greased pan that you're going to bake it in. This saves you the trouble of having to transfer the mix from the doughboard to the pan.

5 cups wheat flour	2 teaspoons brown sugar
½ cup shortening	1 tablespoon salt
1¾ cups milk	

Mix all ingredients. Knead well.

Now pretend you're a steamroller and flatten that dough as thin as possible. You can use a rolling pin or a jar, but be sure to flour it well and often. Cut off your excess dough and save it for the following batch.

Bake at around 400°. When the edges start to brown, flip it very gently. When it starts to stiffen, flip it again. Finally, when it's board-stiff and you can use it to patch the dinghy, remove it carefully. You've just made hardtack.

To store the flatbread delicacy, break it into manageable pieces and store it in a dry, airtight container. If it remains dry it should last forever.

What do you eat with it? That's no problem. Hardtack goes well with anything. Your real problem will be trying to keep enough on board.

Robert Moffett

• EASY WHOLE WHEAT PANBREAD

2½ cups whole wheat flour or
3 cups whole wheat pastry flour or
3 cups white flour
½ cup bran flakes or rolled oats
2–3 tablespoons honey
1 teaspoon cinnamon
½ teaspoon nutmeg
1½ teaspoons baking powder

1 teaspoon vanilla
1 egg (optional)
½ cup milk (I use powdered)
½ cup butter, margarine or oil
Any or all of these:
½ cup chopped walnuts
½ cup raisins, currants or dates
¼ cup coconut flakes

Mix well, then turn into a greased skillet, cover with a lid and fry for 20 minutes or until brown on the bottom. Flip over and brown the other side for about 5 to 10 minutes. Then enjoy!

When whole wheat flour is not available: For every cup of white flour add ¼ cup bran flakes and ¼ cup wheat germ.

Sarah Dahlstrom

• HOECAKE

Being a Southerner and accustomed to buttermilk biscuits for break-fast, I could not give them up when living aboard with only a 2-burner gas stove.

Hoecake was the answer. It conserves gas, is faster and easier than yeast bread, and provides a hot, tasty bread for breakfast and leftovers, hopefully, for later.

Put ¾ cup reconstituted dry milk in a 2 quart mixing bowl, add ¼ teaspoon vinegar to sour the milk (optional, the bread is fine without it), 2 tablespoons wheat bran (to increase the fiber content) and 1 to 1¼ cups self-rising flour.

Mix gently with a rubber spatula. Stirring will make the bread tough; a minimum of mixing is necessary. The dough should be the consistency of stiff cake batter (adjust amount of flour).

Spread on a hot greased griddle or skillet. Reduce the heat. When the bottom is brown, turn and brown the other side.

Break or cut into pieces and eat with butter, honey, jelly or eggs. I like my hoecake steaming hot, smeared with crunchy peanut butter.

The whole thing only takes about 5 minutes to prepare and cook, and any leftover can be used for sandwiches, French toast, etc.

Dry buttermilk would be ideal for making this, but I have not yet found it in the local stores.

Sara Eoff

• CRUISING CORNBREAD

7½ ounce package cornbread mix (the type that needs only water)
8 ounce can creamed corn
2 tablespoons water

1 tablespoon sugar
1 tablespoon unprocessed bran (optional)
¼ cup shredded or diced cheese
¼ cup chopped onions

Mix all ingredients together by hand. Pour into a greased 8 inch square pan (add crumbled, crisply fried bits of bacon and/or chopped green pepper to batter if you like). Bake at 400° about 25 minutes or until done.

This cornbread can be baked on top of a stove by using a very low flame and baking the cornbread directly in a heavy frying pan. It will be necessary to turn the entire loaf when it's not quite done. Keep frying pan covered during baking.

Lynette Walther

• SWEET BANANA BREAD

1¾ cups sifted flour
2 teaspoons baking powder
¼ teaspoon soda
½ teaspoon salt
⅓ cup liquid shortening

⅔ cup sugar
2 well-beaten eggs
2 cups mashed ripe bananas (the riper the better)

Stir together the flour, baking powder and salt. Add the sugar slowly to the shortening and work until light and fluffy, then add the eggs and beat well. Add the flour mixture alternately with the bananas, beating after each addition until smooth. Turn into a well-buttered bread pan and bake about 70 minutes at 350°. Makes 1 large loaf.

Jarrett and Stan Kroll

• MANGO BREAD

½ cup butter or margarine
1 cup sugar
3 eggs
2 cups flour
¼ teaspoon salt
1 teaspoon baking soda

1 tablespoon vanilla
2 or 3 mangoes, peeled, seeded and chopped or mashed
1 cup pecans or walnuts, chopped (optional)

Cream butter and sugar. Add eggs, blending well. Stir in flour, salt and soda. Add remaining ingredients, mixing well. Pour into a loaf pan and bake at 375° about 45 minutes till done.

Karen Rogers

• SPICE BREAD

One way around the stale bread situation for long cruises is to make a bread that resists becoming stale or moldy. One such bread is called Pain d'Epices in Belgium, where it is part of practically every meal of the working people. It can be eaten plain or toasted, with butter or honey or applesauce. The honey in this recipe can be replaced by sugar syrup, but I'm not sure if the proportions change or not. Since this is made with baking soda and not yeast, it is a lot simpler to make than many other breads.

Dissolve 5 teaspoons baking soda in 1 cup hot water and set aside. Mix 3 tablespoons melted butter or margarine, 1 egg, 1 pound honey, 4 teaspoons spices and 4 cups flour. Add a bunch of raisins if you like. Mix in baking soda and water; turn into 2 well-greased metal ice-cube trays and bake in a preheated oven at 350° for about 45 minutes. Test with toothpick and remove as soon as it is done.

Spices: the usual recipe calls for 1 teaspoon each of cinnamon, allspice, ginger and cloves, but if you don't have all these along, you can mix and match as long as the total is about 4 teaspoons.

John F. Millar

• HOMEMADE TORTILLAS

Buy a Mexican-made cast iron tortilla press and a 5 pound paper sack of Quaker pure corn meal.

Mix in a bowl 2 or 3 cups cornmeal with 2 heaping tablespoons flour. The flour is not essential but helps bind the cornmeal. Add slurps of water and mix to a dough consistency.

Using a large spoon, measure out enough to make 1 flat tortilla and dust with flour to make handling easier.

Place between 2 pieces of wax paper or plastic wrap in the tortilla press, then press. Hola! Instant tortilla.

Lightly grease a frying pan and cook the tortilla over a moderate flame, turning to lightly brown each side.

Bill Stelling

• SNACK CRACKERS

These crackers are very good and nutritious.

2 cups whole wheat flour
1 teaspoon salt
½ cup sesame seeds

¼ cup raw wheat germ
¼ cup vegetable oil
½ cup cold water

Blend together the first 4 ingredients, then add oil and mix with a fork. Pour in water, mix and continue to add water until the dough is soft and workable.

Turn onto a floured surface and knead for 10 minutes or more.

Pull off a golf-ball-sized piece and roll into a ball. Using a floured rolling pin, roll out the dough as thin as possible without tearing. Repeat until you have used all the dough.

Cook in an ungreased cast iron skillet until light brown on the bottom. Flip and just barely brown the other side. Cool thoroughly on a towel, then store in an airtight container.

To vary flavor:

Use 1 cup whole wheat and 1 cup finely ground rye, corn, buckwheat, oats or rice.

Replace the raw wheat germ with non-instant dry milk or soy powder. Replace sesame seeds with poppy, sunflower, shredded coconut, finely ground nuts or soy grits.

Sally Rinehart

• BREAD STICKS

2½ cups biscuit mix
¾ cup warm water

1 package active dry yeast
¼ cup melted margarine

Dissolve yeast in warm water. Mix in biscuit mix. Beat. Knead on floured surface. Divide dough and roll into 18 thin strips. Spread half the margarine on a baking sheet and place strips of dough on sheet. Brush tops with the rest of the margarine and sprinkle with caraway seed. Cover and let rise in a warm place for 1 hour. Heat oven to 425°. Bake for 15 minutes. Turn heat off and leave bread sticks in the oven for 15 more minutes.

Biscuit Mix

Make up this large quantity and store remainder for future.

8 cups flour   4 teaspoons salt
5 tablespoons baking powder   1½ cups Crisco shortening

Blend dry ingredients and cut in Crisco.

Barbary Chaapel

• MASTER MIX

My master mix is similar to a biscuit mix you buy at a store. It is simple and economical for shipboard life and has a variety of uses.
It *must* be stored in an airtight container.

Mix together:

10 cups all-purpose flour   1¾ cups non-fat dry milk
⅓ cup plus 1 tablespoon baking   1½ tablespoons salt
    powder   1 tablespoon cream of tartar
¼ cup sugar

Cut in 1 pound vegetable shortening (not oil) until the mix has the consistency of cornmeal.
Use in the following recipes:

Waffles

(Makes 6–8)

3 cups mix   1 egg
1½ cups water

Blend well, cook in waffle iron.

Pancakes

(Makes 15)

3 cups mix
1½ cups water
1 egg

Dried or canned fruit or berries
(optional)

Blend and cook on griddle or skillet. Sprinkle fruit over pancake just before flipping.

Biscuits

(Makes 12)

3 cups mix   ¾ cup water

For a delicious treat add these herbs:

1 teaspoon celery seed   ½ teaspoon dill weed and thyme

Blend with 10 strokes, knead. Bake in hot oven (450°) 10 minutes or in a skillet on stove top using flame tamer.

Muffins

(Makes 12)

3 cups mix   1 egg
3 tablespoons sugar   Fruit or berries, if desired
1 cup water

Mix water and eggs, add dry ingredients. Pour into greased tins. Bake (450°) 25 minutes.

Cake

(Makes 2 8-inch layers)

3 cups mix   2 eggs
1½ cups sugar   1 teaspoon vanilla for yellow
1 cup water   1½ cups cocoa for chocolate

Combine ingredients. Beat 2 minutes. Bake 30–35 minutes at 325°.

Gingerbread

1 pan, 8 inches x 8 inches x 2
 inches
2 cups mix
¼ cup brown sugar
½ cup water

1 egg
½ cup molasses
1 teaspoon cinnamon
½ teaspoon ginger and cloves

Beat egg, water and molasses. Blend in dry ingredients. Bake 40 minutes at 350°.

Drop Cookies

(Makes 36)

3 cups mix
1 cup sugar
⅓ cup water
1 egg

1 teaspoon vanilla
1 cup nuts, raisins, chocolate chips,
 drained crushed pineapple or
 coconut

Blend and drop on cookie sheet (or in skillet using flame tamer) 10–12 minutes at 375°.

Sally Rinehart

YEAST BREADS

• EASY HOME-MADE BREAD

1 cup milk
¾ cup shortening
½ cup honey
2 teaspoons salt
¾ cup warm water

2 packages active yeast
3 eggs slightly beaten
4½ cups unsifted all-purpose flour
1½ cups whole wheat flour
1 teaspoon soft butter or margarine

In a small saucepan, heat milk until bubbles form around edge of pan. Remove from heat, add shortening, honey and salt, stir till melted. Cool to lukewarm.

Sprinkle yeast over the water in a large bowl, stir until dissolved. Stir in milk mixture and eggs. Combine flours, add 4 cups flour mixture to yeast mixture. Beat by hand or mixer until blended and smooth; then, with a wooden spoon, beat in the rest of the flour until smooth.

Cover with wax paper and let rise in a warm place (85°) away from drafts. When doubled in size, punch down dough and place in a well-greased 3 quart casserole, cover, let rise till double and bake in 350° oven till done.

Dolores Zimmerman

• WHOLE WHEAT BREAD

Because this recipe uses both whole wheat flour and honey, the bread keeps well if kept wrapped—if you don't eat it all while it's hot, which often happens on board *Bantry Bay!*

I use a Sears bread-maker which is a very useful device. This is a large pot with a clamp-on lid. A large handle on the outside of the lid cranks a stirring bar inside. It makes bread-making simple and easy to clean up. Having a pot with a lid that can't fall off is another boon on a boat.

Mix together:

1 package yeast
2 tablespoons honey

2 cups warm water

Let stand for 20 minutes then add:

1/4 cup melted margarine and/or
    bacon fat
1 cup warm water
1 1/2 teaspoons salt
A big glop of sage honey—at least
    1/2 cup (sage is best, but plain
    will do)

1 cup rye flour
3 cups whole wheat flour
3 cups hi-gluten flour
1 cup all-purpose flour

Mix well, then turn onto a floured board and knead until smooth, adding flour if necessary to prevent sticking. Let rise in an oiled bowl, covered, in a warm place until doubled in size.

Knead again, divide into 3 or 4 loaves, depending how large you want them (large or huge), place in greased pans and let rise again.

Bake in 400° oven for 15 minutes, reduce heat to 375° and bake for 25 minutes more.

Whole wheat flour may be substituted for rye and all-purpose for hi-gluten if necessary. Your bread will be a bit more crumbly.

Beth Schwarzman

· NO-KNEAD YEAST BREADS

My family loves fresh-baked yeast bread, but baking can be a monumental task in a tiny galley.

I found some no-knead recipes, and now the crew of *Xamanek* enjoys fresh bread again.

Casserole Bread

2 cups warm water	1 tablespoon sugar
1 tablespoon yeast	4 cups white (preferably
2 teaspoons salt	unbleached) flour

Dissolve salt and sugar in warm water, add yeast. After 5 minutes, add flour. The dough will be sticky. Let rise till double in size. Stir down and place in 2 well-greased small loaf pans. Sprinkle top with salt and let rise again until double the size. Bake for about 45–60 minutes at 375°. Allow to cool in pan for 10 minutes, then remove and continue to cool until ready to eat.

This is the basic recipe. If you are a garlic lover, add 3 shakes or so of garlic powder. Dried minced onions (2 tablespoons) will make onion bread. Add these to yeast water to rehydrate. A tablespoon of dill weed or any other herb such as basil or oregano will produce tasty variations.

Whole Wheat Bread

2 cups warm water	2 tablespoons molasses
1 tablespoon dry yeast	1 tablespoon salt
1 tablespoon honey	3½ to 4 cups whole wheat flour

Put honey and molasses in warm water. Add yeast and allow to work for 5 to 10 minutes. Mix salt and flour and add to yeast mixture. Stir as vigorously as possible. Start with 3½ cups and gradually add the last ½ cup if needed.

Again, the mixture will be sticky. Put in 2 small well-greased loaf pans. The pans should be about ½ full. Let rise to top of pans and bake at 350° for 45 to 60 minutes or till crust is dark brown.

I test with a knife to make sure the center is cooked. If no dough sticks, it is done.

Brush the top with oil or butter and cool for 10 minutes, loosen from sides, remove from pans and cool upside-down for another 20 minutes. (By this time the crew will be wild with the aroma that has developed and will most likely devour half of your efforts.)

Variations on this recipe can be the addition of other flours—rye, barley, buckwheat. Start with substituting 1 cup of the alternate flour for 1 cup whole wheat flour. I often add sesame seeds (½ cup) for a nutty flavor. If you have sesame oil, it is best for the top.

Sprouted wheat or triticale (high protein wheat and rye hybrid) can be stirred into the dough as well.

Demaris Fredericksen

• SALTWATER BREAD

Baking on board really is part of the fun of cruising for me.

This recipe makes 3 large loaves.

2 packages active dry yeast,
    dissolved in ½ cup warm water
    and set aside

Mix together:

⅓ to ½ cup sugar, molasses or honey

½ cup melted butter or cooking oil

2 cups scalded milk (fresh or powdered)

½ cup cold saltwater

4 eggs (fresh or powdered)

Add dissolved yeast, then mix in 9 to 10 cups flour (white, wheat, or a combination of the two. I like to use 1 cup wheat germ in place of 1 cup flour).

Knead dough for 5 to 7 minutes, cover with clean cloth and let rise for 1½ hours. Punch down and let rise for another 30 minutes. Divide dough and put in greased pans. Bake at 350° until golden brown.

Terri Foulger

• WHOLE WHEAT PRESSURE BREAD

This moist whole wheat bread will become your favorite all around bread.

1 cup warm water	4 cups whole wheat flour
1 can condensed milk and	2 cups unbleached white flour
1 cup evaporated milk and water	1½ tablespoons salt
(mixed)	3 tablespoons corn oil
3 tablespoons or packages dry yeast	Corn meal
½ cup fortified food yeast	6 quart pressure cooker
½ cup honey or date sugar	

This makes 2 medium loaves.

The most important item to bread baking is yeast rising. In 1 cup lukewarm water (75°–115°) dissolve one tablespoon honey, then add 3 tablespoons dry yeast. Set this mixture aside to work up a head. (Make sure it does, or start a new batch.)

Next, scald 1 container (14 ounces) condensed milk with 1 cup evaporated milk/water mixture (careful not to burn it or let it boil over on to the top of the stove, yech!). When the scalded milk has cooled to yeast temperature, combine and add remaining honey or finely ground date sugar, fortified food yeast (vitamin B blast), corn oil and salt. Stir this rich brew for at least 10 minutes before adding any flour. (Sometimes I use a rotary beater to make it smooth.)

Slowly add whole wheat flour, making sure from now on that the bread mixture does not get too dry to stir. Now add 1 cup unbleached white flour (slowly) until thoroughly mixed in. Let it sit and work for 1 hour while you oil and cornmeal your pressure cooker bread pans.

Gradually add white flour until dough starts to leave the sides of the bowl. Turn out onto a floured breadboard or counter top. Knead in just enough white flour to stop the dough from sticking to your fingers (leave it a bit sticky). The moister you keep the dough, the better the final product. Put the dough into the pans and let double in volume (1–1½ hours). Be careful about letting the sun raise your bread because it causes uneven rising.

After the bread has doubled in size, very carefully put the pan(s) into the preheated pressure cooker, leaving the bottom rack in and the pressure rocker off. Take a look at your super bread in 40 minutes to see if it's done (allow 40–60 minutes). Soon you'll be able to tell when the bread is done (or burning) by the permeating aroma in the air.

Variations:

20% Oat Bread—Substitute 2 cups cooked rolled oats for 1 cup each whole wheat and white flour. Cooked oats help the moistness as well as adding flavor. Mix the cooled oats into the super brew before adding the flour. Try adding 1 cup finely chopped nuts. This mixture is my favorite.

Thick and Moist Top Crust—After 30 minutes of cooking, gently open the pressure cooker and pour ½ cup water into the bottom, being careful not to get any directly on the bread. Put the cover back on and wait for the bread to bake completely.

Applesauce and Oat Bread—Start with 20% Oat Bread. Now scald 1 can condensed milk and when cooled add it along with 1 cup applesauce to the super brew. Eliminate 1 cup mixed evaporated milk. See if you can wait for it to cool before slicing.

Tim O'Toole

• CRUMPETS

We have become avid tea drinkers aboard *Discovery II,* and crumpets are a favorite teatime treat.

1 teaspoon sugar	½ cup butter or margarine
½ cup lukewarm water	3 to 4 cups flour
1 tablespoon yeast	¾ teaspoon baking soda
2 cups milk (fresh, canned or powdered)	1 tablespoon hot water

Dissolve sugar in water and sprinkle with yeast. Let foam for 10 minutes. Scald milk and add butter. Cool to lukewarm and add yeast mixture.

Beat in flour to make a soft dough. Cover and let rise until bubbly. Mix soda in hot water and beat into batter. Let dough rise until doubled, then spoon into 3 inch crumpet rings on a hot, buttered griddle or heavy fry pan.

Cook until dry and bubbly on top. Remove rings and brown other side. Split and butter to serve. Yields 12 crumpets.

(You can make your own crumpet rings from empty 8 ounce fish or fruit cans by removing tops and bottoms.)

Carol Hogan

• BEER CHEESE BREAD

On *Harvey Gamage* we often served this easy bread with a hearty stew to our 40 crew and passengers.

1 can beer	½ pound Swiss, Cheddar or
½ cup water	American cheese
2 tablespoons sugar	5 cups all-purpose flour
1 tablespoon salt	2 packages dry yeast (2 tablespoons)
2 tablespoons butter	

Warm in a saucepan the beer, water, sugar, salt, butter and cheese (cut in pieces). Cool to lukewarm.

Mix 2 cups flour with the yeast in a bowl. Add warm cheese mixture and beat for 3 minutes with a spoon. Stir in the remaining flour to make a fairly stiff dough.

Knead for 5 minutes. Put in bowl to rise until double in bulk (about 1 hour in a warm area).

Punch down, divide in half. Then either put into 2 greased bread pans or shape each piece into 2 11-inch x 5-inch rectangles. Divide each into 3 strips connected at one end and braid. Place in greased pans. Let bread rise again till double.

Bake in a slightly preheated oven (5 minutes preheating is sufficient) at 350° for 40–45 minutes or until bread is deep brown and sounds hollow when tapped on the bottom. Remove from pans and cool at least 5 minutes.

The amount of cheese used is variable; it is really just an addition to the basic bread. One of the apprentices I taught to cook used whole wheat flour. It didn't rise as well, but it tasted good.

Aprille Kniep

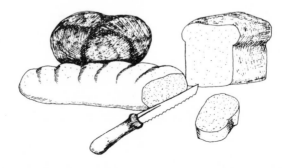

• SWEDISH RYE

Our favorite bread is Swedish rye. A couple of years ago we read in *"People & Food"* about the Optimus Mini-oven, which is designed as a camping oven. We ordered one direct from the Optimus Company and use it constantly on our 2-burner kerosene stove.

2 tablespoons margarine	1 package yeast
1 cup warm water	1 teaspoon salt
2 tablespoons molasses	

Mix all above together in a large bowl until the margarine is melted, then add:

1¼ cups rye flour
1 tablespoon caraway seeds

Beat the mixture for 2 minutes, then add 1¾ cups white flour. Knead mixture for 10 minutes. Let rise in a warm place (diesel compartment on a cold day or in the sun in the cockpit) for ¾ to 1 hour.

Punch down, shape into a long sausage and fit into the Mini-oven pan. Let rise again until the pan is almost full, then bake over medium flame for about 35 minutes.

The bread is shaped like a sponge cake with a hole in the middle, but it is so much better than store bought!

Alice Marzluff

CHAPTER 10

DESSERTS

CAKES

• CHERETA FRUIT CAKE

When we left England in 1976, I was 11 and Christopher was 10. After St. Martin we sailed to Bermuda in time to watch the Tall Ships arrive, ready for the race to Newport.

We saw the Tall Ships again in Boston, and from there we cruised the East Coast of the U.S. south to Miami by way of Long Island Sound, the Delaware, Chesapeake Bay and the Intracoastal Waterway, then on to the Bahamas.

This recipe has been passed down from my grandmother. We never go to sea without one. We have found that fruit cake and soup are just the thing for gales and storms.

½ pound margarine	1 teaspoon mixed spice
½ pound sugar	3 eggs
1 tablespoon black treacle (molasses)	1 tablespoon water
¾ pound self-rising flour	¾ pound dried fruit (preferably raisins, sultanas and currants)

Cream the margarine and sugar. Add black treacle. Add eggs beaten with water and then flour mixed with spice, alternately. Add the fruit with the last of the flour—if the fruit is coated with dry flour, it will be distributed throughout the cake instead of dropping to the bottom. Mix well. Bake at 350° for 1 hour and 20 minutes in a large cake tin or for 40 minutes in 2 bread tins.

Wendy Laws

• HOLDING GROUND MUD CAKE

One day when *Windsong* was anchored in Prickly Bay, Grenada, Colin came below and peered into the pan in which I was stirring with smug satisfaction. "Hmmmmm," he said with his nose in the air. "I haven't seen such good holding-ground mud since we left Long Island Sound."

Good mud, indeed! What was in the pan is perhaps the richest, most gooey and delicious chocolate cake you could hope to concoct. Yet it requires only 1 pan, 1 spoon, ingredients found on any cruising boat, and takes a mere 5 minutes to prepare.

If you make it on board and serve it plain or with a dollop of whipped cream, your crew will think you're a genius. If you double the recipe and make it in layers at home, even the most discerning dinner guests will hail you as a gourmet chef. Here's all it takes:

1½ cups flour	5 tablespoons cooking oil
3 tablespoons cocoa	1 tablespoon vinegar
1 teaspoon soda	1 teaspoon vanilla
1 cup sugar	1 cup cold water
½ teaspoon salt	

Put the sifted flour, cocoa, soda, sugar and salt in the sifter and sift it directly into a square cake pan. Artfully pour in the oil, vinegar, vanilla and water. Mix up the whole muddy mess until it's smooth. Bake at 350° for ½ hour.

Pat Day

• APPLE CAKE

4–6 sliced and peeled apples	1 egg
¼ cup sugar	1 teaspoon vanilla
½ teaspoon cinnamon	½ cup flour
1 tablespoon butter	½ teaspoon baking powder
½ cup sugar	

Arrange apples in buttered 9 inch pie pan, sprinkle with sugar and cinnamon. Cover pie pan with foil and bake at 400° for 15 to 20 minutes. Cream butter and sugar together, add egg and vanilla. Add flour and baking powder. Spread this batter over baked apples and return to oven for 20 more minutes without foil cover.

For stove-top cooking: Place foil-wrapped pie pan on rack in heavy pot, cover tightly and cook until apples are tender. Spread batter over apple slices, replace on rack without foil and replace tight cover. Cook over low heat until batter is baked.

Chris Lantis

• GINGERBREAD WITH APPLE SNOW SAUCE

1 package gingerbread mix	Nutmeg
1 package Dream Whip	3–4 tablespoons Amaretto
1 can apple sauce	(optional)
3 tablespoons lemon juice	

Bake gingerbread according to package directions. Whip Dream Whip and gently fold in apple sauce, lemon juice, nutmeg to taste and Amaretto (or other liqueur). Chill or let stand in a cool place (it will firm up).

Serve gingerbread (warm preferably) with sauce spooned on top.

Janet Jacobs

• MINI-OVEN CAKES

I read an article in an outdoor magazine about a fellow who had climbed a 14,000-foot mountain. The article pictures him on the mountain peak baking a cake in a back-packer's aluminum oven. I was a little skeptical, but when I saw the Optimus Mini-oven in a chandlery I bought it and went directly home and tested it. It worked!

Streusel Coffee Cake

½ cup butter or margarine
¾ cup sugar
1 egg, beaten
2 teaspoons baking powder

¼ teaspoon salt
1½ cups flour
½ cup milk

Cream butter and beat in sugar and egg. Add portions of milk alternately with portions of dry ingredients. Pour into greased pan.

Topping

½ cup butter or margarine
½ cup sugar
2 teaspoons cinnamon

1 teaspoon vanilla
1 cup chopped nuts (any kind)
1 to 1½ cups flour

Cream butter and sugar. Add vanilla, cinnamon and nuts. Add flour gradually, stirring while adding. Use enough flour to make a crumbly mixture. The more flour added, the smaller the crumbs.

Bake the cake mix for 15 minutes over a low flame. Add the topping and bake 15 more minutes or until golden brown.

Dianna Schwierzke

• PRESSURE COOKER CAKES AND PIES

My pressure cooker is a lifesaver.

My method for baking cakes and pies is this: Put shallow rack (provided with most cookers) on bottom of pressure cooker. Oil a round pan that fits snugly in the cooker and put on top of the rack inside the cooker.

For cakes, flour the pan after oiling. Pour in the cake batter, secure the pressure cooker cover tightly and leave the pressure regulator *off* the vent pipe. Have the burner heat quite high to start with until steam comes out of the vent pipe—usually 15 minutes or so. Reduce heat so that only a steady flow of steam emerges from the vent pipe for the last 15 to 30 minutes. When not much steam comes out, the cake should be done. When near the end of baking time, the cover can be taken off to check on the cake to keep it from burning on the bottom.

I use this same method for baking pies. The length of baking time may need to be adjusted depending on what type of stove is being used.

The crust that I patted out for my pies is my mother's crust recipe.

Double crust:

1 cup shortening	2 teaspoons sugar
2 cups flour (½ to ¾ cup whole wheat and/or wheat germ mixed in with white)	1 teaspoon baking powder
	1 teaspoon salt

Mix all ingredients with fork. Add ¼ to ½ cup cold water and mix again.

Joyce Berdie

• TEATIME CAKES

For the crew of *Vela* teatime isn't teatime without freshly baked cake, even on long ocean passages.

Once again, the pressure cooker came to the rescue! The method is simple—give your cake double the specified amount of baking powder or baking soda and roughly double the cooking time.

Do *not* use weights on the cooker. Before adding flour, put the cooker with water and its trivet on the stove so that it is boiling merrily by the time you pour the mixture into the cake tin. The result will be a not-completely risen cake, but one that will keep well for several days as a result of its moist cooking process.

That took care of baking cakes in port or when becalmed. Now I had to find a method of baking under way, and that meant reducing, in some way, the preparation time.

My first success was:

Fruitcake

1 cup raisins	1 teaspoon cinnamon
½ cup shortening	3 tablespoons desiccated coconut
1 teaspoon nutmeg	1 teaspoon cloves
1 cup sugar	1 cup water

Put all in a pan, bring to the boil and simmer for 2 minutes. Allow to cool.

Combine:

1½ cups all-purpose flour, 2 teaspoons soda and a pinch of salt. Stir into the raisin mixture. Pour into a greased and floured baking tin and place on trivet in pressure cooker. Reduce heat to maintain a gentle escape of steam through the vent for the duration of cooking. Allow 1½ hours cooking time.

What could be simpler? And with the added bonus of omitting eggs.

The fruitcake was so well received that I boiled and baked what turned out to be:

Caramel Cake

⅔ cup sugar	1 tablespoon honey
1 teaspoon vanilla	½ cup shortening
⅔ cup water	2 tablespoons desiccated coconut

Bring all to the boil, simmer until dissolved and let cool.

Combine a generous 1½ cups all-purpose flour, 2 teaspoons soda and a pinch of salt. Stir into the cooled mixture, pour into a greased and floured baking tin and place on trivet in pressure cooker. Bake at reduced heat for 50 minutes.

Spurred on by my success, I experimented and came up with a sponge cake smothered in chocolate icing.

Eggless Sponge Cake

½ cup sugar	Few drops vanilla
1 teaspoon honey	⅔ cup water
½ cup shortening	

Dissolve ingredients over low heat. Allow to cool. Stir in a generous 1½ cups all-purpose flour, 2 teaspoons baking powder and a pinch of salt. Pour into a greased and floured baking tin and place on trivet in pressure cooker. Cook for 50 minutes over reduced heat.

When cool, draw a length of thread sideways through the cake to cut it in half. Spread with icing. Sandwich together, serve and wait for the applause!

Annie Larsen

• HAZELNUT CAKE

We spent our working lives in Papua, New Guinea, where we owned 6 boats over the years. Then we decided to give up our careers for a while in order to get the cruising urge out of our systems while we were still young and fit. We now feel we should have started much earlier.

Now in Greece, we have the beautiful world of islands, clear blue water for swimming and the glorious sunny weather, which compensates for the frustrating sailing conditions generally found in the Med.

I cook on a Swedish Origo, stainless steel, 2-burner alcohol cooker which is not pressurized. No oven.

1 cup butter or good margarine	4 eggs
1 cup flour	3 teaspoons baking powder
1 cup sugar	1 cup hazelnuts, finely ground

Cream butter and sugar. Gradually add eggs, sift in flour and baking powder and add hazelnuts. Mix well and pour into a Teflon coated saucepan (7½ inches diameter). Close lid and place on cooker on high settting. Cook for 5 minutes. Then turn heat to medium and cook for 10 minutes. Continue cooking on low setting for 45 minutes. Check with a toothpick to see if cake is cooked. Turn out onto a cooking rack or plate. Let cool.

This cake is best eaten the following day when the hazelnut flavor has fully developed.

Christina Croft

• BANANA CAKE

½ cup margarine	4 tablespoons milk with ¼ teaspoon
1½ cups sugar	lemon juice added
2 eggs	1½ cups flour
4 crushed bananas	½ cup chocolate chips, peanut
1 teaspoon baking soda	butter chips or nuts

Melt margarine, add sugar and mix well, add eggs and mix well, add bananas and mix again. In separate container, mix soda and sour milk and add to above. Add flour and chocolate chips or nuts and stir well. Pour into a greased and floured loaf pan. Bake at 375° in an oven or place on a trivet in a Dutch oven and bake on top of stove over medium heat for 1 hour.

Beverly Salkin

• BARKLEY SOUND CARROT AND PINEAPPLE CAKE—FOR 20

We train Royal Canadian Sea Cadets and have been doing so since 1980. Mail reaches us every 6 weeks with the change of cadets. Sixteen fly home and 16 fly in to the ship.

Obviously, the storing, planning, preparation and cooking of meals takes up a goodly proportion of one's weeks. We have the space aboard for storing dried and tinned goods for 6 months.

The remarkable catering feat undertaken by *Our Svanen* last year was sailing from Mexico to Maui. With 22 people aboard and 23 days at sea we catered 1,518 meals. We consumed 250 gallons of freshwater. *Our Svanen* has no refrigeration and no deep freeze. We ate well-balanced meals, baked our bread each day and caught fish frequently.

Cook aboard is a 17 year old staff cadet. At 0400 the bread is baked, at 0700 breakfast is prepared for 2 watches. At 1700 dinner is served, at 1900 cookies are baked for the night watch. Cadets are excellent bakers. They make fine pastry, good bread and great cookies.

Here is a favorite recipe we have aboard:

Mix together:

1½ cups flour	3 teaspoons baking soda
3 cups sugar	3 teaspoons cinnamon
3 teaspoons baking powder	1½ teaspoons salt

Mix into this mixture 2 cups cooking oil and 6 eggs.

Beat in:

3 cups finely shredded raw carrot	3 teaspoons vanilla
1½ cups crushed pineapple	

Beat well and hard for 5 minutes. Pour into well-greased and floured large pan. Bake at 350° for 35 minutes. Ice with honey and butter and sprinkle with chopped nuts.

Margaret Havers

FRUIT DESSERTS

• MELON UNDER THE STARS

Slice and cube a honeydew melon and place in a large serving dish. Lace with 2 ounces Amaretto and 4 ounces chopped walnuts. Give everyone toothpicks and enjoy in the cockpit while gazing at the stars!

Fran Hanners

• FRUIT COMPÔTE

Place cut-up sections of grapefruit, orange and banana into the ship's most fanciful glassware. Drizzle Grenadine over fruit and chill.

Barbary Chaapel

• PEARS HÉLÈNE

Place drained pears in individual dishes, rounded side up. Cover with hot chocolate sauce, which can be canned, bottled or, better still, easily made by you. Just melt 4 ounces chocolate over hot water, add ½ cup hot water and 1 teaspoon instant coffee powder. Stir in vanilla to taste.

Norma Lemon

• PEARS 'N PORT WINE

Drain the syrup from a can of pears, and combine the syrup with 1 cup port wine and a few cloves. Bring to a boil and continue boiling until reduced in volume by almost half. Cool and pour over pears. Serve with canned cream, whipped with a few drops of lemon juice.

Judy Harrison

• CHERRY SMASH

2½ cups canned cherries (No. 2
    can) drained, sour and red ones
½ cup sugar
½ cup cherry syrup
1 tablespoon margarine

1 cup enriched flour
1 teaspoon baking powder
¼ teaspoon salt
½ cup sugar
½ cup water

In a medium saucepan combine cherries, ½ cup sugar and syrup. Heat to boiling. Add butter. Remove from heat. Sift remaining dry ingredients into a mixing bowl. Add water and mix well. Pour into well-greased, 9 inch square pan (or the nearest size you have aboard). Top with hot fruit mixture. Bake at 400° for 40 minutes.

LEMON-LIME PIE

6 eggs
¾ cup sugar
½ cup melted and cooled margarine
    or Butter Buds
⅓ cup lemon juice

⅓ cup lime juice
2 tablepoons grated lemon rind
    (dried)
1½ tablespoons cornstarch
Confectioners' sugar

Beat eggs, sugar, margarine, juices, rind and cornstarch. Pour into premade graham cracker crust. Bake at 350° for 25 minutes. Dust with confectioners' sugar.

Dorothy Walsh

• PINEAPPLE CRÊPES

2 eggs
1 cup flour
⅔ cup melted butter or margarine

1½ cups milk
4 tablespoons rum

Beat eggs in bowl, add remaining ingredients. Pour a scant ¼ cup batter into small skillet. Cook over medium heat about 2 minutes or until top is set. Turn crêpe and cook on other side about 30 seconds. Place cooked crêpes on paper towel to cool. They can be stacked with wax paper in between until ready to serve. Makes 12 crêpes.

Crêpe Filling

8 ounce package Philadelphia
    Cream Cheese

1 cup chopped fresh or canned
    pineapple, well drained
4 tablespoons rum

Combine all ingredients. Spoon 2 tablespoons filling across center of each crêpe. Roll up and place 2 or 3 crêpes side by side for each serving. Any leftover filling may be spooned over the top.

Wanda Parker

• APPLE BROWN BETTY

1 cup dry bread crumbs
¼ cup sugar
½ teaspoon cinnamon
1 teaspoon lemon juice concentrate

3 apples, sliced
¼ cup melted margarine or butter
2 cups water

Combine the first 4 ingredients. Select a bowl that will fit loosely in the pressure cooker. Place alternate layers of apples and crumbs in the buttered bowl. Pour melted butter over top and cover firmly with aluminum foil. Place cooking rack, water and bowl in cooker. Cook under pressure for 15 minutes. Good while warm with fresh cream or cold alone while standing watch.

Jill Gaither

• APPLE PANDOWDY

2 sticks pie crust mix
20 ounce can apple slices, drained
½ cup brown sugar, packed

3 tablespoons butter
6 tablespoons maple syrup

Prepare pastry for 1 2-crust pie as directed. Stir together apple slices
and brown sugar and put into pastry-lined pie pan. Top with butter and
3 tablespoons syrup. Cover with top crust, make slits, seal and flute.

Bake for 15 minutes at 425°, then remove and drizzle remaining syrup
on top. Cover edges with foil to prevent excessive browning. Bake for
25 minutes longer. Serve warm with additional syrup if you wish.

Debbie Bertland

• APPLE COBBLER

1½ cups biscuit mix
1 egg
¾ cup sugar
4 tablespoons melted shortening or
    oil

3 to 4 apples, sliced thin (skin and
    all)
½ cup milk (powdered milk and
    water)
1 teaspoon cinnamon

Grease a baking dish and add apple slices; top with sugar and cinnamon. Dot with butter.

In a bowl blend the biscuit mix, shortening, milk and egg until it
becomes a batter. Drop by spoonfuls on top of apples until they are
covered. Dust with cinnamon.

Stove-top or Dutch oven: Cook 25 to 30 minutes over medium heat.

Oven: Bake at 400° for 10 minutes; then lower to 350° until done.

Lynne Orloff-Jones

• BOERENMEISJE

This Dutch apple dessert is easy to make aboard and can be eaten at
any time; it is not heavy and does not hurt your stomach.

First, make the "applemoes" (stewed apple). Boil 8 good cooking
apples in a little water until it is a good stew or sauce, whatever you call
it. Watch out that it isn't too watery!

Add some drops of fresh lemon and some sugar—not too much, the "broodmantel" (bread coat) will sweeten it. Cool until just warm.

For the broodmantel cook together ½ stick unsalted butter, 4 slices stale whole wheat bread, crumbled, and about 6 tablespoons brown sugar until it is a dark brown crumbly mass.

Serve the applemoes covered with the broodmantel and a little ground cinnamon. To make a real "boerenmeisje" top it with whipped cream— if you have it.

Eet smakelijk!

Karin Roemers

• PEACH COBBLER

1 can peaches	Bisquick
½ cup brown sugar	Brandy to taste
1 teaspoon cinnamon	1 teaspoon vanilla

Combine peaches, juice, brown sugar, cinnamon and vanilla in a pot. Bring to a boil, stirring occasionally. Sprinkle Bisquick to cover. Place lid on pot and reduce heat. Allow 15 to 20 minutes cooking time. Serve hot with milk poured over it.

Sandy Turner

• MANGO CRISP

½ cup butter or margarine, melted	1 cup rolled oats
6 cups sliced mangoes	½ teaspoon each cinnamon and
½ cup brown sugar	nutmeg
½ cup flour	

Spread 2 tablespoons butter in a 1½ quart baking dish. Arrange mango slices in an even layer. Combine brown sugar, flour, oats, cinnamon and nutmeg. Blend in remaining butter with fork until mixture is crumbly. Sprinkle evenly over mangoes, then press lightly with a fork to cover the entire top. Bake at 375° about 40 minutes till fruit is tender.

Karen Rogers

• BERRY DUMPLINGS

We often find just enough berries to cover the bottom of a pan, and that's all.

So put the washed berries in a pan with enough water just to cover. Mix together 1 cup flour, 1 tablespoon dry powdered milk, 1 cup sugar and a small amount of water.

Drop by spoonfuls on top of the berries and cook covered over a low flame. Don't burn.

Isobel Crittenden

• DESSERTS ON THE GRILL

When we have guests aboard *Entre Amis* while cruising in the Abacos, we are likely to use our covered charcoal grill on the aft rail. Steaks or chops cook quickly, and the charcoal continues to burn, wastefully. After some experimenting we found we could put dessert on the grill to bake while we ate the main course, making use of the charcoal without heating up the galley.

Six aluminum-foil cups, 3 inches in diameter, whether store-bought or molded from heavy-duty foil on a jar bottom, distribute the heat better than a pan, in which the bottom tends to burn.

Baked apples were our first success and then individual pineapple upside-down cakes. We soon discovered that any fruit bottom and several toppings allowed for numerous variations.

For the fruit bottom, put 1 teaspoon brown sugar and 1 teaspoon margarine in the bottom of each aluminum cup. Add fresh or drained canned fruit to cover the bottom. We like pineapple slices, peach halves or slices, apricot halves and apple slices.

Any of the following toppings work.

Quick Cake

Mix together:

1 cup flour	¼ cup milk or canned fruit syrup
½ cup sugar	¼ teaspoon salt
¼ cup shortening or margarine	1 teaspoon baking powder
1 egg	½ teaspoon vanilla

Beat vigorously and spoon on top of fruit.

Crisp

Mix together:

½ cup flour
½ cup brown sugar
¼ cup margarine

1 teaspoon cinnamon or ½ teaspoon
  nutmeg or cloves and ½
  teaspoon cinnamon
¼ teaspoon salt

Mix with fork or pastry blender. Crumble on top of fruit.

Biscuit

One biscuit on top of each fruit cup. Sprinkle with cinnamon sugar.

Shortcake

Mix together:

1 cup biscuit mix
1 tablespoon sugar

¼ cup milk
1 teaspoon soft margarine

Knead and shape into biscuit-like tops for fruit cups.

Shortpie

1 cup biscuit mix
¼ cup margarine

3 tablespoons hot water

Stir vigorously with fork until dough forms a ball. Shape top crusts for fruit cups. Prick with fork.

Bake any of these uncovered in covered grill until done, usually the duration of the main course.

Elaine Heine

• HOT FRUIT COMPÔTE

Use any fresh fruit on hand. Chop up pineapples, section 2 oranges, slice 2–3 bananas, add ¾ cup seedless grapes, ½ cup grated coconut, 1 cup sliced apples. Sauté fruit mixture in a generous amount of butter until everything becomes coated. Add bananas last as they cook very fast. Add cinnamon, a touch of vanilla and a good swig of your favorite liqueur! Serve warm with Brazilian coffee.

Susan Siegel

• CORTOLA

This is a Brazilian sweet course and apparently means "Top Hat." we were given it on our first meal ashore after arriving at Recife from the Cape Verde Islands. I remember making a pig of myself and asking for a second helping.

For each person: Split a banana and fry it, place the fried banana on a piece of toast, cover with a slice of cheese and place under a grill until the cheese melts. Cover generously with sugar mixed with ground cinnamon to suit your taste. Serve immediately while the toast, banana and cheese are hot, and the sugar mix on top is cold.

Jock McLeod

• BANANAS FLAMBÉ

Peel enough bananas to fill your largest frying pan and cut in half lengthwise. Over a low flame, melt 4 or 5 tablespoons butter and put in the bananas. Sprinkle with 2 ounces lemon juice and ¾ cup sugar, turning the bananas occasionally until lightly browned. Just before serving, add a little warmed brandy and ignite it.

Jarrett and Stan Kroll

• TONGAN BAKED PAPAYAS

Split a husked brown coconut in half by striking it in the middle with a hammer or machete.

Grate the coconut meat either by removing it with a small sharp knife and shredding it with a cheese grater or by using a Polynesian style coconut grater. Save the empty coconut shells.

Take the fine pieces of shredded coconut and place them in a clean cloth about 1 inch square. Gather and twist the piece of cloth, squeezing the milk into a bowl until all of the milk has been extracted.

Peel some green papayas and cut the tops off about ⅓ down. Cut these tops into small squares and set them aside.

Clean inside the papayas and place each carefully into half coconut shells. Fill shells with the coconut milk and papaya squares.

Place in a Dutch oven. It is a good idea to add a bit of water to the bottom to prevent sticking if milk should spill into the pan.

Bake for 35 minutes at medium heat or until the papayas become soft and golden. Baked papaya is eaten right out of the coconut shell. One papaya per person is more than enough as this dish is quite filling.

Lidia Feldman

PIES

• KEY LIME PIE

A little background on this famous pie is in order. The true basic ingredient is the Key lime, which is native only to the Florida Keys. They are yellower in color than Persian limes, the kind most commonly found in markets. They are also smaller, rounder, juicier and more pungent.

However, Key limes are at a premium, even in the Keys, since they are not really grown commercially. Because of this, restaurants and individuals make the pie from locally bottled lime juice or regular limes.

Nellie and Joe's famous "South Florida Lime Juice" is especially for lime pies and mixed drinks and is made in Key West and sold all over the Keys. Nowhere on the bottle does it claim to be Key lime juice, but if it is good enough for them, it is good enough for me!

Also, true Key Lime Pie is not green, as most would imagine, but yellow, the color of egg yolks. The lime juice doesn't have enough color to make the pie green—green pies mean greed food coloring. Conchs, as the descendants of the original Key settlers are called, are very specific about the color.

This recipe is easy to follow, and the pie is delicious. The type of crust used and meringue topping can be optional, but the recipe given here is an authentic one. Meringues are less than perfect for cruising fare due to their sensitive nature and dependence upon perfect timing, so I eliminate this last step and still get no complaints from the crowd. Don't shy away from making this pie topless.

Preheat oven to 375°.

Crust:

1¼ cups graham cracker crumbs
¼ cup sugar

¼ cup softened or melted butter

Combine the crumbs, sugar and butter and mix with fingers until crumbly and well blended. Press into 9 inch pie plate, bake 8 to 10 minutes, then place on a rack to cool.

Filling:

5 egg yolks
1 cup canned sweetened condensed milk

½ cup lime juice
1 teaspoon grated lime rind

Lower oven to 350°. Beat egg yolks until fluffy. Gradually add the milk, juice and rind. Pour into the cooled crust and bake for 15 minutes. Remove from the oven to cool while preparing the meringue topping.

Topping:

5 egg whites
½ teaspoon cream of tartar

1 cup sugar

Raise oven to 425°. Whip egg whites until frothy. Gradually add the cream of tartar and sugar, beating constantly to form stiff peaks. Spread the meringue over the pie, covering all the way to the edges to allow for shrinkage while baking. Bake for 5 to 6 minutes or until meringue is nicely browned. Remove to wire rack to cool. Serve chilled if possible.

Terri Naylor

• OATMEAL PIE

This resembles pecan pie and is very easy to make. It makes a delicious dessert to satisfy that craving for sweet things that seems to be part of cruising.

⅔ cup old-fashioned oatmeal
⅔ cup light Karo syrup
⅔ cup granulated sugar
2 eggs, beaten

¼ pound margarine
1 teaspoon vanilla
Pinch salt

Mix all the ingredients thoroughly. Pour into an unbaked pie shell and bake at 325° for 45 minutes or until set and browned.

Earl Bowers

• MARVELOUS PLÁTANOS PIE

A fortunate accident led to what we dubbed the Marvelous Plátanos Pie. Actually, the recipe also had an element of desperation in that I had developed an obsessive craving for apples on a tedious 2 week passage from Mexico to Costa Rica. Experienced cruisers had promised us apples would be available in Costa Rica but failed to mention they were available only in the inland capital at about 50¢ apiece. My dreams of apple pie evaporated, until one morning I left some plátanos frying too long. The result was a somewhat caramelized texture and a flavor faintly reminiscent of baked apple. It was all the incentive needed to try baking an "apple pie."

I used firm but not green plátanos, layering and fanning the slices in a pastry-lined pie plate. A mixture of lime juice, water and honey adds the few tablespoons of liquid needed to make up for the plátanos' lack of moisture. If canned apple juice had been available I would have substituted a few tablespoons of that to add to the intrigue. I otherwise pretended it was apples I was using so sprinkled on the usual cinnamon, nutmeg and brown sugar before adding the top crust.

Even baked in our stove-top oven the result was heavenly and became a frequent treat that often fooled guests as to its contents. Try it and enjoy! Stay flexible and open and who knows what you might discover in your galley.

Katie Dickerson

• PEACH PIE

If there's a will to eat fresh sweets, there's a way. I baked this in our ancient alcohol stove when anchored just behind the *Queen Mary* in Long Beach.

¾ cup sugar
½ cup peach juice
½ teaspoon cinnamon
¼ cup flour
2 16 ounce cans peaches, drained and sliced

¼ cup raisins
¼ cup walnuts, coarsely chopped
1 tablespoon margarine
2 pastry crusts

Combine sugar, peach juice, cinnamon and flour in saucepan and cook until thick. Add peaches, walnuts and raisins.

Pour into 9 inch unbaked pastry lined pie pan. Dot with margarine and top with second pastry crust.

Bake at 400°–450° for 45 minutes.

Sally Graham

• AVO PIE

We became addicted to Avo Pie while visiting sailing friends in Hawaii, where avocados seemed to come aboard in herds.

Mash 1 avocado until very smooth or press through a sieve. Blend in 8 ounces cream cheese, softened at room temperature, ¼ cup honey and 1 tablespoon fresh, or less bottled, lemon juice.

Dollop this heavenly concoction into a baked graham wafer crust. Decorate with banana slices and get ready to fend off the ravenous hordes. Chilling (when possible) improves this cool green mouth-melter pie.

Jaak Barnsley

• MANGO PIE

1 to 1¼ cups sugar
1 teaspoon cinnamon
2 to 3 tablespoons flour
1 tablespoon lemon or lime juice

3½ cups peeled and seeded
mangoes, sliced
Pastry for 2 9-inch crusts

Combine sugar, cinnamon and flour. Sprinkle juice on mangoes and blend thoroughly with sugar mixture. Pour into a pastry shell, top with the second crust and cut slits to let the steam escape. Bake at 425° for 10 minutes then at 350° for 30 to 40 minutes, till crust is browned.

Karen Rogers

• SUMMER PIE

This makes a cool dessert for a summer meal. Make it at home to take along or whip it up in a secluded anchorage.

2½ cups graham cracker crumbs
¾ cup melted butter

Pinch nutmeg

Mix and press into a pie plate and bake for 10 minutes at 325°.

Filling:

½ cup butter
2 cups powdered sugar

2 eggs

Beat until fluffy, place in cooled pie shell and chill.

Topping:

1½ cups graham cracker crumbs
1½ cups Cool Whip

1½ cups crushed pineapple, drained

Fold together pineapple and Cool Whip and spread over chilled filling. Cover with crumbs. Chill until ready to serve.

Eveline Roberge

PUDDINGS AND MUNCHABLES

• PLENTIFUL PUDDINGS

One of my hobbies on board is cooking—I really love it, and Mom lets me plan a budget and menus and cook anything I like, as long as our meals are balanced.

5 Minute Rice Pudding

1–2 cups leftover rice
Handful raisins (optional)
2 teaspoons cinnamon
1 egg (powdered or regular)
¼–½ cup flour

2½ cups milk (we use low fat dried milk but any other will work fine.)
½–¾ cup sugar

Mix flour, milk and egg in a pot over low flame. Stir until thickened. Add remaining ingredients and stir until well combined. (If pudding is too thick, add more milk; if too thin, more flour and stir over a low flame.)
Serve warm to 4 people.

Pressure-Cooked Bread Pudding

2 cups stale bread broken into crumbs
4 tablespoons margarine (powdered, canned or regular)
½ teaspoon salt

3–4 cups warm milk (dried or evaporated and water)
½ cup sugar
2 eggs (powdered or regular)
1 teaspoon vanilla
Raisins (if desired)

In a buttered bowl that fits into a pressure cooker place bread crumbs, margarine and milk. Add remaining ingredients and stir to blend. Cover bowl with tinfoil. Place 2 cups (salt or fresh) water in bottom of pressure cooker, then put in bowl. Cook 30 minutes under 5 pounds pressure. (Be careful that water does not go past sides of bowl.) Serves 4.

Colleen Seyer

• COCONUT PUDDING

1 cup thick coconut cream
1 cup milk
2 eggs

¼ cup sugar
1 teaspoon vanilla

Mix cream, milk and sugar until sugar dissolves. Add eggs and vanilla. Mix well. Place rack in bottom of pressure cooker. Put 2 cups water (salt or fresh) in pressure cooker. Set bowl containing custard on rack and cover it. Cook the pudding under pressure with the regulator gently rocking for 15 minutes. Enjoy the pudding hot or let it cool.

Sue McBride

• RICE CUSTARD

Stir in a double boiler or over low flame:

2 cups milk (evaporated or
    reconstituted powdered is fine)

2 eggs, beaten until smooth
¼ to ½ cup honey or sugar

Continue to stir until thickened. Add:

1 to 2 cups cooked rice
Chopped apples, raisins or currants
1 teaspon vanilla, lemon juice or
    rum

½ teaspoon each of cinnamon,
    nutmeg and mace

Serve hot or cold.

Banana Custard

Follow directions above for basic custard. Cook 15 minutes, then cool. Before serving, add flavoring of choice, 1 cup cooked rice and 1 large banana, sliced.

Carol Mulligan

• MUNCH BUNCH SWEETS

The "Munch Bunch" enjoyed eating almost as much as they enjoyed sailing. By the time they met in Larnaca, Cyprus, their miles at sea totaled 110,000.

No one bothered to count the meals: It's hard to tally non-stop eating. The winter layover meant school and not much sailing—but it didn't affect the munching. To satisfy the sweet tooth, they often concocted goodies from the always and everywhere available sweetened condensed milk. The easiest of these was:

Boiled Can Pudding

Remove label and lid from a can of sweetened condensed milk. Cover the open end with a piece of foil and use string or rubber band to keep it tight against can. If you have lots of fuel/power, place can in a pot with enough water to come about ⅔ up the side of the can. Cover pot.

Boil gently for 3 hours. Or use a pressure cooker (with water, as above) and cook under pressure for 30 minutes. Cool.

Remove bottom lid and use it to push pudding through can slicing off desired servings. (It is RICH, so start with small servings.) You may gild the lily with sauce—chocolate, butterscotch, orange, maple. (Dentists love this!)

Not quite so easy, but allowing a lot more variety, were:

Magic Bars

½ cup butter or margarine
1½–2 cups crumbs (graham cracker, corn flake, stale cookies, etc.)
1⅓–1½ cups shredded coconut
1 cup chocolate chips or ¼ cup chopped maraschino cherries

2 cups marshmallow pieces or miniature marshmallows (optional)
1 can condensed milk
1 cup chopped nuts

Melt the shortening in a 13 inch x 9 inch baking pan (or one of similar volume; we used an 11 inch round). Spread the crumbs over the melted shortening. Press down firmly. Sprinkle coconut over crust.

Sprinkle the chocolate chips (or cherries and marshmallows, or just cherries) evenly over the coconut. Pour the condensed milk evenly over the top. Sprinkle the nuts evenly over the condensed milk; press lightly into the mixture.

Bake at 350° about 25 minutes or until lightly browned around edges. Cool before cutting into 48 (1½ inch x 1½ inch) squares.

Turning munching into partying, the Bunch often made:

Molasses Taffy

1 can condensed milk   Pinch salt
½ cup molasses

Combine ingredients in heavy, shallow saucepan. Cook over medium heat, stirring constantly, to soft-ball stage (236°F)—about 30 minutes. Pour onto buttered pan or platter. LET COOL enough to handle. Butter fingers; pull candy until shiny and light in color. Twist into rope. Cut into 1 inch pieces.

For fancier occasions (such as the weekly potluck barbecue), they sometimes prepared:

Magic Fudge Macaroon Pie *(It makes its own crust)*

3 ounces unsweetened baking   ½ cup flour
    chocolate   1 teaspoon vanilla
½ cup butter or margarine   ⅔ cup condensed milk
3 eggs, slightly beaten   2⅔ cups flaked coconut
¾ cup sugar

Melt chocolate and shortening over low heat. Stir in eggs, sugar, flour and vanilla. Pour into greased 9 inch pie plate. Combine condensed milk and coconut. Spoon over chocolate mixture, leaving a ½ inch to 1 inch space around edge. Bake at 350° for 30 minutes. Cool before cutting and serving to 10–12 adults, 6–8 of the Bunch.

(The Munch Bunch were Don Sandstrom, Yvonne Sewell, Dana Berlin, Nick Berlin, Erik Sandstrom, Kirstin Hanna.)

Joanne Sandstrom

• CHOCOLATE MOUSSE

Makes 2–4 portions:

6 eggs whites (at galley temperature)   1 tablespoon vanilla or rum
6 ounces semi-sweet chocolate or ¾   ¼ teaspoon cream of tartar (not
  cup chocolate chips   essential

Place chocolate in top of double boiler with vanilla or rum and heat over boiling water only until soft. Separate 6 eggs. Put whites into a large bowl (not plastic). Add cream of tartar to the whites and beat vigorously until stiff but not dry (6–10 minutes by hand). Stir chocolate until cool and smooth, then gently blend into the beaten egg whites (as you would stir varnish). When barely mixed, spoon the mousse into a serving bowl and, if possible, chill.

Alexis Strickland

• LEMON SYLLABUB

I'm not a trained cook—I just like food! *Dabchick* is a "narrow boat" and cooking aboard is never dull, with the view from my galley window constantly changing. I have kingfishers, herons and swans; ancient churches, stately mansions and canal-side pubs; golden meadows, woods and hills. All at a gentle 3 miles an hour. One favorite dessert is lemon syllabub—a recipe from the England of Elizabeth I.

Just under 2 cups heavy cream   Juice and grated rind of half a
1 heaped tablespoon fine sugar   lemon
  2–3 tablespoons sweet sherry

Mix lemon juice, rind, sugar and sherry. Separately whip cream until it begins to thicken, then gradually add other ingredients while gently whipping. It should not be too thick. Chill a little, which will thicken it further. Serve with boudoir biscuits or sponge fingers.

Joyce Fox

• HEALTHY COOKIES

1 cup butter
1½ cups honey
2 eggs, beaten
½ teaspoon salt
2 teaspoons vanilla
1 teaspoon baking powder

3¾ cups whole wheat flour
⅓ cup dry skim milk
1 cup sunflower seeds
1½ cups peanuts, chopped
1½ cups raisins
1½ cups chocolate chips, if desired

Cream the butter, then add honey and cream together. Beat in eggs, salt and vanilla. Stir in baking powder, milk, flour, and blend. Stir in seeds, nuts, raisins and chips.

Drop by teaspoonfuls onto unoiled cookie sheet. Bake for 10 to 12 minutes at 375°. Store in airtight tins.

Ann McDuff

• RAINY DAY COOKIES

Cooped up on board one rainy, blowy day and wondering if the rain would ever stop, these freshly made cookies cheered us all up.

Mix in 1 bowl in this order:

½ cup peanut butter
¾ cup white or brown sugar
1 teaspoon vanilla

1 tablespoon water
1 egg (if unavailable, add 2 more
    tablespoons water)

Stir till smooth, then add:

¾ cup whole wheat or white flour
¾ cup oatmeal or rolled oats
½ teaspoon salt

½ teaspoon baking powder
⅓ cup non-instant powdered milk

Mix, then spoon onto a hot oiled skillet with an asbestos pad to even out the heat. Dip a fork in flour and press each cookie flat. Brown on each side, remove and cool. Delicious!

Gary Lepak

• TZU HANG COOKIES

We always seemed able to produce these with good strong tea, whatever the weather or the emergency. They were almost as much a part of *Tzu Hang* as her tiller.

1 stick Oleo (whatever that is)
2 cups sugar

½ cup milk (scant)

Let boil gently for 4 or 5 minutes. Remove from heat.

Add:

¾ cup peanut butter
1 teaspoon vanilla

6 level tablespoons cocoa

Then fold in 3 cups quick oats, drop by spoonfuls onto waxed paper and allow to cool.

We have never fully understood this recipe, which is possibly the reason why the cookies are always different, but always good.

Miles and Beryl Smeeton

• MOCK PEANUT BUTTER CUPS

This is for those times at sea when the America's Cup you're craving is made of Reese's Peanut Butter and there's not a candy store within 100 miles!

The main ingredients are honey, peanut butter, cocoa powder and spray-dried, non-instant milk powder—the kind found in food co-ops and health food stores.

Mix together equal parts honey and peanut butter. Add a little cocoa powder and enough milk to get it to the consistency you want—thin enough to spread on bread or cake; thick enough to roll into little candy balls.

No cooking needed. Just mix and eat. You can add chopped nutmeats, granola, sunflower or sesame seeds, raisins or chopped dates and coconut.

Possible substitutions: Maple or pancake syrup for the honey, butter for the peanut butter, vanilla, rum or flavored liqueurs for the cocoa powder.

Charlotte Criste

• DINGHY DINGS

12 ounce package semi-sweet
   chocolate chips
14 ounce can condensed milk
2 tablespoons butter

2 cups dry roasted peanuts
10½ ounce package miniature
   marshmallows

In a double boiler melt chocolate chips with milk and butter. Off heat add nuts and marshmallows. Spread in a wax paper lined 13 inch x 9 inch pan. Chill several hours. Remove from the pan; peel off the paper and cut into squares. Store at room temperature.

Joan Young

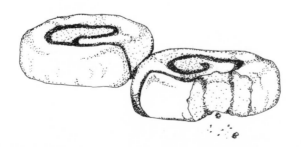

• NO-BAKE COOKIES

Boil for 1 minute:

1 stick margarine or butter
2 cups sugar
1 teaspoon salt
3 heaping teaspoons cocoa or

3 squares semi-sweet chocolate
½ cup milk (fresh, powdered or canned)

Then add 3 cups quick-cooking oatmeal. Let set for 10 minutes. Stir once, then add at least ½ cup nuts, coconut, raisins, etc. Spoon onto greased paper. These keep well in an airtight container.

Dorothy Reeve

• CHOCOLATE CHIP PAN COOKIES

½ cup shortening or margarine
1 cup brown sugar
1 egg
½ teaspoon vanilla
½ cup whole wheat flour
½ teaspoon baking powder

¼ teaspoon salt
½ teaspoon cinnamon
1½ cups Old Fashioned Quaker Oats (uncooked)
½ cup chocolate chips

Mix together shortening, sugar, egg and vanilla. Add flour, baking powder, salt and cinnamon, then mix again. Add oats and chocolate chips and mix thoroughly. Spread mixture to cover bottom of greased 9 inch x 13 inch cake pan, using spoon or fingers. Bake in preheated 350° oven for 12 minutes.

Linda Soltysik

• UNBELIEVABLES

I'm just a landlubber, but I'm also a traveller and recently returned from an expedition to the Galapagos.

I read my son's *Cruising World*—love the recipes and even try some. I hope the readers will try this. It is unbelievably good.

Mix together 1 cup crunchy peanut butter and 1 cup sugar. Stir in 1 egg then drop in spoonfuls on a baking sheet. Bake at 325° for 12 to 13 minutes.

Doris Pierce

• PEANUT BUTTER KRUNCHIES

Simmer 1 cup white sugar in 1 cup light syrup until the sugar dissolves. I use Karo, which is also good for pancakes or waffles, but any syrup should do. In fact, maple syrup might add an unusual and delightful flavor. Do not let this boil, or it will harden into a rock on cooling. Add 1 cup peanut butter and stir until melted. Add this mixture to 5 cups Special K cereal or try any other cereal you like. Mix well until all the Special K is coated and mold into a 9 inch x 12 inch pan. Melt ½ bag Hershey's chocolate bits and pour over Special K mix. Cut into bars and allow to cool.

Debbie Smith

• PECAN BALLS

These are great for parties or for a super snack for the night watch.

1¾ cups pecan halves
2 cups all-purpose flour
1 cup butter or margarine, chilled
    and cut into 1 inch pieces

¼ cup (packed) brown sugar
1 tablespoon water
2 teaspoons vanilla

Preheat oven to 300°. Chop pecans finely. Put all remaining ingredients into a bowl and, with a knife, cut in the butter to blend with other ingredients until the dough is mixed and sticks together. (A food processor could be used for these two steps.)

Add pecans to dough and mix together with hands. Form into ¾ inch balls, place on ungreased cookie sheets and bake for 30–35 minutes. Roll in confectioners' sugar while still hot. Store in airtight tins when cool.

Makes 5 dozen balls but think of making a double batch—they go fast!

Gene Sieck

• COCONUT SQUARES

Fog-bound, anchored off uninhabited McGlathery Island, we had time to explore the island, dig clams, walk through the woods and pick wild raspberries. Back on board *Sea Wedel* and ravenous, I made quick, top-of-the-stove Coconut Squares for dessert.

In a bowl combine:

1¾ cups graham cracker crumbs
½ cup shredded coconut

1 cup chopped walnuts or pecans

In a saucepan boil together for 1 minute:

½ cup margarine
1 egg

1 cup brown sugar
1 teaspoon vanilla

Stir constantly. Remove from heat, stir in crumb mixture and press into a greased dish. Set in icebox to cool.

Served with fresh wild raspberries for dessert our dinner in the fog became a feast!

Irene Westbye

• CHOCOLATE-SCOTCH BROWNIES

6 ounce package chocolate chips
6 ounce package butterscotch chips
¾ cup evaporated milk
3 cups finely crushed vanilla wafers

2 cups miniature marshmallows
1 cup chopped nuts
1 cup flaked coconut
1 teaspoon instant coffee

Melt chocolate and butterscotch chips over low heat. Reserve ¼ cup of this mixture for topping. Add evaporated milk to melted mixture, mixing well. Combine wafer crumbs, marshmallows, nuts, coconut and instant coffee. Add chocolate mixture and mix all well.

Press evenly into buttered 9 inch square pan. Spread reserved chocolate mixture over top. Cool until firm. Cut into 1 inch squares. Enjoy!

Dorothy Reeve

CHAPTER 11

BEVERAGES

COOL DRINKS

• CINNAMON SUN TEA

Thoroughly dry the peel from ½ orange. Break into small bits. Select a container with a tightly fitting lid and pour in 1 dram oil of cinnamon, coating inside surfaces. Add 1 cup black loose tea and the orange peel. To make sun tea, fill a tea ball with the mixture and place in 1 quart water in the sunshine for about half a day.

Barbary Chaapel

• LIME COOLER

This drink can be a snack, a dessert or a pick-me-up. Break 2 eggs into a container, add a 14 to 16 ounce can of sweetened condensed milk, ½ cup fresh lime or lemon juice and a gurgle of good rum. Stir and serve.

That's the basic recipe. Now you can use it as a base for adding anything you like from cream to cracker crumbs.

Earl Copeland

• TEN-DAY KAHLUA AND BALLOON WINE

Some of the things that make cruising more pleasant are the luxuries we often feel we can't afford. When cruising we often indulge in our favorite liqueur, Kahlua, which is homemade before leaving port. Here's how:

Ten-Day Kahlua

1 quart strong coffee	2 vanilla beans
3½ cups sugar	1 fifth vodka

Put 5 or 6 tablespoons good instant coffee (I use Folgers, Nescafé, or freeze-dried) in 1 quart boiling water. Add sugar, stir until dissolved and allow to cool.

Thoroughly clean 2 quart-sized liquor bottles. Mix the vodka with the sweetened coffee. Pour into bottles and suspend vanilla beans inside by a thread. If you can't find vanilla beans, pure vanilla extract can be used. Start with ½ teaspoon per quart and gradually add more until it suits your taste.

Allow 10 days to develop flavor. Remove the vanilla beans and as we say in Hawaii—"Geev um!"

Encouraged by the Kahlua success and on the lookout for other ideas, we began to explore wine making. Here is the recipe for a simple type of wine.

Balloon Wine

2 quarts grape juice (Welch's bottled works well)	4 cups sugar
	Dash of dried yeast

Mix all ingredients in a sterile gallon jug. The important thing in wine making is to make sure that everything used is sterile so that no other organisms work but the yeast! Wine yeasts are best because they work from the bottom of the brew rather than the top, but a regular bread yeast will make a wine that tastes mighty good at sea.

An airlock is essential—and the easiest one is a balloon. Simply put a large one over the orifice of the jug and secure with a rubber band. As the wine works, the balloon will expand. It will continue to expand for 5 to 10 days, depending on temperature, and then go down to its original size.

When finished working, the wine will clear and the sediment will collect on the bottom. At this time the wine can be carefully poured, or even better, siphoned, into smaller, sterilized bottles.

They say wine improves with age, but so far we haven't been able to test that hypothesis as we seem to drink it before it's had time to age.

There are many variations of this recipe using other kinds of juices—apple, cranberry, prune, cherry, plum, etc. The main thing is to make sure the juice is pure, with no additives, as they might cause unpleasant flavors.

As you get more into wine making, you'll probably want to refine your techniques. I would suggest a book on the subject, WINE MAKING, by H. E. Bravery (Arc Books Inc., New York).

Keep a record of what you used and what you did so you can repeat successes. Wine and liqueur making can be fascinating occupations in port—and when cruising, the rewards cannot be overemphasized!

Demaris Fredericksen

• HAPPY HOUR DRINKS

16 ounce can pineapple juice
12 ounce can 7-Up
4 to 6 ounces dark rum

2 to 4 ounces cream of coconut
(according to taste)

Place in a covered jar, shake well and serve over ice. This is a great cocktail to take along on dinghy rides at dusk!

Fran Hanners

• SANGRIA AND PIÑA COLADA

A good thirst quencher even without refrigeration is sangria utilizing a dry red wine and canned fruit cocktail. (I serve the children just the fruit in a paper cup). The remaining half can, juice and all, is divided between 2 8-ounce glasses to which the wine is added.

Another drink that serves both adults and children is Domino Pineapple Coconut Drink, a pre-sweetened mix in a 10 quart cannister. It can be served plain for kids and with a shot of rum for adults, garnished with pineapple or cherries if desired, for a memorable piña colada

Leona Bodie

• BUBBLES ABOARD

During our years of summertime cruising, we've found carbonation to be a magical "ingredient" that adds sparkle to our drinks and a tingle to our palates. Bottles and cans of club soda, tonic and soft drinks to last the summer overflow the lockers, rivaling beer for stowage space.

In provisioning *Everfair* for an extensive cruise, something had to go: We could either exchange our 8,500 pounds of cast iron ballast for aluminum cans, give up carbonated drinks, or find a less space-consuming way to add that sparkle to our drinks. We chose the latter and, so far, have found two ways to have bubbles aboard.

We purchased a siphon bottle that uses CO_2 cartridges to produce a quart of carbonated water. This costs less than a quarter per quart of club soda—and we like the flavor better than bottled soda water.

We bought 1-gallon plastic jugs of tonic and ginger ale syrup from a company that sells home soda fountain equipment (look in the Yellow Pages under "Beverages"), but the syrups come in several other flavors from your local bottling company.

For refreshing sugar-free drinks, we enjoy our club soda plain or add ½ teaspoon of such extracts or flavorings as mint, peppermint, strawberry or vanilla.

Our second method of making our own carbonated drinks uses yeast to make root beer so good that it reminds us of our high school days, stopping after class for a frosty mug or float at the local A & W.

Root Beer Afloat

1 cup sugar
1½ teaspoons root beer concentrate
7¼ cups lukewarm water

¼ teaspoon active dry yeast
dissolved in
¼ cup lukewarm water

Combine the sugar and root beer concentrate and add enough of the water to dissolve the sugar. Pour into a 2 liter container. Add the rest of the water and the yeast dissolved in water. Shake to combine and cap tightly. Place the bottle on its side in a warm place (70° to 80°) for 2 days and then in a cool place (40° to 45°) for 2 days.

Important: Leave at least 1½ inch space at the top of the bottle. Plastic 2 liter soft drink bottles will not seal tightly enough, and the carbonating action of the yeast will force the caps to leak. After combining the ingredients, we divide the root beer between 2 40-ounce glass (liquor) bottles and tighten the caps firmly. Using 32 ounce bottles does not allow you to leave enough space at the top. You can also use corks wired in place.

We recently experimented with another recipe for a delicious carbonated drink you can make aboard using yeast. This recipe is great for the Dominican Republic, where fresh ginger was 13 centavos (10¢ U.S.) per pound!

Ginger Beer

For each quart you will need:

1 jar or bottle larger than 32 ounces with a lid that can be tightly sealed	Peel of 1 medium lime or 2–3 small limes
1 large piece ginger root (about 1 ounce), peeled and crushed	½ cup sugar
⅓ cup lime juice	3¾ cups boiling water
	¼ teaspoon yeast
	¼ cup lukewarm water

Combine the crushed ginger, lime peel, juice and sugar in the jar. Pour in the boiling water. Cover loosely and let cool to room temperature. Dissolve the yeast in the lukewarm water and add.

Seal the jar as tightly as possible and let stand at room temperature overnight. Chill, strain, serve and enjoy!

When *Everfair* visited Puerto Rico, we discovered the Del Pais brand of fruit syrups, which come in every imaginable flavor from lemon-lime to tamarind. Although the directions call for mixing 1 part syrup to 3 parts plain water, we like to use our seltzer bottle for a refreshing carbonated drink.

Bonnie Owra

• LUNCH PUNCH

This punch is cool, refreshing and not too heavy, ideal for a long, leisurely lunch at anchor in one of the beautiful bays of Antigua.

6 sprigs marjoram, bruised	2 bottles sparkling red wine
2 tablespoons fine sugar	2½ cups soda water
1 cup rum	3 limes, thinly sliced
1 bottle still white wine	Cracked ice

In a bowl, cover marjoram with sugar and rum and let stand for 30 minutes. Add still wine and chill. Add sparkling wine and soda water just before serving. Remove marjoram and float limes on top.

Fill glasses ¼ full of cracked ice and pour punch over.

Janice Pickering

• GOOD NIGHTCAP

We first had this drink one cool and windy night in Provincetown, Cape Cod.

Put ice in a glass and pour over some Galiano. Squeeze the juice of a lime wedge into the glass, then run the wedge around the rim of the glass before dropping into the drink.

Sleep well!

Nancy Pittman

• LONG, COOL DRINKS

When *Ramblin' Rose* is safely anchored in a quiet harbor in the Great Lakes and the setting sun is warming the evening sky with passionate hues, we like to unwind with cool, tropical drinks. The main difference between our crew's evening get-together and celebrations on other boats is that we prefer to leave alcohol out of our drinks.

Pineapple Piranha

½ cup crushed pineapple
4 ounces pineapple juice
4 tablespoons canned cream of
    coconut

½ teaspoon lemon juice
7 ounces water

Whir all the ingredients in blender and serve over ice. Garnish with shredded coconut, maraschino cherry or pineapple cube. This, and following recipes, makes enough for 2 full drinks.

Strawberry Spinnaker

½ cup frozen (or fresh) strawberries
½ cup canned peaches (or apricots)
2 tablespoons powdered sugar

1 teaspoon lemon juice
2 teaspoons grenadine syrup
5 ounces water

Whir all ingredients in blender and serve over ice. Garnish with shredded coconut. This is a BIG favorite with the children.

Tahitian Orange

2 tablespoons orange preserves (or any light-colored jelly with "zip")

2 tablespoons frozen orange juice (or powdered orange drink)
1 tablespoon powdered sugar
6 ounces water

Whir all ingredients in blender. Serve over ice with floating slices of orange, lemon or lime. This is a tangy pleaser.

Banana Barracuda

1 banana
3 tablespoons canned cream of coconut
3 tablespoons dry powdered milk

2 tablespoons powdered sugar
1 liberal pinch shredded coconut
6 ounces water

Cut banana into chunks and whir with all other ingredients in blender. Garnish with maraschino cherry or chopped nuts. This is *Ramblin' Rose's* most-asked-for drink—sweet, creamy and cool!

We find it convenient to make all drinks before we set sail and then store them in Styrofoam containers. We've toyed with the idea of freezing the drinks beforehand and later serving them as "slushes".

Terry and Sue Daul

• RUM RUNNER PUNCH

For 20 people, mix together:

40 ounces rum
½ bottle white sugar syrup
½ bottle grenadine syrup
15 ounces lime juice
20 dashes Angostura bitters

¼ tin pineapple juice (large)
¼ tin orange juice (large)
Cherries
Grated nutmeg

Serve over ice cubes.

Sonya Elliot

• ANNAMARIE

This is a light summer cocktail that looks as cool as it tastes. It was made using my favorite ingredients—hence the name.

Into a 4 or 5 ounce wine glass, put 1 ice cube, 1 ounce lemonade, 1 ounce dry gin, 1 ounce Dubonnet Blonde and small wedges of lemon and lime.

If ice is not available, double the lemonade. While this changes the flavor slightly, it does maintain the cool light feel of the drink.

Anna Patrick

• MIMOSA

1 part French champagne   1 part orange juice

Serve with or without ice. This is very popular, especially when you have something to celebrate!

Geri Carlbom

HOT DRINKS

• DISPELLING THE SHIVERS

The first 2 recipes utilize apple cider, which is fresh and plentiful in the fall from the apple orchards that dot the New York shore of Lake Champlain.

Mulled Cider

2 cups water
3 cinnamon sticks
¼ teaspoon nutmeg

1 teaspoon whole allspice
½ cup (packed) brown sugar
1 tablespoon grated orange peel

Bring to boil, reduce heat and simmer 20 minutes. Strain.

Add:

2 quarts apple cider
3 tablespoons lemon juice

½ cup orange juice
1 cup light rum

Cranapple Cider

2 quarts apple cider
1 quart cranapple juice

¼ teaspoon cinnamon
¼ teaspoon nutmeg

Heat to boiling point.

Spicy Tomato Broth

In pan combine:

2½ cups beef broth
1¼ cups tomato juice
1 small onion stuck with 6 cloves
3 tablespoons sugar

½ teaspoon Worcestershire sauce
¼ teaspoon Tabasco
⅛ teaspoon baking soda

Heat over moderate heat for 5 minutes. Discard the onion.

Glückliche Ehe *(Hot Brandied Chocolate)*

In a pan combine:

5 cups hot chocolate   ½ cup brandy
2 cups hot strong coffee   Sugar to taste

Heat to boiling point. A dab of whipped cream or Cool Whip on top is a super bonus.

Joan Young

• HOT SPICED WINE

½ gallon red wine (Gallo Hearty   1½ cups sugar (or to taste)
   Burgundy works well)   1½ teaspoons whole cloves
1 quart water   3 sticks cinnamon

Mix water, sugar and spices in a large pot and bring to a boil. Boil for 5 minutes. Add wine and heat. Do not boil. Taste the mixture every minute or so and remove the spices when it suits your taste.

Janice Cunningham

• RAINY DAY HOT DRINKS

While wintering over in Gibraltar, there are many days when hibernating on your boat is the only sensible thing to do.

It's nice to be able to offer a variety of hot drinks without fussing in the galley. I want to engage in the latest gossip about the weather also, so these instant hot drinks are just the answer. Mixed ahead of time, on another rainy day, they can be stored back in the instant coffee jars.

Suisse Mocha

1 cup instant coffee
½ cup sugar
1 cup nonfat dry milk

2 tablespoons unsweetened cocoa
⅛ teaspoon baking powder

Mix well. Use 2 rounded teaspoons in 1 cup water. Yield: 20 cups.

Café Vienna

½ cup instant coffee
⅔ cup sugar
⅔ cup nonfat dry milk

½ teaspoon cinnamon
⅛ teaspoon baking powder

Mix ingredients well. Use 2 rounded teaspoons in 1 cup water. Yield: 20 cups.

Café Cappuccino

½ cup instant coffee
¾ cup sugar
1 cup nonfat dry milk

½ teaspoon dried orange peel
⅛ teaspoon baking soda

Mash orange peel with bowl of spoon. Mix well. Use 2 rounded teaspoons in cup water. Yield: 20 cups.

Russian Tea

2 cups sugar
½ cup instant tea
2 cups Tang

1 teaspoon cinnamon
½ teaspoon ground cloves

Mix together. Use 3 heaping teaspoons in 1 cup water.

Italian Mocha Espresso

1 cup instant coffee
1 cup sugar
4½ cups nonfat dry milk

½ cup cocoa
½ teaspoon baking soda

Mix well. Use 2 teaspoons in ½ cup water. Yield: 36 cups.

Wendy McKee

• MOCHA COCOA

Some chilly nights and/or good books demand a special, unusually rich hot cup of brew. This is the best we've found to date. Place appropriate servings of instant coffee and cocoa mix into a hefty mug along with 1 stick of cinnamon. Fill with boiling water and let stand for 3 minutes while you adjust the cabin light and fluff up your pillow. Remove the cinnamon stick after a suitable tang has been leached therefrom, and enjoy. (Use fresh ground coffee to start with and this brew is unsurpassable.)

Jack and Pat Tyler

• KARAKAL TEA

At anchor after a day's sailing, a hot drink is welcome. We are teetotalers by conviction and do not have any taste for tea or coffee. So another answer must be found. This is ours. It can be mixed up dry ashore and stored in an airtight container for use as needed.

Mix in a large bowl:

1 cup instant iced tea with lemon mix	1¼ cups sugar
2 48-ounce packages orange crystals	½ teaspoon ground cloves
2 48-ounce packages lemonade crystals	1 teaspoon cinnamon

When ready for a drink, put 1¼ tablespoons of this into a coffee mug and add boiling water.

David Keith

• STEW POT TEA

This was a discovery I made accidentally on a recent delivery from Buzzard's Bay, Massachusetts, to Plymouth, England.

In accord with the "Follett Cooking at Sea Philosophy" one *never* washes the stew pot. So . . . by the time we were suffering from frostbite in the clutches of the Labrador Current, our pan had achieved a nice patina that added greatly to the taste of the delicious meals emerging from our galley.

We had just finished an especially good dinner of sautéed onions mixed with a tin of Snow's New England clam chowder, and there was a good residue left in the pot. Tea seemed to be the logical end here, and I put in a few cups of water.

As it came to boil, 3 bags of Twining's English Breakfast tea were carefully introduced and left to steep for about 4 minutes.

The result has been named Follett Chowder Tea and is delicious beyond one's fondest dreams.

Tom Follett

• HOT BRANDIED LEMONADE

I am not a rum drinker, so I had to find a drink to take the place of hot toddies. Brandy and lemon are two favorites of mine, so that seemed a logical place to start.

This is a very warming drink on a cold, wet day. Try it sometime when you're at home nursing a cold. I'm not sure it cures colds, but it sure helps you cope with the symptoms!

Into an 8 ounce mug pour:

Juice of 1 lemon or equivalent
amount of reconstituted lemon
juice

1½ ounce brandy
1 tablespoon honey, or more to
taste or 2–3 teaspoons sugar

Top with boiling water and stir until honey is dissolved. A slice of lemon adds to the tartness and appearance.

This drink is particularly easy to prepare aboard while under sail if you have a pump-action Thermos container that will maintain water temperature at close to the boiling point for 12 hours or more, depending on conditions.

Anna Patrick

• SUPER HOT BUTTERED RUM

Liquid brown sugar is far more versatile aboard a boat than crystals. Drop in 6 cloves and a couple of cinnamon sticks and let it sit for a few days.

For a super hot buttered rum—put 2 teaspoons liquid brown sugar, 2 ounces rum and a pat of butter in a mug. Fill with boiling water and enjoy!

Louise Auger

CHAPTER 12

HOLIDAY FEASTS

• AN OLD-FASHIONED CHRISTMAS
ON BOARD

With just a bit of advance planning before leaving civilization, Christmas aboard can have all the nostalgia and cheer of back home, even at an isolated anchorage.

We carry a tiny collapsible artificial tree, a small box of carefully wrapped bulbs, some felt decorations and wide rolls of rainproof red and green ribbon. This is standard cruising equipment, well worth its space on December 25.

Small brown paper bags filled ¼ way with sand with a candle stuck in the sand create a magnificent Christmas Eve effect when placed on the foredeck.

Considerable forethought should go into provisioning if you plan a holiday away from civilization. Gourmet items are well worth their price for a once a year celebration. Our holiday cache always includes tinned candies, cookies, fruitcake and candy canes. Our son, Mike, who joins us at Christmas, always looks for the perennial beer sausages in his sock on Christmas morning!

Snow Goose's menu usually looks something like this:

Honey-fried chicken
Baked beans
Potato salad
Hot mulled peaches
Orange cranberry relish   Chicken dressing
Green and black olives   Cinnamon rolls
Butterscotch pie
White wine   Espresso coffee
Eggnog

After everyone has had a hand at stringing stale popcorn for the tree, it's the day before Christmas Eve and time to make the batch of cinnamon rolls. I use Pillsbury Hot Roll Mix. Sift in ⅛ cup cinnamon-sugar mixture. Follow directions on package for dough, then roll it out flat. Spread on margarine (Parkay Liquid) and sprinkle ¼ cup cinnamon-sugar mixture over that. Roll dough into a long roll, cut into slices and place in greased pan to which you've already added 1 tablespoon caramel syrup and 4 chopped pecans.

Caramel Syrup Mixture

1 cup light corn syrup   ¼ cup margarine
1 cup dark brown sugar

Heat slowly until dissolved.

Let the dough rise according to package directions. Bake at 400° for 15 minutes. After removing from oven, turn the pan upside down onto large serving plate to be sure the caramel drips off. Your own roll recipe may be adapted for cinnamon rolls. A stove-top oven may be used, also.

We prefer to be traditional and have chicken even if it has to be canned. Drain the can and save the broth as extra flavor for the Stove Top Stuffing Mix. Then very carefully lift the chicken out of the can, just as carefully cut up, lightly flour and brown in margarine until you have a nice crisp bird. Honey may be lightly drizzled on during this process and salt and coarse ground pepper added.

Hot mulled peaches are simple. Simmer a can of peaches in its juice along with a cinnamon stick, 1 tablespoon margarine and ½ cup of any spirits you have aboard. We generally use rum or wine.

The baked beans take some extra time, so plan ahead.

1 pound dried navy pea beans,
     soaked overnight and parboiled   ½ cup light Karo syrup
½ pound canned bacon, diced   ½ cup dark brown sugar
1 medium onion, chopped   Salt and pepper to taste

Either bake these in a small roasting pan in the oven or in a pressure cooker according to the cooker's directions. If they are done in the oven, bake uncovered at 200° about 6 hours. A little water may be added to avoid dryness. Don't be tempted to add or subtract ingredients. It's perfect!

Hellmann's Mayonnaise is the secret to superior potato salad. Add it lavishly to 2 cans whole potatoes, drained, 4 hard-cooked diced eggs, 1 small diced onion, a sprinkling of celery salt, 1 tablespoon white vinegar, about 4 tablespoons sugar (taste it) and of course, salt and coarse ground pepper.

A real homemade butterscotch pie is sure to bring back childhood Christmas memories. For those without the light magic touch for perfect pie dough from scratch (like me), Pillsbury Piecrust Mix is the next best thing.

Butterscotch Pie Filling

2 cups milk
3 eggs, separated
3½ tablespoons cornstarch
1 cup dark brown sugar

4 tablespoons melted margarine
¼ teaspoon salt
½ teaspoon vanilla

Scald milk in double boiler. Beat egg yolks. Mix cornstarch and brown sugar. Stir in beaten yolks. Add hot milk gradually, then margarine and salt. Pour into top of double boiler and cook until thick. Cool. Add vanilla. Pour into pre-baked pastry shell. For the meringue: Beat 3 egg whites stiff, add gradually 3 tablespoons sugar, then spread over filling, touching all edges of pastry. Brown in 450° oven about 3 minutes. For those without ovens this pie is superb even without the meringue. A stove-top oven will do to bake the crust.

Ocean Spray makes a very good orange cranberry relish, and Borden makes eggnog that is available in cans.

Merry Christmas!

Barbary Chaapel

• ROAST WILD PIG WITH SAUERKRAUT

Along the southeast coast of the U.S. there are many islands where wild pigs abound. You'll find the natives are friendly there, and if you drop enough hints, sooner or later you'll end up with a pork roast.

Drain sauerkraut and replace juice with a white wine. Add 1 scant teaspoon caraway seeds, 3 tablespoons honey and a chopped onion. Cook 20 minutes.

Make small slits throughout the meat and insert slivers of garlic. Rub roast with seasoned salt, cover with apricot jam and then with prepared sauerkraut. Wrap in foil and roast until done.

This recipe can be cooked in a pressure cooker if you don't have an oven on board.

Serve with buttered noodles or rice, a salad and vegetable.

Jack Koneazny

• TURKEY AND STUFFING CASSEROLE

Turkey parts are cheap so we have turkey throughout the year, not just at holidays. Pressure cooking will turn tough and often stringy meat into tender morsels.

2 pounds turkey parts	1 cup celery, chopped
2 cups bread crumbs	¼ cup butter
1 onion, chopped	Poultry seasoning

Place turkey in pressure cooker with 1½ cups water. Bring to pressure and cook for 25 minutes. Cool for 5 minutes, then place under cold water to reduce pressure and open.

In a skillet, melt the butter and sauté celery and onion. Add seasoning, then add bread crumbs and mix well. Moisten with broth from cooking the turkey.

Place turkey pieces on rack in pressure cooker with ½ cup turkey broth on the bottom. Place stuffing on top of turkey and cook for 10 minutes without pressure. Make gravy out of leftover broth.

Living aboard without an oven doesn't stop us from having traditional holiday desserts.

To make pumpkin pudding, buy a large can of pumpkin and follow the directions on the can for pie, disregarding the part about a pie shell. Place pudding in a small glass bowl on rack in pressure cooker and cover bowl with tinfoil. Add water to cover rack and cook, covered, without pressure for the same amount of time as for baking in an oven.

Tamar Collier

• PEKING DUCK

Being Chinese-food fanatics, we felt that Peking Duck was the only proper way to celebrate Thanksgiving. We were rafted up with friends and hiked in a pouring rain to the nearest supermarket to buy a duck and all the trimmings.

The night before the feast, to leave all of our time the following day for preparation of the duck, Richard made the delicate Mandarin pancakes that are a part of the completed dish.

2 cups sifted flour	1 tablespoon sesame, vegetable or
¾ cup boiling water	peanut oil

Measure the flour into bowl. Make a well in center of flour and pour in boiling water, stirring quickly until dough is formed (add more water if needed). When cool enough to touch, knead dough on lightly floured surface until smooth and elastic, 3 to 5 minutes. Cover with damp towel for 30 minutes.

Divide dough into 3 equal parts and shape each part into a roll about 12 inches long and 1½ inches in diameter. Cut each roll into 1 inch pieces. Flatten into a 2 inch circle. Brush 1 circle with oil and cover with an unoiled piece. On a lightly floured surface, starting from the center of the pieces, roll the 2 pieces together to make a thin 5 to 6 inch circle. Roll together all the remaining pairs of pieces in the same manner.

Heat an unoiled frying pan over moderate heat and pan-fry the pancakes on 1 side and then the other. The cooked side should blister and be parchment colored. The 2 pancakes can then be pulled apart and stacked. They will be very thin and soft. Cover at once with foil to keep edges from drying out. Chill in the icebox, tightly wrapped in foil, overnight.

Next morning we borrowed from our friends a portable stove-top oven that had temperature indicators up to 500°. Then we cleaned and dried the duck, inside and out. To serve 4–6, you need:

4½ pound duck	½ cup water
3 tablespoons molasses	

After the duck is cleaned, fasten the neck cavity shut and wrap the duck tightly in aluminum foil. Place on a rack over a large roasting pan in your preheated 425° oven for 1 hour. Mix the molasses and water. Remove duck from oven and let cool slightly. Reduce oven temperature to 375°. Discard the foil and drain all fat from the duck, inside and out. Prick skin of duck in several places, baste with molasses mixture and return to oven for 40 minutes until skin is golden brown. Turn the duck once midway through this 40 minutes.

Remove duck from oven and brush with molasses mixture. Return to oven for 20 minutes. Turn duck and brush again. Return to oven for 20 minutes. The skin is one of the major treats of this dish. When the duck is done, cut the meat and skin into 2 to 3inch pieces and discard the bones.

Be aware of the enormous amount of grease that seeps out of a duck, especially during the first hour, and provide a large enough pan to catch the drippings. We learned this the hard way. Our grease caught on fire at the end of the first hour. Wet towels were hastily thrown over the oven to smother the flame, and our poor duck emerged from the ordeal unscathed, thank goodness. But be careful!

While the duck was cooking, we made Peking Duck Sauce for the dish and sliced some scallions.

4 tablespoons soy sauce	2 tablespoons sesame oil
2 tablespoons sugar	¼ cup water

Mix all ingredients in a pot. Bring to a boil and serve at room temperature. (An alternative or additional sauce can be made by thinning down some plum jelly with water.) Cut scallions into 2 inch pieces, slicing each end into thin strips. Place in a bowl of cool water for about 20 minutes before serving. This will curl up the ends.

At this point we were ready to serve, so we transferred our food to our friends' 30-footer, where we would all have room to sit down and enjoy our food.

Peking Duck is eaten as follows: Each person takes a Mandarin pancake and spreads it with sauce. He or she then places the duck, some skin, and scallion upon it and rolls it up. It's delicious!

Priscilla Campbell

• LOBSTERS AND LIMES

Aboard *Maverick* we tried to give the guests a taste of the Caribbean islands. Fresh food and fruits and vegetables native to the area were used whenever possible, and we usually had a West Indian cook.

The organilla ran the ship. This was a small Spanish hurdy-gurdy that lived on a shelf inside the doghouse. It was built in Barcelona and played six tunes that no one could quite recognize, but it was used by the cook to call hands and guests to meals.

Lobster Casserole

This recipe feeds 20. The quantities can be divided for smaller crews.

Fry 5 chopped onions, 4 chopped green peppers and 2 large cans of mushrooms (drained) in butter for 5 minutes. Spread in 2 buttered baking dishes (9 inches × 12 inches × 12 inches).

Spread 4 cups soft bread crumbs over vegetables (8 cups all together). Cut up the meat from 4 or 5 cooked lobsters and scatter on top of bread crumbs, ½ for each dish.

Make a sauce: Melt ⅔ cup butter, remove from heat and add 1 cup flour. Slowly stir in 5 cups milk. Return to heat and cook, stirring, till sauce thickens. Add canned evaporated milk to make the proper consistency for a medium-thick cream sauce.

Add 1 teaspoon Cayenne pepper, 1 teaspoon dry mustard, salt and pepper to taste, 3 tablespoons Worcestershire sauce, ¼ cup parsley and, at the last minute, ¼ cup sherry.

Pour over the lobster, sprinkle with dry bread crumbs and dot with butter. Bake about 30 minutes at 350° or until bubbling hot.

Carrot Pudding with Lime Sauce

For Christmas or New Year's—serves 6 to 8.

½ cup grated apple	1 cup brown sugar
1 cup chopped raisins	½ cup nutmeats
½ cup flour	½ cup butter
1 cup grated carrot	1 teaspoon salt
1 cup grated potato	1 teaspoon baking soda
1 cup currants	1 teaspoon mixed spices

Mix all together and bake in a greased pan, covered, for 3 to 4 hours at 250° or steam for the same time in a double boiler or pressure cooker for 60 minutes.

Flame with heated rum or brandy and serve with lime sauce, custard sauce or hard sauce.

Lime Sauce

Mix ½ cup sugar, ⅛ teaspoon salt and 2 tablespoons cornstarch in a saucepan. Gradually stir in 1 cup boiling water. Cook until thick and clear. Remove from heat and stir in 2 tablespoons butter and the juice and grated rinds of 2 limes.

Add a drop of green food coloring if you wish. This makes 1¾ cups. It is also good on gingerbread.

Dee Carstarphen

• THANKSGIVING TREATS

Months before leaving I tested recipes that could be adapted to our new liveaboard lifestyle. This meant modifying old favorites by substituting canned and dehydrated products for fresh, frozen or refrigerated. And I had to learn to cook at sea level again.

Being able to prepare traditional Thanksgiving and Christmas foods helped create a holiday atmosphere in a tropical climate away from friends and family.

Pecan pie and steamed cranberry pudding are so tasty and easy that we enjoy them year round.

Pecan Pie

1 prepared piecrust
¾ cup pecan halves
½ cup honey
½ cup brown sugar

2 eggs, well beaten
2 tablespoons margarine or butter
1 tablespoon flour
½ teaspoon vanilla

Mix together all ingredients except pecans. Pour into piecrust. Place pecans on top and bake, covered, over low heat for 1 hour or until center is set. A flame diffuser helps create an evenly distributed heat. The pie can be baked in an oven at 350° for 40–45 minutes. (Pecan halves make a crisper texture than pieces.)

Homemade Piecrust

Combine 1 cup flour and ½ teaspoon salt. Cut in ⅓ cup shortening until mixture is as coarse as small peas. Add enough water to form a ball. Gently roll on a floured surface or between waxed paper to fit a 7 to 8 inch skillet (with tightly fitting lid). Instead of rolling, you can press the dough with the fingers into the skillet bringing the edges up the sides 1 inch.

Steamed Cranberry Pudding

½ cup chopped nuts
2 cups raw cranberries, halved
½ cup molasses or honey
1½ cups white flour

or
1¼ cups whole wheat flour
2 teaspoons baking powder
½ cup boiling water

Grease and flour a 1 quart mold or stainless steel bowl. Combine flour, molasses, cranberries and nuts in a mixing bowl. Add soda to hot water and pour over berry mixture. Mix well and pour into prepared mold.

Cover with aluminum foil, secured with string. Place on a trivet in a pressure cooker with 4 cups water. Place lid on cooker and allow steam to escape from vent for 1½ hours. Do not use steam control.

Remove from heat, let stand 5 minutes, then open. A heavy pan with a tightly fitting lid may be used or the pudding may be cooked at 5 pounds pressure for 45 minutes.

Serve with brandy or rum sauce or simple sauce.

Brandy or Rum Sauce

1 tablespoon flour	½ cup or 5 ounce can evaporated
1 cup sugar	milk
	½ cup margarine

Combine all ingredients in a small saucepan and heat over a low flame until thickened, stirring constantly. Remove from heat and mix in 1 to 2 tablespoons brandy or rum.

Simple Sauce

1 cup dehydrated cream	1 to 2 tablespoons water
⅓ cup honey	

Mix all ingredients thoroughly, using enough water to reach desired consistency Add 1 to 2 tablespoons brandy or rum.

Dehydrated cream is available in stores specializing in food for emergency storage or for backpacking and camping. It is extremely versatile, adding richness to packaged pudding mixes and cream sauces made with dried milk. A small amount added to canned stew turns it into stroganoff.

Dehydrated margarine is also a staple in our galley.

Cranberries keep well without refrigeration for up to 7 days. Any leftover from the pound purchased for the pudding can be chopped and combined with apples, celery and nuts for a salad. Leftover sauce makes a delicious topping, or the extra berries can be chopped and added to waffle, pancake or muffin batter.

Judy Ross

• VEGETARIAN HOLIDAY DISH

My favorite party menu centers around a meatless and much-simplified version of the Greek dish, moussaka. Basically it consists of layers of eggplant, cheese and a good hearty sauce.

First sauté several medium-sized chopped onions in oil in a large heavy pot. Add 1 cup sliced mushrooms and/or green pepper, celery—whatever is available. When they look done, add about 3 cups of a mixture of cooked beans and brown rice. Pinto, kidney or navy beans will do just fine. Mash the mixture all up. Pour in a can of tomato paste and enough wine, vegetable juice or water to make it easy to stir.

Now's the fun part: seasoning. Usually I put in 1 tablespoon molasses, 1 teaspoon each oregano, paprika and parsley, and a shake of nutmeg and cumin. Salt and pepper to taste. A shot of Worcestershire sauce goes well, if you're in the mood. Let it all simmer for 15 to 20 minutes, stirring occasionally.

Next take a ripe medium-sized eggplant and peel it, then slice thinly. Place a layer of slices on the bottom of a good-sized casserole dish. Pour in half the sauce, then cover with a layer of shredded, mild white cheese. Repeat, ending with a generous topping of cheese.

You can sprinkle paprika and sesame seeds on top. Bake at 350°F for about 45 minutes. Serves 4.

Now prepare a Greek style salad. Chop tomatoes, cucumber and green pepper into a wood bowl. Add lots of thinly sliced onion, then crumble at least ½ cup feta cheese on top. Garnish with black olives and a pinch of dried herbs. Dress with equal parts olive oil and red wine vinegar for a delectable combination of flavors.

Serve with fresh whole wheat buns, a bottle of wine and candlelight to amaze your guests with a simple but completely delicious meal.

Happy eating!

Betty Lou Oliver

• HOLIDAY GOODIES

With a 2-burner alcohol stove as my only cooking appliance, I've put together a collection of recipes that do not need an oven or refrigerator. These are some especially for the holiday season.

Pralines *(You'll love the buttery flavor!)*

2 cups brown sugar
¼ cup cream or canned milk
2 tablespoons butter

Pinch salt
1½ cups pecans or walnuts, chopped

Melt butter, add sugar, cream and salt and stir over medium heat until sugar is dissolved and mixture is liquid. Boil gently for 3 minutes. Remove from heat and stir in nuts. Drop spoonfuls onto waxed paper.

Chocolate Boat Cookies

Mix in a pan:
2 cups white sugar
½ cup margarine or butter

½ cup water

Boil 1 minute. Then add:
½ cup peanut butter
⅓ cup cocoa

3 cups rolled wheat or oatmeal
1 teaspoon vanilla

Mix well, then drop onto foil or waxed paper. Let sit for several hours, if your crew can be distracted, and you will have a tasty, firm, nourishing cookie.

Bourbon Balls

These are best after keeping for 3 weeks, so you may have to make a second lot to store if the crew get to your first batch.

Mix together:

1 cup vanilla wafer crumbs	2 tablespoons Dutch cocoa
1 cup finely chopped pecans or walnuts	1½ tablespoons light Karo (syrup)
1 cup powdered sugar	¼ cup (or more) bourbon, Jamaica rum or brandy

Make into small balls. Roll in powdered sugar. Store in a foil-lined tin.

By substituting undiluted frozen orange juice for the liquor these candies will be a great favorite with children.

Five Minute Fudge

I think this got its name because a hungry crew can eat it in 5 minutes.

Combine ⅔ cup (small can) undiluted evaporated milk, 1⅔ cups sugar and ½ teaspoon salt in a saucepan over medium heat. Heat to boiling and cook for 5 minutes, stirring constantly. Remove from heat. Add 1½ cups small marshmallows, 1½ cups chocolate chips, 1 teaspoon vanilla and ½ cup chopped nuts. Stir for 1 or 2 minutes so the marshmallows are melted. Pour into a buttered 9 inch square pan. Allow to cool. Cut into squares and enjoy.

Dorothy Reeve

• SHERRY WITH EVERYTHING

There should always be 2 bottles of sherry in the kitchen or galley—not cooking sherry—but 1 bottle of dry sherry and 1 of medium dry sherry. A judicious addition of sherry can enhance the flavor of ordinary dishes.

For example, ¼ cup dry sherry, added at the last moment, will improve tinned consommé and most other soups except cream soups (add cream instead).

Steak and kidney pie is always better for the addition of 2 tablespoonsful dry sherry just before serving.

Caramel cream, or plain baked custard are luxurious with a spoonful of dry sherry, warmed and poured over before it is taken to the table. This is alleged to be the favorite pudding of King Edward VII. I often wonder if Lily Langtry brought the recipe with her from the Isle of Jersey.

Almond paste for covering Christmas cakes is made with 1¼ cups ground almonds, ¾ cup granulated sugar and ¾ cup confectioners' sugar mixed together with 1 small egg (beaten) and medium dry sherry to make a stiffish paste.

English Trifle

Sponge fingers are sliced and spread with strawberry jam, then sandwiched together and put on the bottom of a serving dish. A mixture of ⅔ medium dry sherry and ⅓ fruit juice or syrup is sprinkled over the sponge fingers—not too much, it should not be soggy.

Cover with drained tinned fruit, then a layer of crushed macaroons.

Make a custard with eggs, milk, sugar and a little cornstarch and allow to cool. Add a tablespoon of medium dry sherry to the custard, then pour over the trifle.

A good layer of thickly whipped cream is added and decorations of blanched almonds, fruits, cherries or angelica are the finishing touch.

What Not To Do With Sherry

Mix half and half with gin. I knew a man who drank this every day before dinner. He died young.

Muriel Wallace

• GRAND MARNIER CAKE

This is a delicious cake for any occasion, but especially at Christmas time.

Cream 1 cup butter with 1 cup sugar until light and fluffy. Beat in 3 egg yolks. Sift together 2 cups flour, 1 teaspoon baking powder and 1 teaspoon soda, then add to batter alternately with 1 cup sour cream. Stir in the grated rind of 1 orange and ½ cup chopped walnuts or pecans.

Beat 3 egg whites till stiff but not dry. Fold into the batter. Pour into a greased 9 inch tube pan and bake at 350° for 50 minutes or until cake tests done.

Combine ¼ cup orange juice, ⅓ cup Grand Marnier, Curaçao or Cointreau and ¼ cup sugar. Spoon immediately over the hot cake, then allow the cake to cool before removing from the pan.

Mary Gammons

• RICH FRUITCAKE

On a long passage, our tastes in food are similar to our tastes ashore with one exception—we both develop an increasing desire for sweet foods. These two recipes are easy to prepare at sea for holiday occasions or at any time we have a craving.

1¼ cups all-purpose flour	1 cup sultanas (white raisins)
1 teaspoon baking powder	½ cup glacé cherries, chopped
1 cup water	(optional)
8 ounce can condensed milk	1¼ cups butter or margarine
1 cup currants	1 teaspoon bicarbonate of soda

Sift flour and baking powder into a bowl. In a saucepan combine all other ingredients (except bicarbonate of soda) and bring to the boil. Add bicarbonate of soda and fold mixture into the flour with a spoon. Put into a greased cake tin and bake at 300° for 2 hours.

Nutties

½ cup margarine or butter	½ teaspoon salt
1 tablespoon syrup	4 teaspoon vanilla
½ cup brown sugar	½ cup chopped nuts
2 cups rolled oats (about 7 ounces)	

Combine oats, salt and nuts in a bowl. Melt margarine, syrup and sugar in a saucepan and add to the oats mixture. Add vanilla and stir well. Spread in a flat baking tin and bake at about 350° for about ½ hour. Cool in the tin and cut into fingers when almost cool.

We find we can stuff ourselves with these goodies when we are at sea and still lose weight!

Marcia Pirie

• CRUISING FRUITCAKE

Our Christmas fruitcake really makes a good dessert or snack for the family as well as a treat to offer a visitor coming aboard. It is not one of the heavily fruited kind, but more of a cake. You may find yourself making one batch for Christmas and one for the boat, as I do.

Line 8 small or 5 large loaf pans with greased brown or waxed paper. Beat together:

1 cup sugar	¾ cup vegetable oil
3 eggs	3 tablespoons brandy

Add:

2¾ cups mincemeat	1 cup raisins
1 cup chopped glazed orange peel	½ cup light golden raisins
½ cup chopped glazed citron	½ cup chopped walnuts
½ cup chopped glazed lemon peel	

Sift together and add:

4¾ cups sifted flour	½ teaspoon salt

Add 1½ teaspoons baking soda to ¼ cup boiling water and mix it into the batter. Divide the batter between the pans. Bake at 350° for 45 minutes to 1 hour. Cool completely.

Wrap the fruitcake in cheesecloth, well soaked in brandy. Wrap again in aluminum foil and store the cakes in plastic bags in a cool place.

It will take a few weeks for the brandy to be absorbed sufficiently to make the cakes taste as they should.

If you want to keep them for a number of months, give them an extra "drink" of brandy every once in a while.

Pauline Dolinski

• CRUISING CHRISTMAS CAKE

Each Christmas I make at least one extra cake, which I drizzle well with brandy and/or sherry, wrap extra well in foil and keep in a cool dark place until our cruising season begins.

Then it comes aboard *Mistress X* in a cookie tin, providing many a dessert and snack.

3½ cups all-purpose flour
1 teaspoon salt
1½ teaspoon each cinnamon and nutmeg
½ teaspoon each allspice, ginger, cardamom, cloves and mace
1 pound butter
2 cups granulated sugar
12 eggs
4 cups golden raisins
2 cups currants
2 cups seeded raisins

2 cups chopped, pitted dates
1 cup each candied pineapple and cherries
1 cup candied citron
½ cup mixed candied lemon and orange peel
½ cup diced candied ginger
1 cup blanched almonds
1 cup pecans, walnuts or filberts
½ cup cranberry sauce or thick jam
1½ teaspoons vanilla
½ cup brandy or sherry

Sift flour, salt and spices together. Cream butter and sugar thoroughly and beat in eggs one at a time. Add flour to fruit and nut mixture, then add creamed butter mixture.

Mix well, then add cranberry sauce, vanilla and brandy. Beat mixture until fruits are well distributed throughout batter. Have cake pans lined with 3 layers of greased paper or 1 layer of foil and turn batter into pan to no more than ¾ full.

Bake in slow oven (275°). Allow from 2½ to 4 hours to bake to dark brown, depending on depth and width of pans. Allow cakes to cool in the paper and store without removing the paper. Keep in a cool dry place, closely covered. Drizzle with sherry or brandy before storing and at weekly intervals for one month.

Makes more than 11 pounds of cake.

Anna Patrick

• SQUASH PIE

A couple of medium acorn or butternut squash should supply more than enough pulp to make a pie. Simply peel, scoop out the seeds and steam (pressure cooker is great) or boil until very tender. Then push the squash through a sieve or blend in a blender so that the pulp is finer in texture and lump-free. Have 2 8-inch pie shells ready or 1 deep dish 9 inch shell.

2 cups sieved squash	½ teaspoon ginger
2 eggs	1 teaspoon cinnamon
1 cup brown sugar (or 2 tablespoons molasses)	¼ teaspoon ground cloves
	1 cup evaporated milk
¼ teaspoon salt	

Mix eggs and squash in a large bowl, stir sugar into mixture and mix well, then add salt and spices and finally stir milk in gradually until the whole is well blended. If the consistency seems too thick, add ½ cup more milk.

Pour mixture into pie shells and bake at 450° for 10 minutes, then lower heat to 325° and continue baking for 30 minutes or until the pie is set and only the center jiggles slightly. Serve warm, not hot, with whipped cream.

Aprille Sherman

• GOURMET BRANDY BALLS

Try gourmet brandy balls for an extra bit of energy while sailing. Also great for reducing the chill factor or for parties.

⅓ cup brandy
2 cups vanilla wafers
½ cup honey
⅓ cup white rum

2 cups shelled walnuts, finely ground
Granulated sugar

Roll the wafers into fine crumbs and mix with the brandy, honey, rum and walnuts. Shape into round, bite-sized balls, then roll in the sugar. Wrap each in plastic wrap. The recipe makes about 5 dozen and the flavor improves with age.

Jack Winston

• DON'T FORGET THE MINCE PIES

In the United States mince pies are a traditional Thanksgiving dessert, while in England they are a Christmas and New Year's treat.

I think I'm a pastry freak, especially when cruising. To me, it's the simplest way of making boring food appetizing.

At home or afloat I use Flako piecrust mix—all you add is water, then bake.

Now for the mince pies. I find Crosse & Blackwell and Borden make excellent mincemeat, available in 28 ounce jars. Some have rum and brandy already added. If not, you can add a couple of tablespoons of each and mix well before using.

Using piecrust mix and mincemeat, you can bake a large mince pie or add a layer of mincemeat to an apple pie before you put on the top crust. My favorites are 2 bite-sized pies made in muffin pans that take only 15 minutes at 425° to cook. Made ahead of time and baked at the last minute, they can be served piping hot when guests drop by.

Happy Holidays!

Barbara Davis

INDEX